The Treasury in public policy-making

The Treasury is the central department in the British system of government. Its objectives include controlling public expenditure, maintaining sound public finances, pursuing tax policies to generate revenue, and encouraging improvements in the efficiency of government.

This book focuses on three main themes:

- the development of the Treasury from earliest times to the present, giving special attention to the last twenty-five years;
- the Treasury's current structure and organisation at both ministerial and official level, including the radical restructuring that was introduced in 1995;
- the Treasury's role in the creation and financing of Next Steps Agencies, including brief case studies of the Civil Service College, the Contributions Agency and the Royal Mint.

This major and original study presents details not otherwise readily available and demonstrates the continuing key role of the Treasury in all aspects of public policy-making.

Richard A. Chapman is Emeritus Professor of Politics, Centre for Public Sector Management Research, University of Durham.

Studies in Public Policy-Making

General Editor: Richard A. Chapman
The Centre for Public Sector Management Research,
University of Durham

Also available in this series:
Public Policy-Making for Local Government
   J. A. Chandler

The Treasury in public policy-making

Richard A. Chapman

London and New York

First published 1997
by Routledge
11 New Fetter Lane, London EC4P 4EE

Simultaneously published in the USA and Canada
by Routledge
29 West 35th Street, New York, NY 10001

Typeset in Times by Routledge
Printed and bound in Great Britain by
Mackays of Chatham PLC,
Chatham, Kent

British Library Cataloguing in Publication Data
A catalogue record for this book is available from the British Library

Library of Congress Cataloging in Publication Data
Chapman, Richard A.
The Treasury in public policy-making / Richard A. Chapman
pp. cm.
Includes index.
1. Expenditures, Public —Great Britain—History. 2. Great
Britain. Treasury. 3. Great Britain—Appropriations and expenditures.
I. Title.
HJ7764.C48 1997
336.41—dc21 97–7500

ISBN 0-415-09639-1

Contents

General Editor's Introduction

The Routledge series Studies in Public Policy-Making is designed to meet the needs of undergraduates reading for degrees in government and politics, social and public administration, and public policy. The books will also be valuable to students preparing for professional examinations in certain public services.

Each volume will focus on a given area of policy-making in British government and will concentrate on three aspects of its subject. First, it will provide information about the institutions involved in its area of policy-making, including details of institutional background, recent changes and present structures. Second, it will explain the process of policy-making in its particular area with information about the interest groups involved, how the various agencies interact and how the policy-making processes relate to the parliamentary calendar and other constraints from the political environment. Third, it will illustrate how the institutions and processes work, or have recently worked, in the case of the development of a particular public policy or policies. The emphasis throughout will be on explaining how public policies are made; the series is not intended to evaluate policies nor will there be any emphasis on the relationship of policies to the programmes of political parties or their ideologies. As there is a limit on the length of each volume, authors have been encouraged to write in a concise style but without assuming that the reader has extensive prior knowledge of the subject.

The Studies in Public Policy-Making series is therefore intended to provide an entirely new resource for students of public administration and policy studies. In a number of compact volumes it will offer original contributions to the academic literature, supplementing the more comprehensive but less detailed coverage of basic textbooks; and it will provide insights and analysis as a result of applying, where appropriate, theories and hypotheses from the most recent scholarly publications. The first volume in the series was *Public Policy-Making for Local Government* by J. A. Chandler.[1] The volume on Education is currently being prepared.

The Treasury in public policy-making is the second volume to be published in the series. Teachers and students may find this volume very useful because it includes a case study of the role of the Treasury in the creation of the Next Steps agencies (with special reference to the Civil Service College, the Contributions Agency, and the Royal Mint). For heuristic purposes it is often valuable to be able to put into the context of academic study a major development in the practice of public administration with which students are already familiar from their reading of newspapers and from reporting and discussions in the broadcasting media.

This study begins with an introduction which considers the role of the Treasury in public policy-making. Chapter 2 presents a short history of the Treasury, intended to draw attention to the most significant events and developments that, in retrospect, seem to have contributed to the role of the Treasury in the last few years of the twentieth century. Chapter 3 explains the internal organisation of the Treasury at the beginning of 1996, when it had just been reorganised as a result of the Fundamental Expenditure Review of 1995. This new organisation structure, with its emphasis on the key objectives of the modern Treasury, represents the most fundamental and radical change in the Treasury's approach to its work during the twentieth century. One of the difficulties in writing a book with the aims outlined here is that much of the work has to be updated, and in some parts entirely re-written, to accommodate the continuous changes and factual details that become significant while the research progresses and the book is being written. The case study in Chapter 4 explains the creation and growing importance of Next Steps agencies in British government, and distils information about the Treasury's role from the large literature on this topic. The short concluding chapter draws together the lessons of the three core chapters in the context of the expectations outlined earlier in the book.

The book demonstrates the continuing key role of Treasury work in all aspects of public policy-making. As the well established *Public Administration* textbook by John M. Pfiffner and Robert V. Presthus put it some time ago:

> The budgetary process is central to administration because control of the purse is perhaps the most effective tool of co-ordination; the scope and nature of the entire governmental operation is

determined by the allocation of appropriations to the various big programs.[2]

Similarly, the Haldane Report in the United Kingdom (1918) emphasised the 'exceptional position' of the Department of Finance 'among all the State Departments'.[3] Indeed, finance, or budgeting, has been one of the focal points of public administration and public policy-making throughout its history as a specific area of study. Nowhere is this more significant than in POSDCORB, the mnemonic invented by Luther Gulick to 'call attention to the various functional elements of the work of a chief executive'.[4] However, from the perspective of this book the mnemonic is as relevant to public policy-making as it is to the work of a chief executive. In the mnemonic, B is for 'Budgeting, with all that goes with budgeting in the form of fiscal planning, accounting and control'; but it is often the case that co-ordinating (the CO in POSDCORB) has in practice to go hand in hand with budgeting. Good budgeting work in government can rarely be achieved without good co-ordination and often it is the staff in the Treasury, if one uses a term more suited to UK terminology, that play the most important role in both these activities.

As General Editor of the series I should, perhaps, add that when the series was being planned the publishers and I recognised that *The Treasury in public policy-making* should be one of the first volumes to be published. A number of books on the Treasury have appeared in recent years, including the memoirs of ministers, accounts by economists, and the major research study by Colin Thain and Maurice Wright, *The Treasury and Whitehall, the planning and control of public expenditure 1976–1993*.[5] All these books have contributed to our understanding of the work of the Treasury. However, they do not present, in a single standard-sized volume, the sort of information that students of public policy and administration often need. The intention of this present book is to meet that need by being a worthy successor to the volume on *The Treasury*[6] written by Lord Bridges for the Royal Institute of Public Administration's New Whitehall Series.

Richard A. Chapman

Acknowledgements

I wish to record my thanks to the following institutions and individuals for help received in various ways. The Economic and Social Research Council awarded me a grant of £3,730 to facilitate relief from teaching so that the project could be started during the Michaelmas term 1991, and the Nuffield Foundation awarded me a grant of £1,700 towards my travel and photocopying expenses. I was very fortunate in being appointed to the Sir Norman Chester Senior Research Fellowship by the Warden and Fellows of Nuffield College, which enabled me to spend the Trinity term 1992 in Nuffield College, and therefore to take advantage of the College library. The Royal Institute of Public Administration (until its demise in 1992) was, as usual, helpful, and I made good use of its library and the services of its Information Division for which I am grateful to Mr I. D. Shelley and Miss Jane Henderson.

Sir Robin Butler and Sir Peter Middleton granted permission for me to contact officials in the Treasury and, to facilitate this, Sir Terry Burns appointed, as liaison officer, Mr John McAuslan (and his successors in this role, Mr Jeremy Heywood and Mr Nicholas Holgate). I wish particularly to thank my liaison officers for their generosity with their time and for their help in reading sections of the manuscript. Mr A. D. Whetnall was helpful in answering questions about the timing of the transfer to the Treasury of functions in respect of civil service recruitment, pay and superannuation; and Mr John Cunliffe helped with information about the working implications of the Chancellor's 1991 announcement concerning the delegation of authority for pay.

Crown Copyright is reproduced with the permission of the Controller of Her Majesty's Stationery Office. This applies to the note at the end of Chapter 4 and to the two appendices.

Officials in the three agencies considered in Chapter 4 were very helpful, and I wish to thank Miss Marianne Neville-Rolfe and Dr Stephen Hickey (Civil Service College); Miss Ann Chant and Mr Martin Towler (Contributions Agency); and Mr A. D. Garrett and Mr R. de L. Holmes (Royal Mint). In addition, Sir Peter Kemp gave me some of his time to discuss the development of Next Steps agencies.

My special thanks must be expressed to the following, who read drafts of the whole, or parts of the manuscript, as indicated, and made helpful comments: Dr Jonathan Boston (Chapter 2), Dr Duncan. Bythell, Mr Nicholas Holgate, Dr Barry J. O'Toole, Mr Paul Rayner (Chapter 4), Professor Henry Roseveare (Chapter 2), and Mr Andrew Thompson (Chapter 2). The responsibility for the final manuscript is, of course, mine alone.

Abbreviations

APEX	Analysis of Public Expenditure
BCCI	Bank of Credit and Commerce International
BP	British Petroleum
C and AG	Comptroller and Auditor General
CPRS	Central Policy Review Staff
CSD	Civil Service Department
DEA	Department of Economic Affairs
DSS	Department of Social Security
EC	Economic Community
EDX	Economic and Domestic Policy (Expenditure) Committee of the Cabinet
EMU	European Monetary Union
ERM	Exchange Rate Mechanism
EU	European Union
FER	Fundamental Expenditure Review (also formally known as the Fundamental Review of Running Costs)
FIS	Financial Information System
FMI	Financial Management Initiative
FSBR	Financial Statement and Budget Report
G7	The 'Group of Seven' leading industrial countries whose representatives meet informally to try to co-ordinate international economic co-operation. Its members are the United States, the UK, France, Germany, Italy, Canada and Japan
GDP	Gross Domestic Product
GGE	General Government Expenditure
HMSO	Her Majesty's Stationery Office
IMF	International Monetary Fund
IT	Information Technology
MINIS	Management Information System for Ministers

MoD	Ministry of Defence
MPO	Management and Personnel Office
NAO	National Audit Office
NCT	New Control Total
NIC	National Insurance Contributions
Neddy	National Economic Development Council
NEDO	National Economic Development Office
O and M	Organisation and Management (also Organisation and Methods)
OMCS	Office of the Minister for the Civil Service
OPS	Office of Public Service
OPSS	Office of Public Service and Science
PAC	Public Accounts Committee
PAR	Programme Analysis and Review
PAYE	Pay As You Earn
PCTA	Provisional Collection of Taxes Act
PES	Public Expenditure Survey
PESC	Public Expenditure Survey Committee
PFI	Private Finance Initiative
PPBS	Planning, Programming and Budgeting System
PRISM	Personnel Record Information System for Management
PSBR	Public Sector Borrowing Requirement
RPI	Retail Price Index
SIB	Securities and Investments Board
TCSC	Treasury and Civil Service Committee
TMB	Treasury Management Board
TUC	Trades Union Congress
UK	United Kingdom
VFM	Value for Money

1 The Treasury in public policy-making

A public policy is a programme for action towards an objective or purpose in the public sector, often chosen from a number of alternatives, within the constraints of political circumstances and ideology, and accepted by those responsible for its implementation. This definition is suggested as a straightforward and basic approach to the study of policy-making. Other definitions could have been proposed and there is no shortage of books and articles on the nature of policy-making in liberal democracies, on how policy-makers actually go about their work and what they should do, or on how students of policy-making can be most effective in relation to the modern methodological expectations of academic research in political science and public administration.[1]

The approach to the role of the Treasury in this book is consequently not to use the opportunity to present yet another typology or methodology, nor is it to subscribe to or follow a particular paradigm, but to explain why the Treasury has been and still is so important in the British system of government and, in doing so, to use as a focus its role in policy-making. Whether or not this means the approach comes within the ambit of 'new institutionalism',[2] or of any other type of methodology (or ideology), does not seem to be a matter of much consequence. On the other hand, it does seem important to recognise that writing about public administration in the United Kingdom has significantly advanced in the second half of the twentieth century. The book on *The Treasury* in the New Whitehall series, mentioned in the General Editor's introduction, was written within the constraints imposed on that series. The series grew from a proposal, made in 1949 from the Institute (later the Royal Institute) of Public Administration, when the then Head of the Civil Service, Sir Edward Bridges, was already thinking that there was 'a serious dearth of published information in permanent form about the working of the Government machine and [that] steps ought to be taken to remedy this deficiency'.[3] Nevertheless, the Treasury at that time wished to ensure that any series in which it co-operated would be 'satisfactory, consistent, and unembarrassing'.[4]

One of the consequences of this approach, an approach which was at the time well intentioned and more enlightened than is often credited in later comments on it, or in reviews of books in the New Whitehall series, was that much of the life and human interest was excluded in favour of a factual account of the structure and organisation of the department. Subsequently, books in that series became a very easy target for unsympathetic critics keen to stress what became known as the institutional approach to the study of public administration. As Professor R. A. W. Rhodes has explained, this approach was characterised by

> a subject matter covering the rules, procedures and formal organisations of government, which employs the tools of the lawyer and the historian to explain the constraints on both political behaviour and democratic effectiveness, and fostering liberal democracy, especially the Westminster model of representative democracy.[5]

It was easy to criticise this approach. For example, it was said by Professor David Easton that it could not explain policy or power because it did not (as Rhodes puts it in his representation of Easton) cover all the relevant variables.[6]

However, critics of writers adopting a primarily institutional approach have often not sufficiently recognised the significance of the constraints within which the books and articles were written. For example, there are the constitutional constraints and administrative culture within which officials work. This is not only important for understanding the day-to-day activities of officials in their offices but also for understanding their attitudes to co-operating with authors, as well as for understanding the approaches they have followed in their own writings for publication (whether or not the name of the author is given). In the British system of government it is ministers, not officials, who are accountable for what happens and for explaining why it happens. Therefore civil servants, including holders of the most senior positions, do not wish to accept personal credit for their ideas and achievements within the administrative system; they prefer, instead, to concentrate on making presentations in terms of a historical and/or legal context.

One of the most clearly recognisable consequences of these constitutional and administrative constraints has been the development of sensitivities in relation to official secrecy. Some aspects of this official secrecy have been relaxed in recent years as a result of the reduction in the number of years official papers are held before public access is granted to them. It has also become possible to gain access earlier than stipulated in the standard rule, which holds files without access for thirty years. Other aspects of this official secrecy are still evident in the somewhat arrogant and class-bound attitudes to be seen in some officials (despite protests from others who are more enlightened and liberal-minded) who feel that 'the gentleman in Whitehall knows best; and that the gentleman who dares to question Whitehall is no gentleman'.[7] It is therefore by no means surprising that books in the New Whitehall series, of which *The Treasury* volume was probably the most important and commercially most successful, avoided all criticism and evaluation and did not acquire a reputation for being stimulating to read.

Books and articles on the Treasury published after the early- to mid-1960s have by no means all suffered from shortcomings associated with straightforward historical and legal explanations of the structure and organisation of the department. Limitations of space preclude an extended bibliographical survey of writings on the Treasury, which could be rather arid and in any case seems unnecessary when references in this book and in publications cited here should be enough to facilitate more detailed and specific study by readers wishing to explore further. Moreover, the use of modern technology to access citation indices and other resources reduces the value of using space in a short book for such purposes. However, three of the most important studies of the Treasury will be mentioned briefly here because they have influenced the present author.

The Treasury under the Tories 1951–1964, by Samuel Brittan, was first published in 1964 and revised in 1971 as *Steering the Economy, the role of the Treasury*.[8] It was the work of a leading journalist who specialised on the economy and it benefited greatly from the assistance Brittan received from the Information Division of the Treasury, and from other help from politicians, including, in particular, the author's brother Mr (now Sir) Leon Brittan, who became a senior minister in Mrs Thatcher's administration. As a leading journalist in this area, Brittan's book displays both his skill as a journalist and his expertise on economic policy. It is also immensely readable and informative, especially for its insights into economic policy in the 1950s and 1960s. Moreover, it provided a sort of counterbalance, as a result of its light-handed style, to the book by Lord Bridges, which Brittan was able to read, in proof form, when writing his own book.

The second book to be mentioned here is *The Private Government of Public Money: Community and Policy inside British Politics*, by Hugh Heclo and Aaron Wildavsky, published in 1974.[9] It is still regarded as one of the most important works in the literature on United Kingdom public administration. One reason for this is that the research was so well resourced. The authors acknowledge the generous financial assistance they received, but they were Americans who were able to get quite remarkable access to British civil servants for extensive and intensive interviews (as they put it), involving some 200 or so 'officials, retired officials, ministers and ex-ministers in almost all departments, and Members of Parliament, past and present'.[10] These advantages made British academics distinctly envious.[11] The book concentrates on the process of expenditure decision-making, but uses the process 'as a spotlight for illuminating the characteristic practices of British central government'.[12] What was so irritating to scholars at that time was the apparent lack of appreciation of their own research difficulties, especially when the authors commented, in a gently chiding fashion, on the curious neglect by scholars of the current practice of Treasury officials and Cabinet members in their interaction with each other and with the world outside. Many of the details in the book are now out of date: for example, the Central Policy Review Staff, created in 1970, was abolished in 1983, and the Public Expenditure Survey Committee and the Programme Analysis and Review Committee were also abolished some time ago, though the public expenditure survey remains in good health. However, Heclo and Wildavsky were able to present insights into the working of civil servants in Whitehall that were unprecedented and went far beyond the revelations of biographies and autobiographies of leading 'political administrators' – a term the authors invented and that is still of considerable significance in the literature. Heclo and Wildavsky commented on how misunderstood officials of the Treasury felt their work to be, but they said they acquired a 'deep admiration for the general calibre of British political administrators' and 'They deserve better than they have received at the hands of academics'.[13]

The detailed scholarly study *The Treasury and Whitehall: the Planning and Control of Public Expenditure, 1976–1993*, by Colin Thain and Maurice Wright, was published as the writing for the present volume was being completed, though Thain and Wright published a large number of working papers and articles as their work proceeded, so the direction of their work and the amount of detail it involved was well known before the book was published. Thain and Wright spent four years on research for their book (1988–92), were well supported by the Economic and Social Research Council, and by other sources of research funding, and produced a comprehensive account of the Treasury's control of public spending during the years on which they concentrated.[14] As they put it in their introduction, the central argument of their book is that the Treasury failed to achieve its short-term and medium-term objectives for public spending during the period from 1976 to 1993 because of the constitutional and practical limitations to the exercise of Treasury control.[15] It is clear from their book that Thain and Wright benefited greatly from the interviews they had with a significant number of senior civil servants who were or had been working on aspects of public expenditure. This gave them insights that would not have been available from printed sources and documents, though coping with the information and comments they received must have required special critical presentational skills because it can become all too easy to present justifications of the positions adopted and decisions made by well-intentioned, friendly and able interviewees. That Thain and Wright have been so successful in their task is a great compliment to them and to those who helped them, but it is unlikely that many undergraduates will be able to afford to buy their book, or even read it in their libraries (few university libraries are likely to be able to afford multiple copies).

After reading these three books in particular, but also a number of other partial studies, which have looked at the Treasury from a variety of narrower perspectives, often autobiographical, there is still the need for a book, as up to date as it is possible to be, that in a single volume explains how the Treasury of the United Kingdom developed from earliest times, what its current functions are and how it is organised to achieve its objectives, and to make an assessment of its importance in public policy-making at the end of a sustained period of office held by governments of one political party. Whilst this makes the task of the present volume less ambitious in one sense, because it is not possible to present the sort of mastery of detail required in a book with a narrower focus; in another sense it is more ambitious because writing books with a wider canvas, that have to present clearly, fairly, and succinctly, information gleaned and lessons learned from a large literature covering an extended period of time, and extensive detail about particular facets of the Treasury's work is, without doubt, a very considerable scholarly challenge.

Therefore Chapter 1 of this book focuses on the origins of the Treasury and, with a selective approach, traces the main features of the history of the Treasury from earliest times to the present day. The intention here is, essentially, scholarship, involving judgment. A work of little more than 20,000 words cannot do complete justice to the great detail presented in major works devoted to short periods, specific events, or the significant contributions of particular individuals or government policies. In making these points the author is not criticising works with a much more limited focus; far from it, he is indebted to many of those contributions to the literature. Major insights and important lessons emerge from those studies, but works of narrow focus have disadvantages as well as advantages, as will be apparent from three titles chosen as examples: *Decision Making: A Case Study of the Decision to Raise the Bank Rate in September 1957;*[16] *Treasury Control of the Civil Service 1854–1874;*[17] and *The Treasury and Whitehall: the planning and control of public expenditure, 1976–1993.*[18] The essay which constitutes Chapter 2 has to be selective in what it chooses to emphasise, otherwise there is no way to get a general appreciation of main trends and what is more important.

The criterion for being selective is straightforward, but the viewpoint has to be the present time. What is attempted is to look back from where we are now and choose what appear to be the more significant elements (e.g. facts, people or trends) that at the time of writing appear to have contributed to the role of the Treasury in policy-making as it may be seen today. This, admittedly, gives rise to questions about determinism and historical method. However, this is not the place for a long, discursive exposition of methodology in the study of history. Instead, it may be helpful to give an indication of the sorts of questions to which it is hoped answers, even if only of a preliminary or tentative sort, will emerge. What are the origins of the modern Treasury and what has been its role in the largely 'unwritten' constitution of the United Kingdom? Where legal frameworks are largely absent, how important have Treasury advice and influence been, and how have they worked in practice? What particular functions has the Treasury performed in the past in relation to the development of accountability in the British system of government? How, and with what consequences, did the Treasury 'colonise' other departments and what effects have the process of 'colonisation' had on the relationships of Treasury officials in other departments? How did the Treasury become the tool of Parliament for exercising control over government expenditure? What role did the Treasury acquire in the recruitment and conditions of service of officials in government? How did the Treasury contribute to the ethos of a unified civil service? What is known about the Treasury's role as a 'court of appeal' on the requests (or demands?) of other departments? How did the Treasury acquire such a rich fund of knowledge and experience about what was going on in other government departments? How did the permanent secretary of the Treasury become so important in the civil service and what effects did particular holders of that office have when they were regarded as key leaders in the civil service? How did (does?) the Treasury exercise control, supervision, and co-ordination over public expenditure, and is it more or less effective than it was? What role has the Treasury played in developing new approaches to management in government?

It will not be surprising, though it is probably worth mentioning here, so that readers know what to expect, that the answers to some of these questions are almost as much to be found in Chapter 3 as they are in Chapter 2. Chapter 3 is, however, primarily intended to be an account of what the Treasury does at the present time, how it is organised to achieve its objectives, and how it relates to other institutions within the public sector. Lord Bridges was right when he recognised the need for explanations about the institutions of public administration but there is no account easily available to students and others who wish to have an outline of how the modern Treasury goes about its work. All authors of books in the field of public administration have to cope with the problems arising from structures and processes of organisation that are continuously changing to meet new needs and the requirements of governments, and it is by no means surprising that the monumental recently published book by Colin Thain and Maurice Wright had to have a cut-off date. In their case it was 1993, and consequently when their book was published in 1995 it could not include information about the Fundamental Expenditure Review of the Treasury, published in that year.

It is important not only to know about the details of the machinery of government but also to appreciate how the policies of the government have their impact on the administrative structures and processes within the administrative system. The sorts of questions which have stimulated the approach in Chapter 3 include the following. How does the public expenditure survey work? How has the Treasury accommodated the requirements of politicians to contract the scope of government? What is the overall aim or mission of the Treasury, how is the mission expressed in more specific objectives, and how is the organisation structured to achieve those objectives? What was the Fundamental Expenditure Review and what effect has it had on the actual work of the Treasury? How is the Treasury emphasising and assisting in the implementation of the government's intention to improve management in the departments of central government and make it more efficient? What have been the practical effects on the work of the Treasury of the government's intention to promote the use of private finance in public services and extend privatisation? How is the new 'team approach' to Treasury work being implemented through the creation of 'standing' and 'project' teams of officials? What have been the practical effects on Treasury work of current management approaches which emphasise outputs rather than inputs? How has the Treasury been able to influence agencies in central government to improve the services they provide in terms of 'value for money'? In what ways is it still true to say that the Treasury is at the centre of the formulation and execution of economic policy? How can Treasury advice and guidance be effective without a secure framework of legal rules and controls? What role does the Treasury play in the context of raising funds for, and distributing funds from, the European Communities (including the European Investment Bank and the European Coal and Steel Community)? How does the Treasury interact with and assist the work of parliamentary committees, and what effects do relationships with Parliament and its organisations have on the status of the Treasury within the system of government?

As with the continuation of the consideration of questions between Chapters 2 and 3, some of the answers to these questions are well illustrated by the details provided in Chapter 4, which is a case study of the role of the Treasury in the creation and continuing work of Next Steps agencies. The chapter begins by explaining the background of the Ibbs Report, *Improving Management in Government; the Next Steps*, and presenting details of the implementation of the approach it advocated. The main impetus was the emphasis by the government on achieving better value for money and the improvement of public services. This was to be done whilst contracting the scope of government and reducing the public sector borrowing requirement. The great attraction of creating Next Steps agencies was that they were to facilitate the introduction into public sector management of what were at the time regarded as business values and business methods: government was to become more business-like, with the delivery of services being more decentralised. The original concern of the Treasury in relation to this approach was to ensure that the creation of agencies did not in practice weaken the overall controls over public expenditure. In addition to explaining general features of the creation of agencies, and the role and responsibilities of the Treasury in their creation, Chapter 4 looks at three agencies in particular. These three agencies are the Civil Service College, the Contributions Agency, and the Royal Mint. They should not be seen as a statistically valid sample but as examples of agencies, to illustrate certain practical features of the working of agencies and their relationships with the Treasury. Nevertheless, they have not been chosen at random: the Royal Mint, an agency within the ambit of the Chancellor of the Exchequer, is an example of a trading fund agency, and is therefore required to earn a prescribed return on current cost assets; the Contributions Agency has large-scale responsibilities relating to the welfare state; and the Civil Service College is a relatively small-scale organisation mainly concerned with providing services to government; both the Contributions Agency and the Civil Service College are covered by the normal supply procedures. Three matters of particular current concern are mentioned in this chapter; these are the appointment of chief executives, staffing arrangements, and financial and parliamentary accountability. An important underlying consideration here is the extent to which the policy of creating Next Steps agencies, which has received all-party support at Westminster, has undermined the unified civil service, a unification process in which the Treasury played such an important role in the nineteenth and early twentieth centuries.

As already explained, all the books in the Studies in Public Policy-Making series contain a case study, intended to illustrate how the process of public policy-making works by considering a tangible example. In the case of the Treasury, the variety of possibilities and their competing importance made the choice far from easy. A detailed study could have been presented on the work of the Treasury in relation to controlling public expenditure, or on its work in a particular annual budgetary cycle, or on any one of the Treasury's more specific responsibilities (such as privatisation, or value for money), or on the Treasury's multitude of contacts with departments and agencies and with European Union institutions associated with the UK's membership of the EU. Each of these possibilities had to be considered, not only in relation to their importance as facets of Treasury work, but also in the context of their practicability in terms of limited research resources – in particular, it appeared impractical to research a topic where the primary methodology involved numerous interviews in London by a researcher with a full-time position in the University of Durham. The Next Steps programme was selected for a combination of reasons. First, it is one of the most important programmes affecting both public policy-making and the executive work of government at the present time. Second, it has received all-party support, so it is unlikely to be suspended or reversed after a general election, so lessons from the experience should be interesting and have a continuing validity for some time. Third, it is a programme that illustrates the key responsibilities of the Treasury in its control of, and in its concern for the continuing good stewardship of, public expenditure. Fourth, it is a topic on which there is an ample supply of authoritative and official publications, so that interview research is minimised. These reasons, in turn, illustrate aspects both of the role of the Treasury in public policy-making and also research constraints generally associated with the study of public policy-making. It may be that in future other case studies of the Treasury's work in this context will be undertaken to deepen and broaden our understanding of the work of the Treasury.

2 History: from earliest times to the present day

In the British system of government, which is not based upon a single key document, known as a written constitution, important elements depend on tradition or convention. This means that over many years the importance of certain institutions and their ways of proceeding have evolved and been refined by experience to the stage where their traditions and conventions have, for all practical purposes, as much stability and authority as they could have in a written constitution. Where detailed arrangements are no longer appropriate for their purpose or have simply become unacceptable, they are replaced with new arrangements as a result of a new convention, or a law, or an authoritative proclamation such as an Order in Council under the royal prerogative.

This is well illustrated by the development of the Treasury from earliest times to the present day. The Treasury is, unquestionably, the most important department of central government, but its importance arises more from the nature of its work and status than from any individual formal statement conferring specified powers. Furthermore, its authority is more often to be found in statements of advice and guidance than in orders and instructions. As Lord Welby said in 1879: 'The Treasury itself is rather an office of superintendence and appeal than an office of administration';[1] but he also referred to the Treasury as being 'the most political of departments'.[2] From a quite different perspective, in 1988, Sir Peter Middleton explained that he would not say that the Treasury had a central veto, but, 'We have an opportunity to make our views known'; and he added, somewhat surprisingly, 'The main single activity we have in the Treasury is catering, if I may refer to the Treasury like that. It is not running the economy.'[3]

This chapter describes and explains the main features in the development of the Treasury. There is no comprehensive and up-to-date history of the Treasury, but there are a number of studies of particular aspects or periods and these are acknowledged in the notes. The most complete single-volume historical study is Henry Roseveare's book *The Treasury: The Evolution of a British Institution*, written in the 1960s. This chapter, which draws upon Roseveare's study for the early history, gives special attention to the quarter of a century since Roseveare wrote.

BEFORE 1688

According to Roseveare, the specialised responsibilities of a Treasurer first emerged from the royal household which governed England after the Conquest in 1066; a shadowy figure referred to as 'Henry the Treasurer' was the first identifiable official with that title.[4] However, the origins of the office as well as its early status and functions are unclear. In contrast, the Exchequer was a sophisticated administrative institution in the twelfth century. It consisted of two parts, the Upper and Lower Exchequers. The Upper Exchequer was the court of the Justiciar, with clerical and baronial members, and carried out the relatively humdrum executive functions of the Treasury. The Lower Exchequer was the central safe-deposit of the Crown, where revenue was received and issued.

The special responsibility of the Treasurer in the Exchequer was the composition of the Great Roll of the Exchequer, or the Pipe Roll as it was afterwards called, which listed the charges to be levied and on which, later, the details of the audited accounts were recorded. The detailed tasks were, however, undertaken by clerics, not necessarily ordained, who were the mainstays of the medieval civil service. Chief among these was the Lord Chancellor's clerk, who acted as his deputy and became known as the Chancellor of the Exchequer. The half-yearly audits were carried out by the Treasurer in the Upper Exchequer, watched by his superiors – the Justiciar, the Chancellor and others, including, on occasion, the King himself. The Upper Exchequer was, in effect, a court of account to which the sheriffs and bailiffs were summoned. This work was done on a chequered cloth on which there were columns for pence (up to eleven), shillings (up to nineteen), pounds (up to nineteen), scores of pounds (up to four), hundreds of pounds (up to nine) and thousands of pounds.[5]

Parliament did not exist when the Exchequer was first established, but by the end of the fifteenth century it was taking an increasing interest in public finance. This was not only because the King's financial difficulties gave Parliament opportunities to increase its authority, but also because it wanted the King to maximise the revenue from his resources and make the best possible use of it so that taxes were as low as possible. Moreover, loans were becoming increasingly significant as kings had to borrow to cover deficits, meet emergencies, and bridge the gap between needing and receiving revenue. The Upper Exchequer therefore became a revenue court where disputed liabilities were resolved, a court of common law, and a court of equity, but these functions were distinct from the appeal tribunals which were called the Court of Exchequer Chamber.

The first lay Treasurer was appointed in 1320, and in 1410 the Chancellorship of the Exchequer also passed finally into the hands of laymen. By the sixteenth century, in terms of formal dignity the Lord Treasurer ranked second only to the Lord Chancellor. Lord Burghley became Queen Elizabeth's Lord Treasurer from 1572 until his death in 1598, and managed to help her maintain a degree of control over household expenditure. However, war, inflation and corruption more than balanced his efforts and the situation became worse with the extravagance of James I. After the exposure of Thomas Howard, Earl of Suffolk, for bribery and corruption, the Treasury was put into the hands of a Commission (not for the first time) in 1618, headed by the Archbishop of Canterbury, as First Lord. This meant that responsibility for the Treasury was entrusted to a Treasury Board of five or six Privy Counsellors. Later, during Cromwell's Protectorate, the whole Exchequer-based system was placed in the hands of Treasury Commissioners who were all Privy Counsellors, constituted as a subcommittee of the Council of State.

After the Restoration in 1660, Charles II, in 1667, again put the Treasury into the hands of a Commission. However, instead of senior counsellors he chose for his Commissioners three younger men of his own generation who were all experienced in aspects of financial administration: Sir William Coventry, Sir Thomas Clifford, and Sir John Duncombe. To these three were added the Chancellor of the Exchequer (Sir Anthony Ashley Cooper, later Lord Shaftesbury) and the Duke of Albemarle (who, as General Monck, had played a significant role in the Restoration). However, power was effectively in the hands of Charles's young appointees who could operate as a quorum of three. Their first decision, on 27 May 1667, was to appoint, as Secretary, Sir George Downing.[6] They did this by a resolution which stands as the first paragraph of the record of their proceedings:

Ordered that the Secretary, Sir George Downing, Knight and Baronet, attending this commission, should keep a book singly for registering the brief notes he should take framing any orders upon or pursuing other [of] Their Lordships' directions, which notes at their next meeting, and before they entered upon any new business, he should acquaint them with and what was done thereupon, and so from time to time, what progress was made upon any directions then unperfected. That he should enter the names of the commissioners present at every meeting and constantly observe this method.[7]

Downing, who gave his name to the street in London where he later built four large houses, was an MP who had been knighted in 1660, and had, while in a diplomatic post in The Hague, observed the success of the Dutch in quickly raising a substantial loan for war preparations at the very low rate of 4 per cent. When he returned to England in 1665 he persuaded the King to ask Parliament for Additional Aid of £1.25 million, instead of borrowing from syndicates of businessmen who 'farmed' the revenues of Customs and Excise.[8] The farming of revenues had brought the Treasury into disrepute, especially when the farmers also made payments direct to government creditors, reducing the Exchequer to a mere accounting agency. Downing's appointment as Secretary was semi-official, with no security and no fixed salary, but he was able to demonstrate its full potential. His particular achievement, in the context of this present discussion, was in the arrangements for the loan to the King which made it statutorily explicit that the money should be spent for the purpose intended – the Dutch war, and also enabled citizens to subscribe by means of Treasury Orders. These Orders were repayable in sequence with half-yearly instalments of 6 per cent interest, and were planned to mature during the period required to collect the tax. Consequently, this created a procedure for curbing the King, who became dependent on the new arrangements for extra-ordinary additions to the royal revenue, and stimulating public investment; but it also conferred new responsibilities on the Treasury and Exchequer. These new responsibilities required a proper system of records and higher standards of administration in the Treasury. Downing was therefore responsible for the first real system of Treasury records and the system of administration which went with them. The series of Treasury Minute Books began in 1667 with the record Downing then made of the first resolution of the Board, but Downing also set up other books of records: the book of warrants (i.e. authorities to pay) drawn on separate branches of the revenue, an order book of directions by the Treasury Lords, and letter books sub-divided according to topic.[9] Downing's innovations also created elements of accountability to the public rather than the King, and this was especially evident in the issue of Treasury Orders. Moreover, they marked the beginning of Treasury control of government borrowing and expenditure. This control was formalised in two important Orders in Council, of 31 January 1668 and 12 February 1668 which, together, recognised the full administrative responsibility of the Treasury for all financial questions.[10]

FROM 1668 TO THE FIRST WORLD WAR

After 1668 the Treasury Commission was succeeded by a Lord Treasurer, and then another, but the last Lord Treasurer, the Earl of Shrewsbury, resigned in 1714 and the office has been in commission ever since. This procedure of creating a Commission led to the First Lord of the Treasury Commission becoming the leading Minister of the Crown. From 1721 to 1742 Sir Robert Walpole, as First Lord of the Treasury, and therefore with the considerable Treasury patronage at his disposal, became the first British Prime Minister (although he was not so described while he held office). The procedure also led to the Chancellor of the Exchequer becoming the Minister of Finance and, effectively, the working head of the Treasury Department, because it became accepted that he could act for the Treasury Board. By convention the Chancellor is the only minister who must be a member of the House of Commons – the Commons having a competence in matters relating to the public revenue which is denied to the House of Lords.

A principle of considerable importance, also related to the growing power of the Treasury, became established early in the eighteenth century. The House of Commons, wishing to prevent irresponsible pressure for public expenditure, resolved on 11 December 1706 'That this House will receive no Petition for any sum of money relating to public service, but what is recommended from the Crown'. This resolution became a Standing Order of the House of Commons on 11 June 1713, which survives to this day. It establishes the principle of restricting financial initiatives to ministers of the Crown – in effect, the Treasury.[11]

The principle of appropriation became regularised through experience rather than deliberate planning. This principle means that money voted to the Crown – in effect the Government, because for all practical purposes the government was carried on by ministers in the King's name – is granted for clearly defined purposes and to be used within a given year. Any sums not spent within the year are surrendered. This annuality of supply, first instituted after 1688 when supplies for the army were approved for one year only, was important for keeping control over the spending of money and it helped to regularise the parliamentary practice of 'redress of grievances before supply'. Parliament's power had, in fact, evolved since the fourteenth century through this procedure, which meant that before it would agree to vote supplies to the King he had to agree to stop doing certain things to which Parliament had objected, or had to agree to do certain things which Parliament wanted done.[12]

Towards the end of the seventeenth century the Bank of England, which had been granted a charter in 1694, issued a long loan to the Exchequer; and new taxes were required to pay for the expensive war of the League of Augsburg, costing nearly £45 million, which, as Roseveare puts it 'sired the National Debt'.[13] From 1691 until 1697 a series of Accounts Commissions imposed a searching audit of government expenditure which resulted in further encroachments on the royal prerogative.

Within the Treasury itself, a hierarchy of clerks developed around the office of Secretary. The most distinguished holder of this post in the eighteenth century was William Lowndes, who was previously a Treasury clerk; he became Secretary in 1695, though he did not have a seat in Parliament until 1724.[14] However, it was during the early years of the eighteenth century that the political and executive offices in government became separated. In 1741 this was regularised by an Act which stipulated that clerks in the Treasury and other departments were to be made incapable of holding seats in Parliament, and it is therefore from this date that one of the most important conditions of an independent, non-political civil service may be traced. This exclusion of Treasury clerks (and others) from Parliament in the eighteenth century was part of the attack on corruption and ministerial patronage, and of the continuous attempts to restore the 'purity' and independence of the Commons from executive control.

The Treasury was located in the old palace of Whitehall until near the end of the seventeenth century when James II had the motley range of sometimes malodorous accommodation rebuilt to designs by Wren. The Treasury moved into its rather splendid new quarters in 1686 but much of it was destroyed by fire in January 1698. Then, with its records intact, it moved first into the house of Lowndes, its Secretary, and later moved back into part of the palace that had survived the fire. Its new permanent home, from 1736, was designed by William Kent. Kent was also responsible for converting No 10 Downing Street. The houses in Downing Street had been privately occupied until 1732 when George II offered the crown lease to Walpole, who accepted it as the office for the First Lord of the Treasury. Kent's conversion was extensive and incorporated a passage-way link between No 10 and the Treasury.[15]

In the early eighteenth century there were two Joint Secretaries in the Treasury, together with four chief clerks who supervised the work of about a dozen under-clerks. The Secretaries were much more than clerks in the modern sense, for they were 'the principal middle men of eighteenth-century government, the "fixers" and contact men, operating in the hinterland of politics and finance'.[16] One of the consequences of this activity was the arrangement agreed in 1715 by which the Bank of England took over from the Exchequer the subscription, transfer and general management of nearly all the government's borrowing transactions. In 1787 an Act created the Consolidated Fund (in effect, the name of the public bank account at the Bank of England), through which the great bulk of the government's money passes.[17] The management of government finance then became increasingly demanding. The management of the Consolidated Fund was an important task which involved making sure that there was sufficient in the account to meet drawings upon it, whilst at the same time ensuring that any surplus was used to reduce government indebtedness. Furthermore, this procedure became increasingly significant for the economy at large and the budget became an important annual feature. The term in fact dates from the 1730s, when it was humorously applied to the wallet or *bougette* from which Walpole, as Chancellor, drew proposals for the year's finance.[18]

The end of the eighteenth century saw three important developments. In 1782 Shelburne, as First Lord of the Treasury, introduced an important reorganisation in the Treasury. Business was to be rearranged among six 'divisions' and fixed salaries were to be paid to officials instead of the variable, though higher, remuneration they had taken from the fees they collected. Second, there was the beginning of Treasury colonisation of subordinate departments. Edward Bishop was sent to the Salt Tax Commissioners; G. T. Goodenough went to the Board of Taxes, as Secretary; and J. Martin-Leake became a member of the new Audit Office Board, which had been created in 1785. Third, audit, to check against abuse, became significant because of the growing size of public expenditure. By the time the full cost of the American war had been absorbed, the National Debt exceeded £240 million and half the public revenue was going in debt charges. Pitt introduced the Income Tax as a war tax in 1799, to help deal with the fiscal problems resulting from the wars with Revolutionary France.

When the war with France broke out again in 1803 the details were reformed with Addington's Income Tax Act of 1803.

The Treasury's position was consolidated and strengthened as the nineteenth century progressed. Parliament continued to exercise pressure for economy and this led to the Treasury issuing circulars to departments to reduce the inflated salaries and increments that had resulted from the war years. From the 1820s the estimates of civil departments were presented by the Treasury, and the Treasury's position was further strengthened after 1861 when it was laid down, although not by statute, that the estimates of departments had to be approved by the Treasury before being presented to Parliament.[19] Consequently, the nineteenth century saw the civil departments conforming to the annual parliamentary estimate and appropriation procedures, which had become firmly established for military expenditure. However, the Treasury style was not to impose its will (it had no authority to do so) but to make recommendations and exercise leadership through, for example, making cuts in its own establishment. Its growing confidence and superiority did, however, arise to some extent from the reforms of the estimates and the audit requirements, but also to some extent from reforms relating to the establishments.

Together with concern for checking on the issue of money from the Exchequer and the due exercise of economy, Parliament also expressed a growing recognition of the importance of checking how money had been spent. Thus, in 1828, the Committee on Income and Expenditure called for the restoration of the 'ancient and wise control vested by our Financial Policy in the hands of the Treasury over all the departments connected with the Public Expenditure', which could only be effected 'by the House of Commons constantly enforcing its application, by holding the Treasury responsible for every Act of Expenditure in each Department'.[20] The Committee therefore advocated clear, uniform accounting systems in all public departments, the simplification and consolidation of public business, and an effectual control by the Treasury over all departments.

Reforms of the 1830s had an important part to play in this. In 1833 the structure of the Upper Exchequer was abolished and the remaining offices associated with it, the Chancellor of the Exchequer, the King's Remembrancer and the judicial court of Exchequer pleas, were finally incorporated into the administrative and judicial systems. The death, in 1834, of Lord Grenville, the last life-tenant Auditor of the Receipt, cleared the way for the formal end of the Lower Exchequer. In place of the Upper and Lower Exchequers a new office was created by the Exchequer and Audit Departments Act of 1866: the Comptroller-

General of the Receipt and Issue of His Majesty's Exchequer. This office was given a permanent, semi-judicial status, independent of the Treasury but responsible to Parliament, and charged with the responsibility for receipts and issues relating to the government's Bank of England accounts, which had by then been drawn together in the Consolidated Fund account. Meanwhile, in the Treasury and departments other reforms were continuing. The Boards of Stamps and Taxes had been amalgamated in 1816, and in 1849 they were joined with the Excise Commissioners to form the Board of Inland Revenue, which became the Treasury's most important auxiliary. However, it was not until after 1857 that double-entry book-keeping was universal in government departments or that accounting years in different departments were brought into harmony.[21]

Two particularly significant reforms were instituted in 1861 and 1866. In 1861 Gladstone, an economy-minded Chancellor of the Exchequer, set up the House of Commons Select Committee on Public Accounts, and by later resolutions this became a permanent part of the machinery of the House. In 1866 the Exchequer was transformed into the Audit Office, with a new position being created: the Comptroller and Auditor General.[22] Although appointed by the Treasury, he was responsible to the House of Commons, with a salary drawn directly from the Consolidated Fund (and therefore not subject to an annual parliamentary vote), and tenure during good behaviour so that he was as secure and independent as a judge. His responsibilities involved receiving daily accounts of the gross receipts of revenue and of issues from the Consolidated Fund, and auditing the annual appropriation accounts submitted by the departments via the Treasury. At the same time as these reforms were instituted, the dominance of the government over the business of the House of Commons was restated. It had been accepted for over 150 years that financial initiatives should be left to the representatives of the Crown, which effectively meant the Treasury ministers, but by 1866 it was clear that this gave the Secretaries to the Treasury and the Junior Lords the major role in determining the manoeuvres of the ruling party. In practice, the 1866 Act gave the Treasury power to control the whole of the civil expenditure and the right to 'judge every measure increasing or tending to increase directly or indirectly, the public expenditure'.[23]

These various reforms, many attributable to Gladstone's impact during his time as Chancellor of the Exchequer, consolidated the relationship of the Treasury to the House of Commons or, more specifically, to its watchdog, the Public Accounts Committee, into that of servant and master. The position was clearly put in one of the fundamental statements of Treasury control, a Treasury Minute of April 1868, which said 'my Lords' acknowledged

> that it would be beyond the functions of this Board to control the ordinary expenditure placed under the charge of the several departments, within the limits of the sums set forth under the subheads of the several grants to Parliament, and that it is only in exceptional cases that the special sanction of the Treasury should be held to be necessary.

However,

> My Lords consider that such sanction should be required for any increase of establishment, of salary or of cost of a service, or for any additional works or new services which have not been specially provided for in the grants of Parliament.[24]

Whilst, in essence, Treasury control, as expressed in this Minute, related only to matters which resulted in increases in public expenditure, much more was involved than a purely negative check on expenditure. This was because the creation of the Comptroller and Auditor General and the reformulation of Treasury control were accompanied by two other reforms. One was the revision of the Treasury's internal organisation and the other was reform of the recruitment and conditions of service of officials.

Within the Treasury, a Treasury Minute of 19 August 1805 had, in effect, separated the political aspects of the Treasury's work from its administrative work. Treasury Board meetings had become a fiction because the twice-weekly meetings had no other functions than obtaining signatures to formally approve decisions that had already been taken by Treasury ministers. The Minute of 1805 therefore created a permanent, non-political post of Assistant Secretary and Law Clerk, to take the minutes of the Treasury Board, draft the financial legislation, and accept responsibility for supervising the Treasury staff. This freed the Joint Parliamentary Secretaries to concentrate on their political and financial duties. The chief clerks, working under the Assistant Secretary, each had individual responsibility for one or more of the Treasury's six divisions. A further major reorganisation, promulgated in a Treasury Minute of 17 October 1834, reduced the six divisions to four, but by then the clerks were becoming increasingly unhappy about their conditions of service and poor pay.[25]

Sir Charles Trevelyan, who had previously served in the Indian Civil Service, where he displayed the qualities of 'a tireless, efficient administrator convinced at the rightness of his own action',[26] was appointed to the Assistant Secretaryship of the Treasury in 1840, when he was only 32 years of age. He worked industriously to reform the Treasury from within and, as a member of a small internal committee, consisting also of W. Gibson Craig and J. Parker, investigated the Treasury establishment. The Treasury Minute in fact appointed them to inquire into

> the present state of the Establishment of the Treasury, and into the arrangements and regulations for the distribution and conduct of the business, in order that such changes may be made as may be required to secure the highest practicable degree of efficiency.

That committee recommended reducing the four Treasury divisions to two and also recommended 'that merit and qualification, and not seniority, should be the prevailing motives in selecting persons for promotion'.[27]

This inquiry in the Treasury was, however, one of a series on which Trevelyan served, looking into the establishment questions of various government departments, as part of his duties at the Treasury – and the Treasury Minute setting up the inquiry referred to the Treasury as 'the central office for the revision of the public establishments'.[28] They included inquiries into the Colonial Office (1849), the Board of Trade (1853), the Department of Practical Science and Art (1853), the Poor Law Board (1853), the Privy Council Office (1853), the Colonial Land and Emigration Office (1853), the Board of Ordnance (1853), the Office of Works (1854), and the Post Office (1854). These inquiries should, however, be seen in the context of their time, for they followed the 1832 Reform Act, the inquiry into the Indian Civil Service, and pressures for reform in the universities of Oxford and Cambridge. They were also a response to the concern about the growth in public expenditure resulting from the increase in the scope and intensity of government activity. Moreover, they led to the famous Northcote-Trevelyan Report of 1854 on the Organisation of the Permanent Civil Service. Gladstone, who commissioned the Northcote-Trevelyan inquiry (by a Treasury Minute dated 12 April 1853)[29] conceived its task as 'to draw up a general Report on the state of the Civil Service with a statement of remedies broader and larger in their nature than could conveniently be treated of in the separate reports of each distinct establishment'.[30]

The Northcote-Trevelyan Report said that the civil service did not attract the ablest, but instead it was sought after by the unambitious, indolent or incapable. Consequently, the service suffered both in internal efficiency and in public estimation. It suggested that the best method of getting good civil servants, and of making the most of them after they were recruited, was to train young men carefully selected by examination and whose permanent appointment would be confirmed only after the satisfactory completion of a short period of probation. In order to ensure that the examinations would be carried out in an effective and consistent manner throughout the service, the Report recommended that a Central Board of Examiners should be established, and the examination should be a competitive literary examination (plus an inquiry into the age, health and moral fitness of the candidates). There should be a proper distinction between intellectual and mechanical work and for the intellectual positions the examination should contain an extensive range of subjects and should be open to all persons of a given age and on a level with 'the highest description of education in this country'; there should be a lower standard to test for the more 'mechanical' clerkships. Once in the service, the recruit should be transferred from one department of the office to another so that he would be given the opportunity of making himself master of the whole of the department's business, then his promotion should depend on merit and not on seniority.[31]

Sir Kenneth Wheare aptly described the Northcote-Trevelyan Report as 'a broadsheet, or broadside; it is a manifesto on Civil Service reform . . . a reformer's tract or pamphlet unaccompanied by the usual apparatus of minutes of evidence, and the like'.[32] Before the Report was published (on 24 January 1854), the Queen's Speech at the opening of Parliament had declared the government's intention to reform the civil service, but no more was said officially about administrative reform until the Civil Service Commission was set up by Order in Council on 21 May 1855, by which time there was widespread agitation for reform because of mismanagement of the Crimean War. It should be noted that this important reform constituting the Civil Service Commission was not made by Act of Parliament, as the Northcote-Trevelyan Report had envisaged, but by an Order in Council. Sir George Cornewall Lewis, who supported the procedure, argued that the setting up of a board of examiners 'would necessarily entail some expense, and however small this might be, it would necessitate an annual vote which would give the House of Commons a practical veto upon the system once in every session'.[33] Indeed, there was no full dress debate in Parliament on the reforms until three weeks after the Order in Council was made.

The system of selection introduced by the Civil Service Commissioners was essentially one of authentication. That is, most departments arranged with the Commissioners for staff to be recruited by limited competition among a selected number of nominated candidates, usually three per vacancy. It was alleged that William Hayter, the Patronage Secretary to the Treasury (1852–58), kept two hopelessly stupid young men handy to compete against any favoured nominee[34] and that he continued to nominate 'at his pleasure' some 240 clerks a year in the revenue services. Only in 1857 did the government declare that the principle of 'limited' competition was to obtain in all departments dependent on the Treasury[35] which, of course, included the Civil Service Commission. However, two further events soon led to the implementation of open competition. First, the Superannuation Act of 1859 enacted that no civil servant should receive a pension unless he possessed a certificate of competency from the Civil Service Commission; and second, following the report, in 1860, of a House of Commons Select Committee on nominating and examining candidates, an Order in Council of 4 June 1870 made open competition obligatory, except for the Foreign Office and a few other specialist posts, throughout the home civil service.

Nevertheless, it was not until 1878 that open competitive examination became the normal procedure for recruitment to the Treasury. The reform of the methods of recruitment and the other structural reforms both contributed to the rise in morale and the growing institutional self-confidence in the Treasury. However, they also contributed to making the Treasury vulnerable to attack. Roseveare's reasoning puts this well:

> Its select size, its distinctive privileges, the marked ease with which it gained access to the highest fruits of public life, and – above all – its claim to unique powers in relation to its peers among government departments, all these were at the source of an articulated hostility which flows through the late nineteenth century.[36]

The most significant attack was, surprisingly, a public one. It came on 30 January 1900 from Lord Salisbury, the Prime Minister and Foreign Secretary – who was, incidentally, the last Prime Minister not to hold the office of First Lord of the Treasury. During the debate on the Queen's Speech Salisbury said:

> and last of all I feel I am laying my hand on the sacred feature of the Constitution when I say there is the Treasury . . . the present Chancellor of the Exchequer . . . is a Minister who has filled the office with the greatest consideration to the powers of the Treasury; but I say that the exercise of its powers in governing every department of the Government is not for the public benefit. The Treasury

has obtained a position in regard to the rest of the departments of the Government that the House of Commons obtained in the time of the Stuart dynasty. It has the power of the purse, and by exercising the power of the purse it claims a voice in all decisions of administrative authority and policy. I think that much delay and many doubtful resolutions have been the result of the peculiar position which, through many generations, the Treasury has occupied.[37]

Salisbury was, however, known to have had a distaste for the Treasury, as his earlier correspondence with the Chancellor of the Exchequer, Sir Michael Hicks-Beach made clear:

That the Treasury should say that any expenditure is excessive or thriftless in regard to the aspects for which it is intended is obviously within its functions. But in practice the Treasury goes much further. It acts as a sort of court of appeal on other departments. Because every policy at every step requires money the Treasury can veto anything: and can do so on proposals which have nothing financial in their nature: and for judgment upon which it has no special qualification . . . in small matters the Treasury interferes too much. In large questions its resisting point is frequently inadequate.[38]

However, in defence of the Treasury, it should be noted that its tasks were increasing in both size and complexity. The charges on the national debt were at their worst in the years before the Crimean War, then absorbing about half the gross public expenditure. In 1842 Peel had revived the income tax, temporarily, for a three-year period, and the tax has continued ever since. The Treasury operated within narrow fiscal bounds with strict public economy and, in terms of its own affairs, exercised leadership in economy to the point where it was probably under-staffed. When these factors are considered alongside others it is not difficult to appreciate the feelings towards the Treasury, especially within the great spending departments.[39]

The increasing confidence and significance of the Treasury is, perhaps, also indicated in another way. As Roseveare says, it is natural to wonder how far the permanent Treasury was really responsible for the 'strikingly consistent orthodoxy of successive Chancellors, regardless of party'.[40] Roseveare explains, for example, how Sir Edward Hamilton, as Joint Permanent Secretary to the Treasury (1902–7), would begin to project the outcome of the year ending 31 March and begin deliberating the possible outlines of the next budget. He adds that, as Hamilton developed his competence there were clear signs that

Chancellors were increasingly inclined to accept his guidance.[41] Indeed, it seems that sometimes the Treasury officials not only shaped the policies but also the politics of their masters. In this increasingly important role of contributing to policy-making, the Treasury received much support from the Comptroller and Auditor General. Together, their tactics disciplined the departments through growing awareness of the need for financial rectitude.

One of the ways in which the increasing control became more evident was through the procedure of virement. By 1885 the Civil Estimates were grouped in seven classes containing a total of 135 separate votes. Some of these votes would, during the year, be financing services which were exceeding their budgets, while others would be underspent. In a system geared to annuality any surplus would have to be surrendered to the Exchequer, but from 1846 a Treasury Minute regularised the procedure for transfers between sub-heads, requiring Treasury sanction before any transfer occurred. This was endorsed subsequently by a resolution of the House of Commons, and the power to authorise transfers between votes in the naval and military departments was conferred by the Appropriation Act of 1846–47. Further Treasury Minutes laid down procedures for this in practice.[42] It is this procedure of transferring funds between authorised purposes for expenditure which is called virement. Ultimately, of course, the approval of these transfers was the responsibility of the House of Commons, but the Treasury acquired this authority to approve transfers after it had made appropriate critical investigations. The Treasury's effective control therefore developed largely from examining details when departments requested authority for increased expenditure. It was always looking for opportunities to stimulate economy, and the basic assumption of Treasury control was that public spending had to be resisted, but the Treasury could not interfere in the affairs of other departments without their co-operation – and the main stimulant for co-operation was a department's need for more funds.

Indeed, this is well illustrated by Maurice Wright's major study, *Treasury Control of the Civil Service 1854–1874*. Wright explains how important in this context were the Treasury procedures to demur and to institute inquiries. He explains that the manner in which the Treasury discharged its responsibility resembled an elaborate game, with rules which were known but were never openly discussed. When the Treasury was not satisfied with a request from a department (for example, relating to increasing the establishment) it demurred in its official reply, requesting further details or more justification. This procedure delayed authorisation to increase expenditure but also had a salutary effect in challenging a department's need and therefore stimulating an exercise which involved careful thought within departments before even asking for additional resources.

Sometimes this would lead to an inquiry by the Treasury, either because the department asked for it or because the Treasury thought it appropriate. Most inquiries were the result of Treasury initiative, even though departments may have formally requested them. As Sir George Hamilton once told Gladstone:

> With regard to our functions in reviewing other Establishments, I wish to observe that when a Department asks for an increased Establishment and the Treasury demurs – as it is its duty unless satisfied as to the necessity for such an increase, it is the Department asking for the increase which usually invites an inquiry – I am not aware that it is our practice to propose such inquiries ourselves.[43]

In practice, of course, this could be interpreted from different perspectives, as reflected in the terms of reference of an inquiry. If the Treasury had a major role in designing the terms of reference the terms were wide: an inquiry in 1856 was instructed 'to inquire into the conduct of business of the Home Office'. However, if a department initiated an inquiry the terms of reference were more narrowly drawn, for example, 'to make recommendations for the consolidation of the departments of the War Office'.[44]

These inquiries had an important overall effect, enhancing the role of the Treasury. First, they enabled Treasury officials to acquire valuable insights into the organisation and establishment of departments under their control. Second, they resulted in better understanding within the Treasury of the work and difficulties facing departments. Third, the officials who would later make recommendations to Treasury ministers when departmental requests were officially presented, were very well informed about the details and justification for requests. Fourth, they contributed to developing within the Treasury 'a rich fund of first-hand knowledge and experience of current administrative practice in the public departments'.[45]

The reasoning behind these developments resulted from the Treasury's interest in economy, which was quite different from efficiency, which was the responsibility of the head of department. The position here was clarified (and subsequently developed) from a Treasury Minute of 14 August 1872 which formulated the rule that the permanent head of a department should be designated as the Accounting Officer. This meant that he was responsible for the Appropriation

Accounts presented to the Comptroller and Auditor General, and since the responsibility extended beyond technical accountancy to the economy and efficiency of the department's work, it was logical that the departmental head should combine the responsibilities. The consequence is, as the position has developed today, that the Accounting Officer has to appear before the Public Accounts Committee to answer for any details within his sphere of responsibility – an important facet linking the executive parts of government to the legislature in a way that is a key element in democratic control within the British system of government.

The internal organisation and status of officials within the Treasury also developed during the nineteenth century. Following a recommendation by Mr G. A. Hamilton, the position of Assistant Secretary was defined and changed to that of Permanent Secretary from 1867. The important Treasury Minute on this change, for many years thought to have been lost, is reprinted in Wright's history of Treasury control.[46] The new title, recognising the more substantive character of the office, in fact allocated no new functions to the position but formalised the existing practice, including the statement that the Permanent Secretary was to have 'particular regard to all increases of Establishments and Salaries in the Public Service'. On his retirement, in 1869, Hamilton wrote to Robert Lowe: 'The office of Permanent Secretary to the Treasury may be regarded as almost the keystone of the whole Civil Service'.[47] However, the position was to be developed to achieve even more significance under Sir Warren Fisher after the First World War.

By the late nineteenth century the Upper Establishment of the Treasury was one Permanent Secretary, one Assistant Secretary, four Principal Clerks, seven first class clerks and twelve second class clerks, organised within five divisions. In 1908 this was increased to six divisions, but without any increase in staff.[48] The position of Permanent Secretary was continuously acquiring more importance, with the complexity and volume of work and with the increases in public expenditure, and this was especially evident with the welfare legislation introduced in the early years of the twentieth century. However, as the Treasury grew in importance, and acquired new sub-departments (like the Parliamentary Counsel's Office created by Treasury Minute on 8 February 1869) it generally took the best candidates in the recruitment competitions. Some of the best Treasury men, after acquiring practical experience, were later sent to positions of seniority in other departments; this further enhanced the standing of the Treasury and gave it a good network for informal communication and co-operation. By the time of the First World War the Treasury staff contained a number of very able men who were to make their mark in the twentieth-century history of the civil service.

One of the further ways in which the significance of the Treasury was enhanced in relation to the rest of the civil service was through its role in developing pensions schemes. The first comprehensive departmental pensions scheme was introduced by Treasury Minute for Customs staff in 1803. In 1810 an Act laid down for the whole service a maximum pensions scale on the Customs model and stipulated Treasury sanction for the grant of any pension; this made the Treasury, in effect, the department with primary responsibility for civil service pensions. The 1810 Act also provided for an annual parliamentary return of salaries and thus made salaries for the first time the direct concern of Parliament.[49] An Act of 1834 launched a contributory pensions scheme but this led to grievances about the plight of widows and to the creation (in 1853) of an inter-departmental body of civil servants to secure redress. Following initial inquiries by a House of Commons Select Committee, a Treasury Commission was appointed to complete inquiries into the Superannuation Acts. Most of the Commission's proposals were incorporated in the Superannuation Act 1859, which also required officials to obtain a certificate from the Civil Service Commissioners in order to qualify for the award of a pension. The overall effect of these provisions after 1859 was to give the Treasury almost unlimited discretion to regulate and control the award of superannuation allowances.[50]

By the First World War there was increasing concern about Treasury attitudes of superiority and Treasury control, because it was felt that control was being administered by inexperienced young pedants who had little insight into the work of spending departments.[51] However, there was a unified system of efficient administration, involving control of expenditure, operated outwards from the Treasury to all parts of the executive work of government.[52] As far as the civil service more generally was concerned, reforms had progressed from the improvement of recruitment and promotions procedures to the development of a class system based on distinguishing between intellectual and more mechanical work, so that an identifiable and unified service was emerging. Also, as far as the Treasury's ministers were concerned, the 1849 Treasury Instruments (Signatures) Act, which reduced the legal quorum necessary to authenticate formal documents from three Commissioners to two, meant that the number of junior Treasury Lords was reduced from four to three. The Chancellor of the Exchequer was already established as the minister responsible for the Treasury's work; the other Lords of the Treasury were recognised as having political but not administrative duties; and the positions of First Lord of the Treasury and Prime Minister were normally held by the same person. Indeed, it is unlikely that the positions will ever again be separated because, with the Ministers of the Crown Act 1937, the payment of a pension to a retired Prime Minister is conditional on holding both offices.[53]

FROM THE FIRST WORLD WAR TO 1962

By the early twentieth century the Treasury was the key department of central government, not because there was a single authoritative statement giving it this position but because it had acquired important responsibilities piecemeal, in an unplanned fashion, over hundreds of years. Its pre-eminent position was in some respects advanced, and in other respects clarified, by important Acts of Parliament, Orders in Council, and Treasury Minutes during the nineteenth century. In particular, its relationship with Parliament and its control over public expenditure were clearly established as, indeed, were its responsibilities for personnel management, either through detailed responsibilities exercised by its own decisions or through the Civil Service Commission which came within its ambit. However, some of these elements of control, and the Treasury's general responsibility for public policies, were consolidated as a result of the First World War and the years immediately following it.

The most important features of the period from the First World War to 1962 may be traced by considering three broad themes. These are: the Haldane Report and reorganisation associated with it; the role of the Head of the Civil Service; and Treasury control and influence over the national economy. These themes will be discussed in turn, though it should be appreciated that they are interrelated and, moreover, they do not constitute a comprehensive account of the history of the period.

According to Roseveare, the initiative which led to the famous Haldane Report on the Machinery of Government[54] can be traced to the Treasury memorandum presented to the Financial Secretary, Edwin Montagu, before he became Minister of Reconstruction in 1917.[55] The memorandum commented on the wasteful overlapping of functions among the old and new departments, and it called for a comprehensive review of government organisation. However, this may be seen as but one of a number of expressions of concern about the administrative confusions of the First World War.[56] These led first to the creation by Asquith, in 1916, of a Reconstruction

Committee of ministers to advise on future peacetime problems and to co-ordinate the work which had already been done by the departments.[57] Second, in 1917, Lloyd George created a separate Ministry of Reconstruction.

The Ministry of Reconstruction Committee on the Machinery of Government, set up under the chairmanship of Lord Haldane had, as its terms of reference: 'to enquire into the responsibilities of the various Departments of the central executive Government, and to advise in what manner the exercise and distribution by the Government of its functions should be improved'. The committee had a distinguished membership including politicians from each of the main political parties (Mr Edwin Montagu, Sir Alan Sykes and Mr J. H. Thomas); two civil servants (Sir George Murray and Sir Robert Morant); and Mrs Beatrice Webb. As none of the politicians played a leading role in the work of the committee, the pace was effectively set by the other four. Haldane had a philosophical background and distinguished record as a Cabinet Minister. He regarded the search for rational principles as an essential preliminary for success in politics and administration and believed that research was as necessary in the social sciences as it was in the physical sciences. Murray was formerly Permanent Secretary to the Treasury, and was described by Violet Markham as 'wise, cynical, humorous, a realist without illusions', and by Beatrice Webb as an engaging 'simple-minded reactionary' who nevertheless was often receptive to 'a lot of new ideas' which he found 'damned interesting'.[58] Morant was a forceful public servant who was responsible for the 1902–3 Education Acts, and who believed in social reform. Beatrice Webb had considerable practical experience of social and political reform, and a knowledge of administrative theory and practice.

The work of the committee has attracted much research and has been the subject of numerous studies from a variety of perspectives.[59] The first part of the report analysed the machinery of government and drew attention to principles which, it recommended, should be applied when allocating functions between departments and when considering their relationship to the Cabinet and Parliament. The second part of the report concentrated on the principal departments and the application of the principles in particular circumstances. In this, primary attention was given to the department of finance, under the control of the Board of Treasury. The report then listed the Board's principal functions as:

(a)   Subject to Parliament it is responsible for the imposition and regulation of taxation and the collection of the revenue, for which purpose it has the assistance of the Revenue Departments.

(b) It controls public expenditure in various degrees and various ways, chiefly through the preparation or supervision of the estimates for Parliament.

(c) It arranges for the provision of funds required from day to day to meet the necessities of the public service, for which purpose it is entrusted with extensive borrowing powers.

(d) It initiates and carries out measures affecting the public debt, currency, and banking.

(e) It prescribes the manner in which the public accounts should be kept.[60]

The report concluded that from this list of functions 'it will be seen that the Treasury is a Department of control and supervision rather than administration'.[61] One of the perceptive lessons that the Haldane Committee drew out of experience was that

the interests of the tax-payer cannot be left to the spending Departments; that those interests require the careful consideration of each item of public expenditure in its relation to other items and to the available resources of the State, as well as the vigilant supervision of some authority not directly concerned in the expenditure itself; and that such supervision can be most naturally and effectively exercised by the Department which is responsible for raising the revenue required.[62]

It also argued for closer personal relations between the Treasury and the other departments and for ending the traditional attitudes that departments have a natural disposition to extravagance and that the Treasury is irreconcilably opposed to all increases in expenditure.[63] It drew attention to the control over expenditure exercised through the preparation of the annual estimates, a control which was, and is, further served by the scrutiny of the Comptroller and Auditor General,[64] and urged more frequent inquiries by the Treasury into the general administration of departments.[65] The report made three special recommendations about 'establishment' work, these were: (a) the creation in all departments where the staff was sufficiently numerous of an establishment officer to study personnel management questions; (b) the maintenance of a system of continuous records about work done, the time involved, and cost incurred; and (c) the creation of a separate branch in the Treasury specialising in 'establishment' work, which would keep in touch with departmental establishment officers and would 'keep itself acquainted with what was being done in business circles outside, and perhaps in foreign countries'.[66] It considered whether there should be any change 'as regards the Department with which the general control of the personnel of the Civil Service is to rest', and decided that as much of the work depended directly on the control of expenditure generally, no other department suggested itself as more suitable than the Treasury.[67]

Anyone with insight into the history of the Treasury and the civil service will appreciate the significance of some of these reflections and recommendations. Indeed, while the Haldane Report did not contain a series of recommendations for uncritical and speedy implementation, it seems shortsighted to conclude, as a Treasury memorandum did in 1949, that 'The Haldane Report has stayed on the shelf since it was written'.[68] Whilst the report seems not to have been formally debated by Lloyd George's Cabinet, attention by the Cabinet and/or public discussion of a report is not the only way to assess its significance. More important, as far as the focus of this present study is concerned, the Report appealed to the higher grades of administrators, and it was subsequently recognised as a useful document because it gathered together in an authoritative format a number of acceptable suggestions for central co-ordination of the civil service. It set the tone for later thinking on central government administration in Britain and viewed Whitehall as a coherent set of government departments rather than a mere grouping of government 'offices'.[69] Furthermore, in a variety of ways it made a significant contribution to the general ethos of British administrative studies in the twentieth century. For example, 'efficiency' was interpreted in the report in qualitative as well as quantitative terms, recognising the importance of ethical and political goals in the practice of public administration.[70] The Haldane Report should therefore be considered together with the development of the role of the Head of the Civil Service and the changes in organisation within the Treasury, both of which were important in the pre-history of administrative reforms introduced later in the century.

The most significant development in the British civil service during the first half of the twentieth century was in the position of the Permanent Secretary to the Treasury as Head of the Civil Service, and the effect it had on the development of a more unified service from what had previously been a number of government departments. It was a development, like others in British central government, to which a variety of factors contributed, but its achievement was particularly associated with Sir Warren Fisher, who served as Permanent Secretary to the Treasury from 1919 to 1939. As Bridges put it in 1964,

'Fisher ... did more than any other man in the last fifty years to give cohesion to the Civil Service and to help to turn the Treasury into a proper instrument to be the Central Department of the British Civil Service'.[71]

As already explained, the change in name for the most senior permanent official in the Treasury dates from 1867. Before then, the position was known as Assistant Secretary. George Alexander Hamilton (who succeeded Sir Charles Trevelyan as Assistant Secretary on 21 January 1859) and the First Lord agreed to this change in May 1867, and it was authorised in a Minute drafted by Hamilton. The reason given was that the functions of the Financial Secretary had increased and consequently so also had the functions of the Assistant Secretary. It was therefore decided by the Treasury Board that 'the office shall now be given a more substantive character than that of Assistant Secretary and they are pleased to direct that its title should be that of "Permanent Secretary"'.[72] As Wright explains, the Permanent Secretary was to have 'particular regard to all increases of Establishments and Salaries in the Public Service', though this was not a new responsibility. The new title for the position continued when Gladstone succeeded Disraeli because no good reason was advanced for changing it and it was felt that the more authoritative title gave increased weight in correspondence with other departments.[73]

By the First World War the position, as it had been defined by Hamilton, had been further strengthened. The Treasury was by that time responsible for approving the whole process of selecting and appointing candidates for the civil service, through powers given by Order in Council to approve proposals from the Civil Service Commissioners.[74] The Treasury also had oversight of all expenditure on civil establishments throughout the public service and worked closely with Parliament as part of its control of public expenditure. Moreover, as a result of these responsibilities, the Treasury was very well informed about the work being done in all government departments. The responsibilities and formal authority exercised by the Treasury and its Permanent Secretary were therefore already stated in various Minutes and Orders in Council, but Fisher brought to the position unusual leadership qualities and a personality not normally expected in a senior bureaucrat. As Sir Horace Hamilton put it in 1951, he had 'a blazing energy, a ruthless determination and a complete absence of fear'.[75] Furthermore, Fisher was appointed in 1919 when the civil service was prepared to accept change and accede to reform proposals resulting from the aftermath of the First World War.

Fisher's career before his appointment to the Permanent

Secretaryship in 1919 demonstrated his single-minded determination, peculiar flair, and ambition. From an early age he decided he wanted to enter the Higher Division of the Civil Service. He joined the Inland Revenue in 1903, soon (in 1907 and 1908)[76] began applying for a transfer to the Treasury, but quickly rose within the Revenue so that in August 1918 he was appointed Chairman of the Board of Inland Revenue. He became Permanent Secretary to the Treasury on 1 October 1919, just after his fortieth birthday. In 1948 Sir James Grigg referred to Fisher as

> one of the most remarkable men the Civil Service has ever produced . . . he did much to unify the Civil Service . . . in 1933 the Civil Service was more united, more efficient and of greater esteem as well as influence than it has ever been before or since.[77]

A useful short biography on Fisher by Hamilton was published in *Public Administration* in 1951,[78] and a thorough biography by Eunan O'Halpin was published in 1989.[79]

Before Fisher's appointment to the Treasury, the department had three joint Permanent Secretaries (Sir Robert Chalmers, Sir John Bradbury and Sir Thomas Heath) but this was widely recognised as being a poor arrangement. Therefore when Fisher was appointed as its single permanent head the opportunity was also taken to reorganise the most senior appointments. The new arrangement consisted of Fisher as Permanent Secretary, together with Controllers of Departments. The functions of the Permanent Secretary were, as stated in the Treasury Minute of 4 September 1919, to include 'responsibility for the organisation of the Treasury, for the general supervision and co-ordination of the work of the Treasury as a whole, and for advising the Board'. He was to 'act as Permanent Head of the Civil Service and advise the First Lord in regard to Civil Service appointments and decorations'. The Controllers, responsible for Finance, Establishments, and Supply Services, were to have the status in the civil service of Heads of Departments and were directly responsible to the Treasury Board.[80] This meant, as Fisher told the Public Accounts Committee in 1936, that the Permanent Secretary to the Treasury was left 'deliciously vague, floating somewhere rather Olympian'.[81] He did his best to work the scheme (which he had no part in designing), but 'it was an extremely unwieldy and top-hampered and unsatisfactory arrangement'.[82] In fact, it was this arrangement which provided unique flexibility and enabled him to concentrate on broad principles, operate in his very individual style, and develop his conceptions for the Treasury and for the civil service.

Fisher's conception of the Treasury was 'a sort of clearing house, or general staff',[83] which stopped taking the best recruits from the open competitive examinations and instead took 'picked youngsters' who had already had experience in other departments. According to Fisher this change was liked by other departments[84] because it meant that Treasury officials had some experience of administrative practice, which was a good training for Treasury work, and meant that they were not just recruits from universities who joined the Treasury without any other experience, and where they further developed a specialist style of criticism.[85] He told the Public Accounts Committee on 30 April 1936, when referring to administrative class civil servants, 'which is the Commissioned rank of the Service', that he always recruited his juniors in the Treasury from other departments.[86]

Although there are earlier references to the Permanent Secretary to the Treasury as official Head of the Civil Service, there was no official and authoritative reference to the position before the Treasury Minute of September 1919. As Bridges has explained, 'over both the duties and the title, what was done in 1919 and 1920 was to substitute for a rather vague informal arrangement something clear, precise and formal'.[87] Fisher, however, regarded this title as of considerable importance. In evidence to the Tomlin Commission in 1930 he wrote that

> until relatively recent years the expression 'Civil Service' did not correspond either to the spirit or to the facts of the organisation so described. . . . Departments did not really think of themselves as merely units of a complete and correlated whole; and in the recognition by each Department of the existence of others there was, from time to time, an attitude of superiority, of condescension, of resentment, or even of suspicion.

This departmentalism he regarded as the antithesis of a 'Service'. He wanted to combine the entities into a service with an '*esprit de corps* and co-operative sense and informed by the spontaneous interchange of experience and knowledge'.[88] According to Hamilton, the phrase that was always on Fisher's lips was 'team work'.[89] O'Halpin has similarly emphasised Fisher's references to the necessity for good faith and teamwork in the civil service, and, as an example, in evidence to the Tomlin Commission, Fisher wrote of the 'evergrowing team sense in all ranks; it pervades the whole conduct of public business'.[90]

One of the functions specified for the Head of the Civil Service in 1919 was to advise the Prime Minister on civil service appointments and decorations. This was later linked to the Prime Minister's consent that was required 'to the appointment (or removal) of Permanent

Heads of Departments, their Deputies, Principal Financial Officers and Principal Establishment Officers'. This was in accordance with Fisher's advice, that in order to achieve economy and efficiency it was necessary to appoint the ablest men, selected from the whole of the civil service. Again, in evidence to the Tomlin Royal Commission on the Civil Service in 1930 Fisher explained how the merits of candidates for high posts was kept under review:

> In the first place, it is completely informal; the less formal it is the greater the likelihood, in my opinion, of the eventual judgment being correct. My colleagues in Departments, whenever they may come into my room, in the course of discussion sooner or later get on to this question, and they are themselves looking out for people. Names are canvassed; it may be that no vacancy is in sight. Thus in the most informal way a trend of opinion gradually forms itself as to the suitability of people, either particularly or generally, for this class of post.[91]

Fisher's style was to work with maximum informality, using semi-official correspondence rather than formal official letters, and relying on seeing people and speaking to them to get his ideas across. It was in this way that his views became widely known and the high standards he upheld became the expected standards of conduct for civil servants. Occasionally these standards were promulgated in an official report or statement, like the famous report on the Francs case.[92] The details of that particular inquiry into alleged impropriety are now less significant than the stand taken by Fisher and his two colleagues who conducted the inquiry 'as three Civil Servants of some experience and jealous for the honour and traditions of the Service'.[93] The report ended with the often quoted statement about the standards expected of civil servants:

> Practical rules for the guidance of social conduct depend ... as much upon the instinct and perception of the individual as upon cast-iron formulas; and the surest guide will, we hope, always be found in the nice and jealous honour of Civil Servants themselves. The public expects from them a standard of integrity and conduct not only inflexible but fastidious, and has not been disappointed in the past. We are confident that we are expressing the view of the Service when we say that the public have a right to expect that standard, and that it is the duty of the Service to see that the expectation is fulfilled.[94]

It was primarily in evidence to various committees and commissions that Fisher made his clearly held views known. Such inquiries also provided opportunities for him to lay down effectively, as Head of the Civil Service, the principles by which he expected civil servants to be guided in their daily work. For example, in evidence to the Tomlin Royal Commission on the Civil Service he said:

> The presentation of integrity, fearlessness, and independence of thought and utterance in their private communion with Ministers of the experienced officials selected to fill the top posts in the Service is an essential principle in enlightened Government; as – whether or not Ministers accept the advice thus frankly placed at their disposal, and acceptance or rejection of such advice is exclusively a matter for their judgment – it enables them to be assured that their decisions are reached only after the relevant facts and the various considerations have, so far as the machinery of Government can secure, been definitely brought before their minds.[95]

Fisher's considerable achievement as Head of the Civil Service was to advance the sense of unity in the service. He built upon the reforms of the nineteenth century, which introduced a common system of recruitment. He encouraged informality and team spirit between departments and between staff. Indeed, this is especially well illustrated by the Civil Service Sports Council, founded in 1921, and which on one occasion Fisher defended because 'It centralises, in the best sense; it makes them (i.e. the fellows involved in the civil service sports movement) feel a Service instead of a lot of Departments'.[96] He also influenced the selection of staff to the most senior posts by making recommendations across departmental boundaries, so that the best talents were developed from the whole of the civil service. Above all, Fisher encouraged and developed a civil service ethic, involving standards of conduct for officials, both in their daily work and in other aspects of their daily lives. On a number of occasions he expounded the role he saw for the civil service: 'There are four Crown Services, the Defence Departments and my own, and we are the Cinderella'.[97]

The position of Head of the Civil Service was therefore effectively established by Fisher and from it the sense of unity in the civil service was developed. Both these developments were advanced further by Edward Bridges, who served as Secretary to the Cabinet during the Second World War and as Head of the Civil Service from 1945 to 1956. Bridges, like Fisher, contributed to its ethos and traditions and set a high standard by his own example of how civil servants ought to behave. However, as O'Halpin has noted, neither Fisher's immediate predecessors nor his successors had anything like his range of activities, with influence extending far beyond the normal expectations of the duties of his office.[98] Bridges was, of course, influenced by Fisher, but his major contributions as Head of the Civil Service were probably the distillation into succinct statements of principle commonsense wisdom arising from wide practical experience and its application to particular cases. When the work of Fisher and Bridges is considered in relation to the civil service in general, it is therefore not surprising that by the middle of the twentieth century the unity of the civil service was, as Hamilton put it in 1951, 'accepted as a commonplace of administration'.[99] It is also not surprising that in 1964 Bridges wrote that 'Throughout the Civil Service there is a great sense that it is a single Service . . . [and] the management of the Civil Service is something which cannot be divided up into self-contained pieces entrusted to different authorities'.[100] It was the leadership of the unified service that became one of the prime functions of the Treasury, under the responsibility of its permanent secretary who was also Head of the Civil Service.

Whilst the Treasury had been internally reformed after the First World War, and the Haldane recommendations to strengthen Treasury control over questions of staffing and organisation were implemented under the leadership of the Head of the Civil Service, the Treasury also enhanced its role in the control and influence of the national economy – and this was especially significant in the period after the Second World War. Indeed, in many respects administrative reform in the period from 1945 to the mid-1960s can be interpreted in terms of working through and applying recommendations for reform, or the practical evolution of reforms, which had been largely set in motion during or as a consequence of the two world wars.[101] In relation to the national economy the Treasury's role was enhanced, on the one hand, by reforming both itself and the wider civil service to make them better equipped to deal with their tasks; and, on the other hand, by taking a more active role in relation to the national economy. These two elements should be seen as closely interrelated not just in the period after 1945, but during the half century from 1914.

The internal restructuring of the Treasury following Fisher's appointment has already been explained, as has the more professional emphasis on accountability; these were accompanied by related changes within all the major departments of government including the creation of Establishment Officers, as recommended by the Haldane Committee. Moreover, these reforms were implemented at a time when staff associations were growing in significance, when Whitley Councils were introduced into the civil service as an enlightened new feature of personnel management, and when, after the Second World War, there was a new emphasis on the importance of staff training and new techniques of organisation and management. The consequence was a new style of management in the public services, pioneered by central government from the Treasury. Nevertheless, the reforms never really satisfied critics that the civil service in general was doing enough, or doing it well enough, to meet the challenges of the times.

The Treasury's overall control of civil service staffing, which had its origins in Treasury control of expenditure, was considerably enhanced after the First World War, not only by the creation of establishment officers in all government departments to work with the Treasury in supervising and organising personnel, but also by the other measures instituted and encouraged by Fisher to develop a unified civil service. This enhancement was further strengthened by the role the staff associations found themselves playing in the new Whitley Councils. Whitley Councils were recommended as a means for improving the relations between staff and management through committees on which both were represented. The National Whitley Council was a large and unwieldy body of fifty-four members, and from its outset in 1919 the Treasury took the lead on the Official Side.[102] However, Whitleyism was, in practice, effective nationally primarily through its sub-committees and informal contacts and, especially, through similar structures in departments. Indeed, this approach to industrial relations was so successful in the civil service that it was admired and copied by other countries.[103]

After the Second World War new emphasis was placed on training, mainly as a result of the work of the Committee on the Training of Civil Servants under the chairmanship of Ralph Assheton, which reported in 1944.[104] This committee was set up in 1943 as a result of a recommendation from the Select Committee on National Expenditure, and its main recommendations became the basis for civil service training in the immediate post-war period. The Training and Education Division of the Treasury was created in 1945, to co-ordinate departmental training and run a variety of central courses, and a National Whitley Council Joint Committee on Training was formed to assist the Treasury in formulating training policies. These developments were important in the pre-history of the Treasury's Centre for Administrative Studies, which opened in 1963, and the CAS in turn was important in the pre-history of the Civil Service College.[105]

The other significant innovation which emerged after the Second World War was the pioneering work to improve civil service procedures and the more effective achievement of objectives through organisation and methods work. The origins of the work have been traced by Roseveare to one of the divisions created in 1919 within the Treasury's Establishments Department. The functions of the division included: 'Routine, i.e. questions of office machinery, the keeping of registers, records and statistics, the employment of labour-saving appliances in the Public Service' and 'Special investigations, as required into methods of work, output, etc.'.[106] However, the Second World War had stimulated as much discussion about the administration of central government as had the First World War, and the O and M Division was formally created in 1941 out of the Investigation Section of the Treasury, and as a response to public criticisms of the civil service on grounds of inefficiency. The main purpose of the O and M Division was to offer advice when called upon by departments. The division flourished and inaugurated the *O and M Bulletin* in 1945, which later became *Management Services in Government*, then *Management in Government*, before it ceased publication in 1984. It also published a manual on Organisation and Methods techniques which became a Stationery Office best-seller.

These new approaches and achievements, mainly emanating from Treasury initiatives (even though it should be acknowledged that some of the initiatives were in response to publicly expressed recommendations and/or criticisms) meant that the Treasury's role and status within central government continued to grow, though usually with the utmost economy and often with inadequate staffing. Furthermore, these achievements during the period from 1914 to 1962 were at a time when the country was facing economic problems of unprecedented magnitude, and the ideology of successive governments, the people as a whole and, surprisingly, all political parties, favoured a more positive role for government. Consequently, where new functions had to be added to the activities of government and there was no obvious department to which they should be allocated, they tended to remain with the Treasury. The effect was that by 1947 the Treasury was responsible for nineteen votes in the annual accounts. These included: the registration of electors; the Treasury and subordinate departments; Privy Seal Office; government hospitality; repayment to the Local Loans Fund; Royal Commissions; the Secret Service; repayments to the Civil Contingencies Fund; scientific investigation; universities and colleges; financial assistance in development areas; rates on government property; and advances to allies.[107]

The country's serious economic problems in the period following the Second World War meant that the Treasury was therefore assuming a new role; it was also attracting new criticism. One of the most far-reaching aspects of its new role, and its approach to dealing with economic problems, was its association with J. M. Keynes. Keynes, then a Cambridge don, made his first appearance in the Treasury as early as Sunday, 2 August 1914, when he assisted in drafting finance papers for Lloyd George. In 1915 a Treasury Minute recorded that he had been assisting the Treasury at the Chancellor's request, but by 1917 he was sufficiently well established for a new unit (called 'A' Division) to be created to contain Keynes and his assistants.[108]

The proportion of the Gross National Product being devoted to public expenditure was growing throughout this period. In 1900 it was 14 per cent; in 1938 it had risen to 33 per cent; and in 1961, to 38 per cent.[109] When it is also remembered that Britain had 1,300,000 unemployed at the outbreak of the Second World War, it is evident that even before that war government policies had a considerable influence on the national economy. It is therefore surprising that such modest resources in the Treasury were devoted to long-term planning – indeed, the Financial Enquiries Branch, headed by Sir Ralph Hawtrey, which dealt with such matters, consisted, according to Roseveare, of little more than a man and a boy.[110]

The Second World War produced a new demand for co-ordination of the national economy. In November 1939 a Central Economic Information Service was established under Lord Stamp, and from this, in January 1941, were developed the Economic Section of the Cabinet Office and the Central Statistical Office. Sir John Anderson became Lord President (virtually 'Prime Minister of the Home Front', in Churchill's phrase) and emerged as the effective co-ordinator of economic policy. With the influence of Keynes, who was back in the Treasury as an adviser from 1940, and the academic economists who worked with him, together with the economic co-ordination of Anderson and his Lord President's Committee, a new policy became acceptable. Emphasis was placed on allocating total national resources in such a way as to maximise the war effort and to prevent the 'frivolous' misuse of such resources by private individuals. National income accounting rather than public revenue accounting became the Treasury's job. This function continued in peace-time, when all aspects of the economy remained highly regulated; even after 1951, when many of these controls began to disappear, the importance of Keynesian tools for demand management (mainly to keep unemployment down) perpetuated the Treasury role in economic, as opposed to merely fiscal, policy. The Cambridge economists, as they became known, made their mark in persuading the Treasury to use the instruments of government, especially taxation and exchange control, the bank rate, the issue of Treasury bills and government stock, to produce a 'managed economy'.

After the War, Herbert Morrison, the Lord President of the Council in the new Labour Government, continued to exercise responsibilities of economic co-ordination; but in March 1947, when Morrison became ill during a period of economic crisis, it was decided to create a new Economic Planning Staff of departmental officials under the chairmanship of Sir Edwin Plowden. The main function of this Central Economic Planning Staff was to develop a long-term plan for the use of the country's manpower and resources.[111] A few months after it was set up, on 29 September, Sir Stafford Cripps was given the new role of Minister for Economic Affairs, with overall responsibility for the Economic Planning Staff, the Economic Information Unit and the Economic Section of the Cabinet Office. However, when Hugh Dalton resigned as Chancellor of the Exchequer on 12 November 1947, he was succeeded by Cripps, who took with him to the Treasury all the responsibilities he had as Minister of Economic Affairs. The new arrangements were made clear by the Prime Minister who announced on 2 February 1948 in the House of Commons:

> the Central Economic Planning Staff under Sir Edwin Plowden, and the staff of the former office of the Minister for Economic Affairs, retain their identity, but now form part of the Treasury organisation and discharge their general co-ordinating functions under the direction of the Chancellor.[112]

To assist him, when Cripps took the additional responsibilities with him to the Treasury, he was provided with an additional Parliamentary Secretary, known as the Economic Secretary to the Treasury, who was to be concerned with 'general economic policy and planning, including the economic aspects of Treasury supply work, overseas financial negotiations, and internal financial planning'.[113] This sequence of events (helped also by such other factors as the nationalisation of the Bank of England in 1946) therefore resulted in consolidating in the Treasury all the responsibilities for regulating the national economy and made the Treasury the centre for economic planning and co-ordination – an aspect of Treasury control which was consolidated under the succeeding Conservative governments.[114]

According to Bridges, in the late 1940s the Treasury's 'prudent housekeeping' was a 'judicious blend' of departmental self-control and Treasury supervision. Bridges championed the Treasury man as arbiter in 'weighing up facts and testing evidence and judging men', against commonsense administrative standards.[115] It was this approach, emphasising the virtues of the generalist, which became the focus for critics both within Parliament and, more generally, outside.

In 1958 a sub-committee of the Select Committee on Estimates inquired into various aspects of Treasury control. It took evidence, reviewed the methods of Treasury control, and made the important recommendation that a small independent committee should be appointed, with access to Cabinet papers, to report upon the theory and practice of Treasury control of expenditure.[116] The Treasury's observations on the report supported the recommendation but pointed out that if the inquiry was to have access to Cabinet papers, the committee would have to be a government inquiry, under the authority of the Chancellor of the Exchequer. It was therefore under these limitations that Lord Plowden was appointed chairman, with a small committee of three businessmen who also had civil service experience, to undertake the task.

The Plowden Committee issued a number of confidential reports and a summary of its conclusions, now known as the Plowden Report, which was published in June 1961.[117] The Report's central recommendation was that public expenditure (which, by then, had risen to 42 per cent of GNP) should be considered 'as a whole, over a period of years ahead, in relation to prospective resources' (para. 12). This required the Treasury to re-direct its energies into controlling the 'policy' and the 'programme' stages (paras 79, 80) and this in turn required 'a wider application of mathematical techniques, statistics and accountancy, to problems of public expenditure' (para. 30). 'Management' was a key concept in the Plowden Report, which recommended the centralised promotion of new techniques and services – scientific, statistical and 'O and M'. The Plowden Report, which marked the end of the post-war period in the Treasury, also marks the beginning of a period emphasising more professional management, a period which stretches from 1962 to the present day.

FROM 1962 TO 1992

The Plowden Report had a number of important consequences for the Treasury in particular, as well as for the public service in general. These include the creation of the Public Expenditure Survey Committee (PESC); a reallocation of functions within the Treasury; a boost to criticisms of the civil service, mainly because of the high status given to generalists in the service and the emphasis on the need for management expertise in the Report; and a major stimulation towards improving the quality of management through training and the development of management techniques. These phenomena were interrelated and affected each other, though they will be outlined in sequence here. Together, however, they had a major impact contributing both to the role of the Treasury in policy-making in the 1990s and also to radical change in the nature of the civil service.

PESC was the committee of principal finance officers of the major spending departments, chaired by a Treasury deputy secretary, which considered reports from the Treasury on the forecasts of departmental expenditure. As an innovation of the 1960s its origins are generally thought to lie in the Plowden Report, although there is also evidence that spending plans covering periods of four or five years were in existence before 1961.[118] The difference after Plowden is essentially that the planning approach was regularised as a system, compared with previous piecemeal attempts and, more importantly, the various plans covering different departments were brought together and considered against a forecast of the growth of national income.[119] From 1965 this process was conducted at Cabinet level against a consideration of how much could be afforded and a decision of priorities between departments. Since 1969 White Papers on public expenditure resulting from the PESC exercise have been published regularly, on an annual basis. In its early years the development of PESC became co-ordinated with the technique of Programme Analysis and Review (PAR).[120] PAR can, in turn, be traced back to early attempts in the 1960s to introduce programme budgeting into the departments of central government. Later, the PAR exercises in departments were complemented by the work at Cabinet level of the Central Policy Review Staff (CPRS) – created after the 1970 White Paper on *The Reorganisation of Central Government*.[121] PAR was intended to ensure that departments had clear objectives and statements of priority that were presented for central consideration before resource allocation began, and CPRS was a specialist unit which was primarily concerned with analysing issues for the Cabinet. Both PAR and CPRS were later abandoned by the Thatcher Government in favour of other approaches which included efficiency scrutinies and a determined effort to reduce the scope of government activity. More recently, PESC also was abolished, and now survives as no more than an interdepartmental circulation list for papers about the running of the public expenditure system and especially the Survey. The current arrangements for the central examination of departmental priorities and resource allocation are explained in the next chapter.

A second major result of the Plowden Report was reorganisation within the Treasury, though it should be noted that the actual reorganisation went further than the Plowden recommendations. Nevertheless, as Sir Richard Clarke has put it, this was the biggest Treasury reorganisation since 1919, and was planned to enable the Treasury to carry out effectively the functions laid down by the Plowden Committee and the new tasks for the chief economic department involved in the government's 'interventionist' policies.[122] From 1962 the Treasury was organised in two sides, each under a permanent secretary – a 'Finance and Economic side', and a 'Pay and Management' side. This meant that for the first time[123] the distribution of duties in the Treasury between divisions and groups was almost entirely on a functional basis. Within the two 'sides' there were five groups: Pay and Management were two groups on one 'side', and Finance, Public Sector, and National Economy were on the other 'side'. Looked at another way, there were about thirty-five traditional divisions within the five groups, though some of them were called by other terms (e.g. one service, one section, and several branches).[124] The somewhat awkward arrangement[125] of a government department with two joint heads which had existed in the Treasury since Bridges' retirement in 1956 continued until 1968 when the Civil Service Department was created.

According to Bridges, the new functional organisation approach increased the importance of securing the fullest day-to-day contacts and proper co-ordination between the groups and sides of the Treasury.[126] The consequences were that, for example, a new National Economy Division 2 was set up with responsibilities for policies connected with economic growth; also, in the new mixed divisions, administrators and economists worked more closely together so that their different training and experience interacted. However, according to Samuel Brittan, despite these intentions and the new functional internal structure, the centre of gravity of economic policy began to shift slightly away from the Treasury.[127] This was partly because of a series of major inquiries set up to consider various problems of social reconstruction, but it was also because of the creation in 1961 of the National Economic Development Council (Neddy) as an organisation concerned with indicative planning and as part of a group of measures for dealing with the balance of payments crisis. The Council in fact first met on 7 March 1962 under the chairmanship of the Prime Minister and subsequently held monthly meetings usually chaired by the Chancellor of the Exchequer. It included other ministers, employers, trade unionists and one or two 'independents'. Neddy was assisted by a number of Economic Development Committees (known as Little Neddies), concerned with particular industries, and by the

National Economic Development Office, which produced briefings for the Director General and for Council members, and supplied staff for the Little Neddies. The centre of gravity of economic policy, and of other fields of Treasury work, shifted much more radically later in the 1960s when, in response to growing criticism of public sector institutions, the Labour Government elected in 1964 made significant changes in the most important institutions of central government. These included creating the Department of Economic Affairs (1964) and the Civil Service Department (1968). Both these major changes in the machinery of government are explained below.

These structural changes, and others elsewhere in the public sector, were in response to public discussion and pressure from the political environment. From about 1960 there was a spate of introspective books and articles critically analysing British institutions and calling for modernisation. These included Thomas Balogh's essay 'The Apotheosis of the Dilettante',[128] published in 1959, Brian Chapman's *British Government Observed* (1963),[129] and the Fabian tract *The Administrators* (1964).[130] In 1964 Harold Wilson, interviewed by Norman Hunt for the BBC, explained that he was worried about what he felt was the amateurism of the central direction of government and he outlined reforms he had in mind if Labour won the general election – including the better use of experts, more transfers into and out of the civil service and a strengthened Cabinet Secretariat.[131] This was soon followed, in 1965, by a Report from the Select Committee on Estimates on 'Recruitment to the Civil Service' which recommended a committee to examine and report upon the structure, recruitment and management of the civil service.[132] Consequently Harold Wilson, re-elected as Prime Minister after the 1966 General Election, set up the Fulton Committee on the Civil Service. Much has been written about the Fulton Committee,[133] and there is no need here to review again its general recommendations. However, for the purposes of the history of the Treasury it is important to note that one of the major findings of the Fulton Committee's investigations was that the civil service had too few civil servants who were skilled managers. Indeed, in its highly controversial first chapter, the Fulton Report strongly criticised what it called the 'tradition of the "all-rounder"' and 'the cult of the amateur'. To overcome the management defects it found, the Fulton Committee recommended more training in management for scientists and other specialists, more specialisation for administrators, and the application of the principles of 'accountable management' in the organisation of executive activities. Its specific recommendations therefore included the creation of a new Civil Service Department, the creation of a new Civil Service College, and the wider use and promulgation of the best management techniques. These features of the Fulton Report were therefore consistent with the approach recommended by informed critics and fitted in well with the emphasis on improving the quality of public service management which had been highlighted in the Plowden Report, but which had also featured prominently in the specialist literature as well as in the media throughout the 1960s.

On the day the Fulton Report was published, in 1968, the Prime Minister announced that a new Civil Service Department (CSD) would be created, covering the previous responsibilities of the Pay and Management Divisions of the Treasury and the Civil Service Commission. He also announced the establishment of the Civil Service College with three centres (one at the non-residential Centre for Administrative Studies in London, one at Sunningdale and one in Edinburgh). The College headquarters was formally opened by Mr Edward Heath as one of his first engagements as Prime Minister, on 26 June 1970, and the Edinburgh Centre was opened in November 1970. The work of the Treasury Centre for Administrative Studies was developed by extending the course for assistant principals from twenty weeks to twenty-eight weeks and instituting five different varieties of six-week courses.

Associated with the criticisms of the Treasury and the civil service there was a growth of interest in the machinery of government. It became fashionable to explain the post-war economic failures of Britain not only in terms of its amateur approach to management problems but also in terms of a faulty administrative structure. Harold Wilson, as Prime Minister of the newly elected Labour Government in 1964, was sympathetic to many of the criticisms and responded by making a number of major structural changes in the machinery of government. One of these was to institute a new Ministry of Technology 'to guide and stimulate a major effort to bring advanced technology and new processes into British industry'.[134] Another innovation, more significant in terms of the present discussion, was the creation of the Department of Economic Affairs (DEA), which was intended to have responsibility for long-term planning and for bringing about 'structural' changes in the economy while leaving financial management to the Treasury. Neither of these new departments lasted long, however, partly because they were not sufficiently carefully planned in advance, partly because of economic factors which the government could not control, and partly because of personality and other problems within the government. Wilson's intention was that the

DEA would be 'concerned with real resources, with economic planning, with strengthening our ability to export and to save imports, with increasing productivity, and our competitiveness in domestic and export markets'.[135] Mr George Brown, the first Secretary of State for Economic Affairs, was an enthusiastic and energetic ambassador for his department, and replaced the Chancellor as the Chairman of Neddy, but it was not always clear where the dividing line came between the responsibilities of the DEA on the one hand, and the Treasury and Board of Trade on the other. This, in turn, did not make for the best interdepartmental relationships.

These difficulties of overlapping functions and shared responsibility between departments were even more significant in relation to the CSD. The CSD was established in 1968 to implement one of the most important recommendations in the Fulton Report, but it was a development that had a surprisingly long pre-history. The most important event in its early pre-history was the 1914 Report of the MacDonnell Royal Commission on the Civil Service which recommended 'the creation within the Treasury, and subject to its administrative orders, of a special section for the general supervision and control of the Civil Service'.[136] This seems to have been the beginning of the idea that control of departmental expenditure on administration should be organised at the centre but separately from the control of expenditure on policy. However, the idea was taken further by the Haldane Committee, which recommended a separate branch within the Treasury, specialising in 'establishment' work, and by the Bradbury Committee which, in 1919, also recommended the creation of 'a special Establishment Division at the Treasury' with responsibilities for close personal relations with departmental establishment officers and for studying the scientific organisation of staff. The Bradbury Committee said it had considered whether this staff should be separated from the Treasury, but concluded that as its functions were essentially those which should be performed by the Treasury, the intervention of a third authority would entail friction and duplication of work.[137]

As has already been explained, Fisher, as Permanent Secretary to the Treasury and Head of the Home Civil Service, played a major role in developing a unified service, with the Treasury as its base department, and under his leadership the Treasury took the lead on the Official Side of the National Whitley Council. However, in evidence to the Tomlin Royal Commission, Fisher clearly stated that in his opinion there was no advantage in the proposal for creating a separate department with its own minister to deal with establishments work, and referred to it as 'a fifth wheel to the coach'. According to Fisher, a minister responsible for such a department would have 'to square the Chancellor of the Exchequer', then 'these Treasury officials come into play, so all you do is to make a much more cumbrous machine, with not a vestige of advantage to anybody'.[138] Bridges had a similar attitude when he was reflecting on the Plowden Report and its effects, in his book *The Treasury* (published in 1964). He wrote: 'I am particularly glad that, in framing the new organisation, the temptation has been firmly resisted to take the management side out of the Treasury and to make it into a separate department'.[139]

For most of the period since the First World War the Treasury continued to be a focus for various sorts of criticism. These criticisms can be traced in a number of official reports, but they were particularly sharply focused in the 1942 Report from the Select Committee on National Expenditure.[140] It found that the period from 1919 to 1939 was marked by an almost complete failure to foster the systematic study of organisation as applied to government departments. However, after a careful review of all the arguments it did not recommend setting up a new department, but instead proposed reforms to increase the confidence of civil servants in the personnel management expertise of the Treasury. In 1963–64 the Select Committee on Estimates again considered this question and its report[141] drew attention to a number of related issues which, later, were further considered by the Fulton Committee on the Civil Service.

Many of the feelings about Treasury arrogance and superiority, mentioned earlier in this chapter, resurfaced. Sir James Grigg, whose book *Prejudice and Judgment* was published in 1948, reflected on his own entry into the Treasury in 1913 and explained how he was sent on missions to other departments 'invariably to see officials very much senior to myself and to lay down the law to them. No wonder the Treasury was disliked in those days!'[42] In the 1960s there was considerable resentment about the quality of personnel management in the civil service (for which the Treasury was blamed) and suggestions for radical change that would shake up the system and make it more amenable to new ideas, but sometimes statements by writers who might have been expected to be sensitive on this issue did not help. Bridges, for example, who had spent all his civil service career in the Treasury, apart from his war-time experience as Secretary to the Cabinet, wrote confidently in 1964 that Treasury staff had 'a rather harder time than most of their opposite numbers in other departments'.[143]

It was therefore not very surprising that the Fulton Committee found that the central management of the Treasury had been 'patchy rather than systematic, with too few staff and too little expertise'[144] and it concluded that the Treasury must accept its share of responsibility for the defects that were revealed. The Treasury, it said, had failed to keep the service up to date.[145] It therefore recommended that the responsibility for recruitment and selection should be more closely associated with the other functions of central management in a single organisation, and the expanded and unified central management of the service should be made the responsibility of a new department created specifically for that purpose.[146] Furthermore, because the Committee saw among civil servants a lack of confidence in the Treasury as the centre of civil service management, a change was necessary to demonstrate to them that a fresh start was being made.[147] However, in the Committee's opinion it was in the interests of the service for the Prime Minister to be seen as ultimately responsible for the total task of managing the service, and the Committee therefore recommended that that responsibility should continue, though day-to-day management should be delegated to a non-departmental minister of appropriate authority who was also a member of the Cabinet.[148] The Committee saw the CSD as becoming the power-house for reform and initiative and made setting up the CSD the first priority in its recommendations; it should have wider functions than those previously performed by the 'Pay and Management' group of divisions of the Treasury, which it should take over; it should absorb the Civil Service Commission; and the Civil Service College, which the Committee also strongly recommended, should be under its general direction. The Permanent Secretary of the CSD should be designated Head of the Civil Service. It said that all the functions that belonged to the Treasury in its role as 'employer' should be transferred to the new department, leaving to the Treasury responsibility for advising the Chancellor of the Exchequer on the overall control and allocation of public expenditure, on financial and fiscal policy and on the general management of the economy.[149]

The CSD was established on 1 November 1968 not by an Act of Parliament but by an Order in Council: 'The Minister for the Civil Service Order' (No. 1656) – a procedure entirely consistent with precedent for regulating the civil service. The proposed relationship between the CSD and the Treasury was set out in Office Notice (68)59 on 25 October 1968, which became known as 'The Concordat'. 'The Concordat' stressed the need for close liaison and consultation between the two departments and proposed the establishment of formal links which, however, the CSD and Treasury seem in 1980 to have agreed did not, in fact, materialise.[150]

The CSD quickly grew and established itself as a significant force within central government. The Civil Service Commission was incorporated within it; the Civil Service College, when it was formally launched in 1970, became part of it; in 1972 the Central Computer Agency was set up within it and brought within the department the old Management Service (Computer) Division of the Treasury, HMSO's Computer Procurement Division and Central Computer Bureau, and the Technical Support Unit from the Department of Trade and Industry. A high profile was maintained by Sir William Armstrong, its first Permanent Secretary and Head of the Civil Service; progress reports on its work were published;[151] a new annual publication, *Civil Service Statistics*, was inaugurated; and a new computer was acquired to be the nerve centre for PRISM (Personnel Record Information System for Management). On 1 January 1981 the staff of the CSD totalled 3,197.[152] These are only a few examples of well publicised developments. The tide of optimism was full and the CSD was popularly expected to work wonders in the civil service.

However, the tide turned in the 1970s. In 1973 the CSD published its last annual report and progress reports published by the National Whitley Council ceased after 1971. In 1976 the Principal of the Civil Service College was retired early and the status of his post was downgraded; the College's Edinburgh Centre was closed in 1973 as a contribution to economies in public expenditure. In 1977 the Select Committee on Expenditure inquired into the civil service and heard criticisms that the department did not have sufficient power to make an impact on departments, and that its ministers, who spent a lot of their time on other duties, never seemed to have mastered its problems. Sir John Hunt, then Secretary to the Cabinet, explained that he thought the case for setting up the CSD at the time it was set up was 'absolutely overwhelming', but that 'the separation of supply expenditure from establishment expenditure between the Treasury and the CSD was always a little illogical'.[153] In its Report the Expenditure Committee suggested that the CSD had 'lost its original drive' and it was 'handicapped by its ambivalent relationship with the Treasury and the inadequacy of its powers'. The Report said: 'It is our view that the separation of control of expenditure from responsibility for efficiency is indefensible. Unless responsibility for expenditure and efficiency is combined at a single central point of Government, there can be no effective control of the civil service',[154] 'we are convinced that responsibility for efficiency and control of expenditure should be vested in a single, central Department'.[155] The Committee's most important recommendation was that the control of manpower and the efficiency of the civil service should be transferred back to the Treasury, and the CSD should be left with responsibility for only personnel, appointments, recruitment, training, pay and pensions.[156] No immediate action was taken and after the 1979 General Election a Conservative Government assumed power. The 1981 Report from the new Treasury and Civil Service Select Committee focused on the CSD, drew attention to the apparent lack of interest in the CSD's work at ministerial level, and recommended that the standing of the CSD should be raised, liaison should be improved between the CSD and the Treasury, and that common services should be shared and some functions transferred.[157]

On 12 November 1981 the Prime Minister announced that the CSD was to be abolished; the Treasury would take control of civil service manpower, pay, superannuation and allowances, and take over responsibility for the Central Computer and Telecommunications Agency; management, organisation, training and overall efficiency including recruitment, training and personnel policy would go to a new Management and Personnel Office under a new Second Permanent Secretary in the Cabinet Office; and the Permanent Secretary to the Treasury and the Secretary to the Cabinet would become joint Heads of the Home Civil Service. An Order in Council (No. 1670 of 1981) to transfer the responsibilities was laid before Parliament on 1 December, but the new arrangements were introduced administratively on 16 November. In 1988 the Management and Personnel Office was abolished and its functions reallocated to the Treasury or to the newly created Office of the Minister for the Civil Service, within the Cabinet Office (OMCS). In 1992 the OMCS was abolished in favour of a new sub-department within the Cabinet Office, the Office of Public Service and Science (OPSS). When Sir Peter Kemp, the Permanent Secretary, who had risen to the grade of Second Permanent Secretary in the civil service without having a university degree, was dismissed soon after the creation of OPSS, his reaction was that Oxbridge had won after all.[158]

Whilst the CSD had to depend on persuasion, the Treasury always retained its control over public expenditure. After the demise of the CSD Sir Robert Armstrong, then Secretary to the Cabinet and Head of the Home Civil Service, explained to the Treasury and Civil Service Committee that the Treasury control of public expenditure

is an established and settled thing that everybody has lived with and knows about. In a sense the Civil Service Department has been struggling . . . because the Treasury have kept this primacy and have . . . in large measure, retained the respect of departments . . . the Civil Service Department does not have that bit of clout in its knapsack.[159]

However, other factors relevant to these developments in recent years should also be noted. Central management work in the civil service was never held in the sort of high regard comparable to policy-making work, and this meant that the CSD was never really attractive to the most able and ambitious civil servants. By 1974 Sir William Armstrong's prestige had suffered when he became personally involved with Prime Minister Edward Heath's corporate economic strategy, and he suffered a nervous breakdown. His successor as Head of the Home Civil Service, Sir Douglas Allen, was much more interested in economic policy than man management. The last CSD Permanent Secretary was Sir Ian Bancroft, who had a particularly unhappy official relationship with Prime Minister Margaret Thatcher. In addition, there was industrial action in the civil service during the 1970s and in those circumstances the department responsible for advocating civil service interests did not find favour with ministers. One of the last, but by no means least important, factors contributing to the demise of the CSD was the view of Sir Derek Rayner, Prime Minister Thatcher's adviser on waste, bureaucracy and efficiency, that all moves to improve fundamentally the efficient organisation of Whitehall would be limited as long as the practical, geographical and philosophical heart of the administration was split between the Treasury in Great George Street at one end of Whitehall and the CSD in the Old Admiralty Building at the other.[160] The present position almost returns the allocation of functions to the Treasury as they were before 1968 – but they are not quite the same, and the Treasury is probably now stronger than it was then, primarily because of the management emphasis in central government that has grown in recent years.

Much of the current management emphasis can, like the other developments of the past thirty years, be traced back to the Plowden Report, for it was the Plowden Report that recommended better use of techniques of management and measurement, and emphasised the importance of improving management throughout the public service.[161] This applied not only to the Treasury's responsibility in allocating economic resources but also to the Treasury's responsibility for the overall efficiency of the public service, and its responsibility for the development of management services and the introduction of new management techniques.[162] Professor W. J. M. Mackenzie expressed the position well in his perceptive and amusing translation of the Plowden Report: 'The functions of policy-making are now concentrated in the Treasury, and it has been given ample power to keep lower management in its place. It is in the hands of the Treasury alone to measure the efficiency of management . . . '.[163]

Since the Plowden Report the Treasury has more or less continuously, in spite of the rise and fall of the CSD, been not only concerned with management efficiency as part of its responsibilities for the control of public expenditure, but also active in promoting new approaches to management that would result in greater efficiency throughout the public service. It has already been explained that PESC and PAR resulted from recommendations in the Plowden Report as, indeed, did the CPRS. However, it should, perhaps, also be noted that it is generally difficult to pinpoint the origin of any particular administrative reforms.[164] The Plowden Report was the product of an 'internal' Treasury committee and some of its recommendations were clearly a boost for already recommended and/or existing policies and practices, though support from the Plowden Committee gave them greater significance and official blessing. The Conservative Government, in power after the 1979 General Election, was pledged to reduce the scope of government, reduce waste, and make government more efficient. This determined emphasis in its approach to government led to the creation of the Prime Minister's Efficiency Unit under Sir Derek Rayner. However, the Efficiency Unit, the Cabinet Office (especially the MPO and, later, the OMCS), and the Prime Minister's Policy Unit have, since their creation, worked together with the Treasury on projects in which they all had an interest.

An example which illustrates this well is the development of the Financial Management Initiative (FMI). This approach to management emerged from an early Rayner scrutiny – a scrutiny being a short-term study of a particular area of work by a small team from the Efficiency Unit. The idea of scrutinies was that although each study is fairly small in scale the effect of scrutinies would, over time, permeate the whole civil service. FMI was therefore an approach to management built upon the experience of MINIS (Management Information System for Ministers), which in turn had resulted from an earlier scrutiny.[165] FMI was designed, to quote the words of the 1982 White Paper:

To promote in each department an organisation and system in which managers at all levels have:

(a)   A clear view of their objectives, and means to assess and, wherever possible, measure outputs or performance in relation to those objectives;

(b) Well defined responsibility for making the best use of their resources, including a critical scrutiny of output and value for money; and

(c) The information (particularly about costs), the training and the access to expert advice that they need to exercise their responsibilities effectively.[166]

In practice, FMI was launched as part of the government's reply to a report from the Treasury and Civil Service Committee, and had Prime Minister Thatcher's strong personal backing. It began by requiring the thirty-one largest departments to produce, by the end of 1983, a detailed appraisal of their current arrangements in the light of the stated FMI principles, and a plan for introducing the changes and systems necessary. The Initiative was promoted and co-ordinated by the Treasury and MPO through a small unit set up for the purpose and consisting of four civil servants and four consultants.[167]

Other management techniques have been stimulated by similar means and they have, for example, included accountable management and performance indicators. There has also been a strong and continuing emphasis on achieving given objectives with efficiency, effectiveness and economy.[168] One of the most important results of introducing these techniques, and of the continuing active co-operation between the Treasury, the Efficiency Unit and the OMCS (and its successors, the OPSS and the OPS) is the creation of executive agencies, and a special case study of their creation is presented in Chapter 4.

FROM TREASURY CONTROL TO MANAGEMENT

This account of the Treasury's development began with the emergence of a Treasurer from the royal household after the Conquest nearly 1,000 years ago, However, although 'Henry the Treasurer' is, according to learned opinion, the first identifiable officer with that title, according to Roseveare 'the origins of the office still remain as mysterious as the migration of eels'.[169] Indeed, the Lord Treasurer (as he was later known) is less important for the purposes of this study than what Roseveare calls the executive routines and judicial problems of the Exchequer. This is because the position of Lord Treasurer was later put into commission, and once this practice became established it was the Secretary to the Commissioners of the Treasury who became the key figure and began to create the procedures which led to the foundation of the modern Treasury. The important break from individual to office was therefore made when the fourth Earl of Southampton, then Lord Treasurer of England, died in 1667; Lords Commissioners succeeded him and Downing became their Secretary. There were other Lord Treasurers after Southampton, but the practice of putting the office into commission has finally and continuously been accepted since 1714.[170] However, it was Downing's appointment that was probably the most significant event in the early history of the Treasury.

Treasury control over government expenditure could only effectively begin when there were appropriate procedures and reliable records. From the beginnings of Treasury control, in fact exercised on behalf of Parliament, the Treasury soon acquired its modern status as the key department of central government. Its power and influence grew from its functions and these functions gave it a special relationship with each of the departments that were dependent on it for the supply of resources. Just as Parliament acquired its powers (e.g. for the redress of grievances) by making conditions on granting supply from taxation, so the Treasury acquired its powers from its role in approving public expenditure.

Over hundreds of years the present arrangements emerged and were improved on a piecemeal basis, a procedure which is entirely consistent with other aspects of the British system of government. Until the twentieth century the Treasury's main functions were prudent housekeeping, but the housekeeping functions became more demanding as the scope of government expanded with the growth of the positive state and the creation of welfare services. Additional functions were assumed when large-scale funding was required to finance the two world wars. This led to changes within the Treasury as it became less concerned with preventing public expenditure and more concerned with ensuring the most prudent and economical spending of money on approved projects.[171] The changes were achieved by increasing Treasury control of the Estimates through the budget, and by Treasury control over procedures and, consequently, over details of public expenditure.

As the twentieth century progressed there were, in addition, ideological changes in the accepted role of government, not only in relation to the scope of governmental activity, but in controlling the national economy. The Treasury itself became more positively engaged in activities that simply did not exist before the important roles conceived for it by Keynes and the Cambridge economists. Other functions were added, as they were considered necessary; new departments were created and later merged into an expanded Treasury. Furthermore, there were changes in the civil service which meant that it developed from staff working in separate and independent departments, into a unified service. One consequence of the development of a unified service was a further enhancement of the functions and status of the Treasury. From responsibility for expenditure, on staff as for other resources, it became a department for the central management of the civil service.

Changes in the Treasury over hundreds of years were rarely achieved by legislation; furthermore, they have rarely been the means to achieving clearly defined long-term goals publicly known in advance. Instead, they have been achieved by a combination of precedents, customs, Orders in Council and apparently straightforward office notices; and they have been made in response to pressures from events, and in response to requirements from government and Parliament. Nevertheless, the changes made by these means are often of fundamental importance, and one of the most significant developments, resulting in a new emphasis most clearly apparent since the Second World War, is the Treasury's role in managing the national economy. It now does this not only in terms of economic policies, through the application of economic theories, and through controls over key institutions concerned with the national economy, but also through a variety of discussions and negotiations and through detailed refinements in the processes of public finance and public sector management. These procedures and arrangements within the modern Treasury, the Treasury's relationships with other institutions, and the constraints imposed upon its daily life from the political environment are considered in the next chapter.

3 Structure and organisation*

The need to raise money for government, and the need to approve expenditure by each of its departments, were the key elements in the development of the Treasury. As the government's finance ministry, it acquired the central role in public policy-making and in running the economy. In addition, but in more recent years, the Treasury has developed new responsibilities in relation to other organisations, such as maintaining an effective legislative and institutional framework for regulating the United Kingdom's banking and financial services sector, and it has also had a growing impact on the country's membership of the European Community. These new responsibilities have extended the powers and influences of the Treasury and added new perspectives to certain Treasury functions in relation to the system of government.

Nevertheless, at all times, and in relation to all its activities, the Treasury continues to be the focus for pressure and influence, not only from other departments and government agencies, but also from non-governmental institutions and interest groups, including many with which it has everyday working relationships. This focus, associated with what is now known as the public expenditure survey, is the key element in understanding the day-to-day work of the modern Treasury. Changes of detail have occurred as a result of the recent integration of the traditional autumn spending round with the budget, but these changes are largely of timing and co-ordination and they have had clear advantages in bringing together tax and spending considerations.[1]

In addition to these continuing responsibilities, the evolution of new procedures, and changes of detail, the government has recently required the Treasury to take a less detailed and more 'strategic'

---

* As some of the terms in this chapter have specialist meanings, there is a glossary in Appendix 1. Readers are encouraged to look at the Appendix before reading this chapter, so that they are aware of the definitions to be found there.

approach to ensuring that departments are efficiently run.[2] The government has also required the Treasury to reconsider much of its work, so that some of it is scaled back or wound up altogether. Indeed, when the Treasury Fundamental Review of Running Costs considered, in 1994, what management and organisational principles to apply, it decided that one of them should be to focus on the Treasury's 'core' activities. By this it meant activities which contributed directly to the organisation's strategic objectives and which, as a result of its skills and management priorities, were ones where Treasury staff enjoyed a clear comparative advantage. It said: 'Even if a "non-core" activity is currently being done perfectly well within the Treasury, our assumption is that it could probably be done more effectively or efficiently somewhere else'.[3]

Together, all these factors mean that in recent years, and especially since about the beginning of the 1990s, the Treasury has been experiencing significant change and has had to develop new structures and procedures to deal with its new tasks and increased pressures. Like other departments, it has become customary for the Treasury to publish a formal statement about its structure and organisation to achieve that purpose. This has been done in greater detail than in the past, and its development and publication is consistent with new approaches to management and with established expectations of accountability in public administration. This information is generally available in a number of Treasury publications and, in particular, is in the Treasury's annual departmental report. Changes in the stated purpose, or aim, are made from time to time to ensure consistency with current practice and also to ensure that its emphasis is in line with the government's philosophy and policies, as well as with its approach to policy implementation. Changes are sometimes modest, as might be expected, though occasionally there are significant alterations with major implications for the structure and organisation of the department. This is well illustrated from recent reports. In 1993 the Treasury's aim was 'to assist Ministers in the formulation and implementation of the Government's economic policy'.[4] In 1994 the overall aim was 'to promote sustained growth and higher living standards'.[5] In 1995 it stated that its overall aim was 'to promote rising prosperity based on sustained economic growth'.[6]

These statements are clearly similar, but the consequences of changes in ideological emphasis, in policy, and in departmental structure and organisation, are apparent and likely to be more evident when there is a change in government. Chapter 2 referred to the 1988 – probably light-hearted – statement of the Permanent Secretary who said that the main single activity in the Treasury at that time was catering. This was because, for accounting purposes, the Civil Service Catering Organisation, later known as Forward, came within the ambit of the Treasury. By 1995 this was no longer so, because the government's emphasis on examining and questioning whether it was necessary for particular activities to continue in the public sector meant that the catering activities had been privatised.

The details of the Treasury's structure and organisation since 1995 are the direct result of the 1994 report of the *Fundamental Review of Running Costs* (popularly known as the *Fundamental Expenditure Review*, or FER). That review was one of a number of departmental reviews set in motion by Mr Michael Portillo when he was Chief Secretary to the Treasury, in an attempt to find ways of balancing the government's books. However, the Treasury review had the advantage of being able to build upon a programme of management change already started by the Permanent Secretary and Treasury Management Board; so Treasury officials may have had a more significant role in its outcome than officials had in comparable reviews elsewhere. The review that was set up in May 1994 therefore considered the objectives of the department and reformulated them to 'articulate more clearly what it is that the Chancellor of the Exchequer has asked the Treasury to achieve'.[7] It then examined the Treasury's current range of activities and considered 'whether these should continue to be done by the Treasury or whether they might more effectively or efficiently be taken forward by other Departments or by the private sector'.[8] The terms of reference for this review clearly came from ministers and were the direct result of the Conservative Government's stated policies to re-examine, and where possible reduce, the scope of government activities.

The fundamental purpose of the Treasury, like all other government departments, is to serve its ministers, and the logical place to begin an explanation of the department's structure and organisation is therefore with an outline of who the Treasury ministers are, and a brief explanation of their current responsibilities. This will be followed by a description and discussion of the current structure and organisation and by comments on relations with other organisations and institutions with which the Treasury has working relationships.

THE MINISTERIAL TEAM AND THEIR RESPONSIBILITIES

As already explained (in Chapter 2), the Treasury is governed, constitutionally, by a Board of Lords Commissioners. This Board consists of the Prime Minister, who is the First Lord of the Treasury, and six other members. The Second Lord is the Chancellor of the Exchequer. The other five members of the Board are known as Junior Lords: they are members of Parliament who have only a slender connection with Treasury business; their main duties are to act as assistants to the Government Chief Whip (who has the title of Parliamentary Secretary to the Treasury). The full Treasury Board now rarely meets; indeed, its last meeting was in 1983, when the then Permanent Secretary to the Treasury was retiring. However, two of the Junior Lords may consti-tute a quorum of the Treasury Board, to relieve the Prime Minister and the Chancellor of the Exchequer of the task of signing those documents which need the approval of the Treasury Board; for example, Statutory Instruments.[9]

The Prime Minister usually takes no part in the day-to-day business of the department, though there is close co-operation between the Office of the Prime Minister and the Treasury, because of the impor-tance of economic policy. Consequently the Chancellor of the Exchequer is the effective Ministerial Head of the Treasury and has overall responsibility to Parliament for all aspects of Treasury manage-ment. The Chancellor also has responsibility to Parliament for a number of other departments and agencies: in 1995 these were HM Customs and Excise, Inland Revenue, Department for National Savings, Registry of Friendly Societies, National Investment and Loans Office, the Paymaster Agency, Central Statistical Office, and the Government Actuary's Department. He is also accountable to Parliament for the Expenditure Votes for Civil Superannuation and Net Payments to European Community Institutions.[10] The 1995 departmental report states that, overall, the Chancellor's Departments were expected to spend around £3,338 million in 1994–95, in addition to some £2,043 million of net payments to European Community Institutions.[11]

In addition to the Chancellor of the Exchequer, the Treasury normally has four other ministers. These are the Chief Secretary (who is a member of the Cabinet), the Financial Secretary, and two others whose titles can vary between the Minister of State, the Paymaster General, the Exchequer Secretary, or the Economic Secretary. Those with the title of Secretary rank as Secretaries to the Treasury Board, but their precise departmental responsibilities vary from time to time and are decided by the Chancellor of the Exchequer of the day. In 1995, for example, the responsibilities were as follows.[12] The Chief Secretary was responsible for the control of public expenditure (including local authority and nationalised industry finance); nationalised industry pay;

and value for money in the public services (including 'Next Steps' agencies). The Financial Secretary was responsible for the largely formal procedure of voting funds by Parliament; other Parliamentary financial business (e.g. concerning the Public Accounts Committee, the Comptroller and Auditor General, the Exchequer and Audit Acts); Inland Revenue taxes (other than oil taxation); general oversight of the Inland Revenue (excluding valuation office); privatisation and wider share ownership policy; European Community business including the Community budget and Economic and Monetary Union; and competition and deregulation policy. The Paymaster General dealt with civil service pay, personnel management, recruitment, relocation and industrial relations; the legislative programme and ministerial correspondence; procurement policy, competitive tendering (including local authorities); public competition and purchasing; Customs and Excise duties and taxes; the general oversight of Customs and Excise; the Environmental Ministerial Group on Women's Issues; and charities (non-tax aspects) including payroll giving and profit related pay. The Economic Secretary was responsible for monetary policy; Treasury responsibilities for the financial system including banks, building societies and other financial institutions; the Department for National Savings; the Registry of Friendly Societies and the National Investment and Loans Office; the Royal Mint; the Government Actuary's Department; the Valuation Office; international financial issues and institutions (other than the European Community); industrial and export credit casework; the Treasury interest in general accounting issues; official statistics and the Central Statistical Office; and North Sea oil and taxation.

As with other departments, Treasury ministers have special advisers – three at the time of writing – who are appointed from outside the civil service, on contract terms, to advise on the political and presentational aspects of Treasury business, drawing on their direct links with parliamentary, party and other political contacts. However, it should be emphasised that these details change from time to time, so for the purposes of this present study they are illustrative only: more up to date information may be obtained from the latest issue of the *Civil Service Yearbook*.

Serving the ministers at the most senior level, at the top of the Treasury's management structure, there is a Treasury Management Board, consisting of the Permanent Secretary and the seven directors – details of their responsibilities are explained later in this chapter. The Treasury Management Board considers major issues of organisation and staffing and has the lead responsibility for ensuring that the

Treasury is resourced, staffed and managed to deliver its objectives as effectively and efficiently as possible. Some members of this top management team carry a greater burden of these overall responsibilities than others: for example, the Financial Management Reporting and Audit Director and the Personnel and Support Director share the lead responsibility for ensuring that the Treasury has the financial provision for staff, information systems and accommodation to do its job properly. Other responsibilities are more widely shared, such as ensuring that Parliament and the public are well informed about the objectives and effects of the government's economic and financial policies (though this area of work is co-ordinated by the Treasury communications team, which is accountable directly to the Permanent Secretary). It is the details of these responsibilities, how the Treasury is structured to meet them, and their relationship to the overall aim of the department that will be considered next.

THE TREASURY'S MISSION AND OBJECTIVES: DEVELOPMENTS FROM THE FUNDAMENTAL EXPENDITURE REVIEW

In order to appreciate the links between ministers and their policies on the one hand, and the organisation structure and management system within the Treasury on the other, it is important to understand how the department's overall aim is developed into the more specific tasks or objectives that become the terms of reference of teams or groups of staff. In the most recent departmental report, and as a direct result of the Treasury's 1994 *Fundamental Expenditure Review*, this is achieved by the mission statement. It is illustrated in Figure 3.1, taken from the 1995 departmental report,[13] which gives details of the Treasury's aim, mission and objectives, and how they are related. As these details differ in a number of respects from comparable information in previous reports it is first necessary to appreciate some of the most significant details of the *Fundamental Expenditure Review* and how the Treasury's previous aims and objectives have been, as the report puts it, 'refined, expanded, and placed explicitly in the context of a more timeless statement of the Treasury's overall mission'.[14]

The 1994 *Fundamental Expenditure Review* was the responsibility of a small team of three Treasury officials under the general guidance of Sir Colin Southgate, the then Chairman of Thorn EMI, the major entertainment and electronics business. It was helped by three project teams, which examined specific issues of a controversial nature. These were: management levels in the Treasury (how many different levels of

AIM

The Treasury's overall aim is to promote rising prosperity based on sustained economic growth

MISSION	OBJECTIVES
In seeking to meet this aim we will:	In seeking to meet this aim we will:
	maintain a stable macroeconomic environment, by
• maintain a stable macroeconomic environment	1 delivering permanently low inflation
	2 maintaining sound public finances
	3 keeping public expenditure to a level that is affordable
	4 pursuing tax policies which generate sufficient revenue, while doing the least damage to the economy and encouraging enterprise
• strengthen the long-term performance of the economy and the outlook for jobs, in strategic partnership with others	**strengthen the long-term performance of the economy and the outlook for jobs, in strategic partnership with others, by**
	5 promoting policies and public expenditure priorities which improve the use of resources and the efficiency of markets throughout the economy, within an affordable level of total public expenditure
	6 maintaining a financial control system which delivers continuing improvements in the efficiency of government
	7 maintaining a framework for government accounting which makes clear how resources are used and provides effective accountability to Parliament
• maintain a professional, well motivated and outward-looking organisation, committed to continuous improvement	8 promoting greater use of private finance in support of services currently provided by the public sector and the privatisation of those parts of the public sector which do not need to remain in public ownership
	9 maintaining a regime for the regulation of financial services which preserves a stable financial system, honest markets and the confidence of investors and depositors, while promoting an open, efficient and competitive financial services sector
	In carrying out all these responsibilities we will
	10 keep abreast of developments in other countries and promote UK economic interests and ideas abroad
	11 ensure that Parliament and the public are well informed about the objectives and effects of the government's economic and financial policies
	and maintain a professional, well motivated and outward looking organisation, committed to continuous improvement by
	12 ensuring that the Treasury is resourced, staffed and managed to deliver its objectives as effectively and efficiently as possible

Figure 3.1 **The Treasury's aim, mission and objectives for 1995–96**
Source: HM Treasury, *Chancellor of the Exchequer's Smaller Departments, Net Payments to European Community Institutions: The Government's Expenditure Plans 1995–96 to 1997–98*, Cm 2817, HMSO, 1995, p. 3

management are required in different parts of the Treasury?); the role and organisation of the Personnel, Finance and Support group (how far should key personnel and other 'support' decisions be taken by line managers and how far should they be determined by the 'centre'?); and the efficient office (how can paper and information handling in the Treasury be made more efficient, through improved working practices and improved IT?).[15] The terms of reference for the review were to consider the coverage of the department's activities, the Treasury's roles and responsibilities vis à vis other organisations, any growth areas of expenditure and how pressures might be contained, the organisation of directorates and the allocation of resources, and the appropriate senior level structure for the department.[16] The review team began work in May 1994[17] and its proposals were published on 19 October.

The review had to take into account the impact of the 1994 White Paper on the Civil Service, which envisaged that the Treasury and the then Office of Public Service and Science (now the Office of Public Service) would adopt a more 'strategic' approach in seeking to improve the department's management and efficiency.[18] As a consequence of emphasising the need for departments to improve efficiency themselves, and of other aspects of taking a more 'strategic' approach, which involved reviews of departments' financial management and control systems rather than controlling detailed aspects of departmental management, the review envisaged a significant change in the roles for the Treasury. For example, the review said it believed that the Treasury's role on public sector pay issues should be confined to approving major changes in departmental pay systems which might threaten the Treasury's public spending objectives. As a result, the review reconsidered the Office of Public Service and Science/Treasury borderline and recommended that a number of the Treasury's activities in the civil service management area should be transferred to the Office of Public Service and Science.

The review also had to take into account two other important factors. One of these was the views of the Treasury Management Board, which was already in the middle of considering a programme of management change, including what became known as its 'picture of the future Treasury'. In March 1994 it had produced a statement of the overall aim of the Treasury ('to be recognised as a professional and effective Finance and Economics Ministry that matches the best in the world'), and a series of bullet points about doing the right jobs well (including a number of points on identifying the right jobs, doing them well, and organising for success), the characteristics of a good place to work, and good relations with the rest of the world.[19] The other important factor taken into account was the Treasury's role in promoting private finance and privatisation: this was an important feature of the government's approach to reducing the scope of government activities, but it had not featured in the Treasury's 1994 set of objectives.[20]

The working principles on which the review operated were to emphasise

- *focus* – that the Treasury should concentrate on *core* activities (i.e. activities which contributed directly to the organisation's strategic objectives and which, as a result of its skills and management priorities, were ones where Treasury staff enjoyed a clear comparative advantage);
- *clarity of responsibility* – that the Treasury will work best if its staff are clear about what they are expected to achieve;
- *outputs not inputs* – that officials should be encouraged to think in terms of the outputs they are seeking to deliver, not the inputs they are contributing to the task.[21]

By considering the work of the Treasury from first principles in this way, the review team produced the mission statement, which it expected to be fairly timeless, together with a set of strategic objectives, which were specific to the present government, but which could be altered to meet changed circumstances or the requirements of a subsequent administration. However, in line with modern approaches to management, the review team said that in their view it was important that the objectives 'should be seen not simply as the objectives of Ministers – they should be "owned" by the Treasury as a whole'.[22]

With the assistance of the study of its Management Levels Project Team, the review recommended that the Treasury establish a number of issue-based teams. The characteristics of these teams would normally be: 'a separately constituted group, with a clear team leader, a specific objective, clear terms of reference, an identifiable timetable, dedicated resources, and a separate budget'.[23] However, it recognised that there were a number of practical issues that had to be resolved in connection with setting up and running such teams, and it therefore recommended that the details should be considered alongside the separate exercise to design and introduce a Treasury-specific pay and grading system, which was introduced from 1 April 1996.

This recommendation for future organisation adopting a team approach, was one of the most original and controversial features of the *Fundamental Expenditure Review*. When fully implemented it is envisaged that officials should be organised in a mix of 'standing' and 'project' teams and that, at any one time, staff might be in a number of teams. Also, management levels should be based on management roles, not grades. This means that people might be in jobs with a number of different capacities at any one time. Furthermore, as long as each team has an accountable leader, common objectives and an understanding of each member's contribution,[24] there would be no need for the most senior official to be the team leader.

Four management levels were identified, introducing a flatter staffing structure than before. These were: *strategic management* of the Treasury (the Permanent Secretary with the assistance of the Treasury Management Board, comprising the heads of the directorates, and 'responsible for determining the Treasury's overall strategy, for allocating resources to the organisation's objectives, for setting up high level cross-directorate teams as necessary and so on'); *sector management*, 'responsible for managing a coherent block of Treasury work, for setting up teams to take this work forward, for ensuring that those teams have clear objectives and adequate resources, and for monitoring and appraising their performance; *team leader*, responsible for the delivery of a clearly defined set of objectives – either on a recurring or regular basis or as a one-off project – by managing, motivating and developing a team of staff within a separate budget; and *team member*, responsible for making a specific contribution to meeting the team's objectives.

The resulting flexibility means that individuals would often work at a number of levels in the organisation, and the different management levels should not be confused with civil service grades. Consequently, teams might be led by officials at Grade 3 level, or by Executive Officers, depending on the nature of the issue, and a particular official might play a different role in a number of different teams at any one time – leading one, participating as a team member in another, and perhaps even managing a 'sector' of other teams. It might even be that the team leader is of a lower civil service grade than some or all of the team's members.[25]

The top management structure at the Treasury now consists of the Permanent Secretary and seven directors, with responsibility for Treasury objectives as shown in Figure 3.2. Together, these officials are known as the Treasury Management Board. In appreciating the significance of this structure, it should be noted that the important work of managing the civil service, with its long-standing historical significance in central government, has been transferred to the Office of Public Service, within the Cabinet Office. It should also be appreciated that, as recommended by the *Fundamental Expenditure Review*, lead responsibility for the Treasury's objectives has been allocated clearly among the directorates. In the opinion of the review team, the adoption of this new standing directorate structure creates a logical set of director

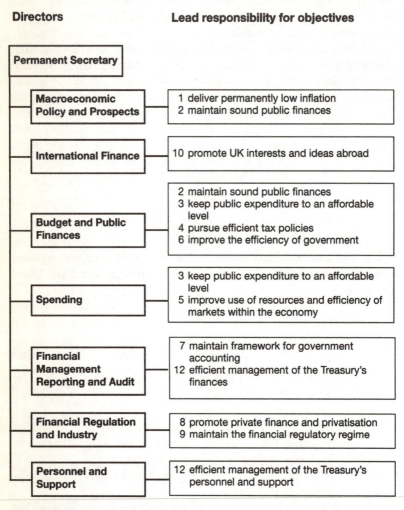

Directors   **Lead responsibility for objectives**

Permanent Secretary

Macroeconomic Policy and Prospects
1 deliver permanently low inflation
2 maintain sound public finances

International Finance
10 promote UK interests and ideas abroad

Budget and Public Finances
2 maintain sound public finances
3 keep public expenditure to an affordable level
4 pursue efficient tax policies
6 improve the efficiency of government

Spending
3 keep public expenditure to an affordable level
5 improve use of resources and efficiency of markets within the economy

Financial Management Reporting and Audit
7 maintain framework for government accounting
12 efficient management of the Treasury's finances

Financial Regulation and Industry
8 promote private finance and privatisation
9 maintain the financial regulatory regime

Personnel and Support
12 efficient management of the Treasury's personnel and support

Figure 3.2 **The new directorate structure**
Source: HM Treasury, *Chancellor of the Exchequer's Smaller Departments, Net Payments to European Community Institutions, The Government's Expenditure Plans 1995–96 to 1997–98*, Cm 2817, HMSO, 1995, p. 22
Note: Objective 11 (informing Parliament and the public about the government's economic and financial policies) is the responsibility of all directors

commands, 'it minimises duplication between directorates while maximising synergies within them; and it reflects likely work pressures and priorities over the period ahead'.[26]

Within the directorates there were, in 1995, about sixty standing teams, as shown in Figure 3.3, to focus on aspects of the Treasury's objectives allocated to their directorate; these standing teams operate throughout the year. However, it was emphasised in the *Fundamental Expenditure Review*, as, indeed, is clear in the history of the Treasury from at least as far back as the last century, that the Treasury is a small department, with a highly esteemed collegial nature. To take advantage of this valuable collegiality, arrangements have been made to supplement the standing teams with teams of cross-directorate officials concerned with particular issues. This, again, was an important feature of the review because the report said:

> Cross-directorate teams of this kind not only make good organisational sense in their own right; they should also provide a clear signal to the rest of the department that such teams – whether established to deal with specific one-off international issues, to deliver a macroeconomic forecast twice a year, or whatever it may be – are very much part of the Treasury of the future.[27]

The *Fundamental Expenditure Review* report outlined the expected responsibilities of directors within the recommended structure. These responsibilities are:

- to establish a set of teams within the directorate to carry forward separately identified areas of responsibility;
- to ensure that these teams have a clear set of objectives and sufficient resources to meet them;
- to act as mentor or sounding board, providing experienced senior adviser input and a more strategic perspective to the work of the teams as appropriate;
- to keep under active and continuous review the deployment of resources within the directorate to ensure that this continues to reflect the directorate's work priorities and pressures;
- to monitor the performance of the directorate's teams against their agreed objectives and budgets;
- to ensure that cross-cutting issues are dealt with effectively within the directorate;
- to represent the directorate's teams as necessary in high level dialogue with external parties – both in the UK and abroad;
- to ensure that staff within the directorate are managed in line with

Directorate management   **Standing team management**

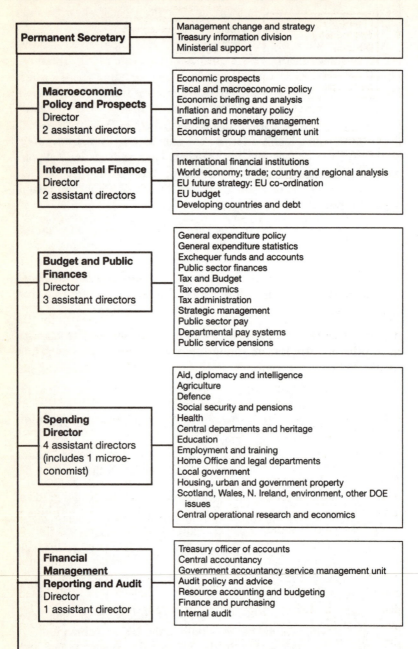

| Permanent Secretary | Management change and strategy
Treasury information division
Ministerial support |

Macroeconomic Policy and Prospects
Director
2 assistant directors
— Economic prospects
Fiscal and macroeconomic policy
Economic briefing and analysis
Inflation and monetary policy
Funding and reserves management
Economist group management unit

International Finance
Director
2 assistant directors
— International financial institutions
World economy; trade; country and regional analysis
EU future strategy; EU co-ordination
EU budget
Developing countries and debt

Budget and Public Finances
Director
3 assistant directors
— General expenditure policy
General expenditure statistics
Exchequer funds and accounts
Public sector finances
Tax and Budget
Tax economics
Tax administration
Strategic management
Public sector pay
Departmental pay systems
Public service pensions

Spending Director
4 assistant directors
(includes 1 microeconomist)
— Aid, diplomacy and intelligence
Agriculture
Defence
Social security and pensions
Health
Central departments and heritage
Education
Employment and training
Home Office and legal departments
Local government
Housing, urban and government property
Scotland, Wales, N. Ireland, environment, other DOE issues
Central operational research and economics

Financial Management Reporting and Audit
Director
1 assistant director
— Treasury officer of accounts
Central accountancy
Government accountancy service management unit
Audit policy and advice
Resource accounting and budgeting
Finance and purchasing
Internal audit

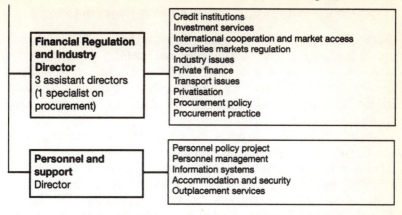

Figure 3.3 **Treasury senior management structure (from April 1995)**
Source: HM Treasury, *Organisation of the Treasury: April 1995*, HM Treasury, 1995, p. 3

the department's human resources policies and receive good training and career advice.[28]

The report specifically mentioned that the role envisaged for the deputy directors was not to act as an intermediate level of management between team leaders and directors but primarily as a substitute for the director, carrying out specific tasks, and operating with the director's full delegated authority.

Each of the standing teams was expected to be 'managed by an explicit team leader who will be accountable to the directorate management for delivering a clear set of objectives, within a given budget'.[29] In order to indicate the level of staff required, in terms of skills, experience and 'weight', for the positions of team leaders, the *Fundamental Expenditure Review* judged them to be of Grade 5 – which, in a more historic context, means equivalent to the old grade of assistant secretary. However, the report also indicated that in future it was envisaged that standing teams might be led by experienced staff of Grade 7 or Grade 6 level, and this would, in particular, reflect the enhanced training, better management, and 'reduced promotion opportunities' expected of future arrangements. This would also be consistent with less importance being attached to 'grade-based' distinctions in future. Above all, this arrangement reflected a key message of the *Fundamental Expenditure Review*: 'that the Treasury of the future must be more managerial, less gradist, less hierarchical and more flexible'.[30]

IMPROVING THE TREASURY: THE NEW DIRECTORATES

Whilst it may be possible to equate the old arrangements of divisions and groups with the new directorates and standing teams, to do so would be to seriously under-appreciate the intention of the recent changes. The new approach to management in the Treasury, including its new structure and organisation terminology, is in fact much more than cosmetic change.

Some of the most important differences have already been mentioned, such as the emphasis on outputs instead of inputs. Others feature in the departmental report, which emphasises, for example, that the new departmental objectives involve other changes from previous statements. These include making it clearer that the Treasury has two distinct objectives in relation to public expenditure: 'first, to maintain firm control over the overall level of public expenditure (objective 3); and second, within that overall total, to promote policies and spending priorities, with other departments, which strengthen the performance of the economy and the outlook for jobs (objective 5)'. They 'narrow down the focus of the Treasury's responsibilities for the "effective and efficient management of the public sector" to the basic objective of maintaining a financial control system which delivers continuing improvements in the efficiency of Government (objective 6)'. They 'make explicit two important policy objectives which were previously left unstated: the Treasury's role in promoting private finance and privatisation; and the Department's responsibility for maintaining an effective and transparent framework for government accounting'. In addition, they give new emphasis both to the need to keep Parliament and the public well informed about the objectives and effects of the government's economic and financial policies, and the need to ensure that the Treasury itself is well managed.[31]

Following the publication of the report of the *Fundamental Expenditure Review* there was a short but important period of discussion and consultation, then, on 16 December 1994, the Treasury published a further document, *Improving the Treasury*,[32] which set out the decisions on the recommendations that had been endorsed by the Chancellor of the Exchequer. In fact, most of the recommendations concerning the aim, mission and objectives of the Treasury, and their effects on its structure and organisation were quickly accepted and implemented. In relation to the review team's re-consideration of the range of Treasury activities, major changes were immediately implemented – in particular there was the transfer of civil service management functions to the then Office of Public Service and

Science. This transfer included central responsibility for civil service pay, recruitment, retirement and redundancy policy, personnel management and statistics, industrial relations, conditions of service and allowances, the central management of the Principal Civil Service Pension Scheme, and responsibility for the delegation to individual departments of pay and grading decisions for staff outside the new senior civil service.[33]

One particularly important feature of the new roles-based management structure is that the organisation has a flatter hierarchy. The previous system was more bureaucratic in the sense that most officials of a certain grade were accountable ultimately to the permanent secretary, but through officials of more senior grades than themselves. The new arrangements for flatter hierarchies have enabled significant reductions to be made in staff numbers at senior management level – for example, on 1 January 1994 the Treasury had twenty-four officials in Grades 3 or 4 and sixty-four officials in Grade 5; by 1 April 1995 these were reduced to fifteen at Grade 3 or 4 and fifty-three at Grade 5.[34]

However, in order to appreciate how the new organisation structure fits together with the Treasury objectives, it is necessary to see how the various directorates operate in practice. The following outline contains details drawn from the 1995 departmental report. More complete (and more up to date) details may be found in subsequent reports; and it should be remembered that details of responsibilities, as well as the Treasury's objectives, change from time to time, and major changes are always likely when there is a change in government.

The *Permanent Secretary* has direct responsibility for three team leaders: those who run the strategy branch, the Treasury communications team, and the ministerial private offices. The first of these has two main responsibilities: 'to help directorates and teams to ensure that their policy advice to Ministers and the department's management and resourcing more generally are informed by an explicit and "strategic" view of likely medium and long-term developments' and to act as the secretariat to the Treasury Management Board.[35] The ministerial support team serves the five Treasury ministers (although the Treasury budget carries in addition part or all of the salary costs of the Prime Minister, and the twenty-one government Whips). The work of the team is involved with all aspects of their support, including such matters as correspondence to ministers from MPs (this amounted to some 25,000 items in 1993).[36] The Treasury communications team – the press office – is concerned with all aspects of public relations. These include such facets as advising ministers on the likely questions that might be raised (through the press, television and radio) on economic policy, and advising ministers and officials on matters of day-to-day presentation of economic policy. It also deals with interpreting statistics on the UK economy and presentation of the budget.

The directorate responsible for *Macroeconomic Policy and Prospects* is directed by the Chief Economic Adviser to the Treasury, and has six standing teams, as shown in Figure 3.3. It is their responsibility to focus on the delivery of permanently low inflation and some aspects of maintaining sound public finance. The main priority here has been to manage monetary conditions to keep underlying inflation in the range 1–4 per cent, and to bring it down to the lower half of that range by the end of the 1992–97 Parliament. Since April 1994 the Chancellor of the Exchequer has published the minutes of the monthly meetings he has with the Governor of the Bank of England and these minutes are widely commented on in the media. This means that the information now available from the Treasury, together with information available from the Bank of England's Quarterly Inflation Report, makes the UK's monetary policy one of the most open in the world. In terms of monitoring and forecasting, the Treasury publishes forecasts of economic prospects twice a year; and receives reports from the Panel of Independent Forecasters on the current position of and future prospects for the UK economy. It holds meetings with economists from industry, the City and academic institutions. The Treasury also maintains a model of the UK economy and publishes details about it. It is thought that by bringing together into this single macroeconomic directorate all the work on inflationary and monetary policy the Treasury's ability to deliver permanently low inflation will be strengthened. It should also enhance the value of the Treasury's specialist macroeconomists, who, instead of being narrowly focused around the forecasting cycle, are instead more available to concentrate on the Treasury's key macroeconomic policy objectives.[37]

As far as the Treasury's second objective (see Figure 3.1) – maintaining sound public finances – is concerned, this is achieved: by monitoring cash flows and the Public Sector Borrowing Requirement; by developing ways to fund and manage debt that support monetary policy; and by liaising with the Bank of England, which advises the Treasury on how to achieve its strategic objectives and carries out day-to-day transactions on the Treasury's behalf.

The *International Finance Directorate* has five standing teams, headed by three officials who have overlapping responsibilities, as shown in Figure 3.3. Consequently, staff working in this directorate are typically members of several teams. The lead responsibility of this directorate is to focus on promoting UK interests and ideas abroad. This involves promoting UK interests within the European Union, in international discussions on export credit policies and in international organisations. There is a very considerable and steadily increasing volume of work associated with the European Union: this includes such matters as reducing fraud and waste; improving financial management in the Community, considering how best to achieve reform of important EU policies, especially in the context of future EU enlargements to include the countries of central and eastern Europe; pressing for further trade liberalisation by the EU; and ensuring that UK interests are fully pursued at EU Council meetings and at meetings concerned with European finance and budgeting. On the international front, this directorate works on such tasks as analysing and forecasting the world economy; providing support through debt rescheduling for countries with external financing difficulties following sound economic policies, to maximise ultimate debt recoveries; and promoting in international groups and organisations measures to ensure an open world financial and trading system.

In order to carry out these tasks not all staff are located within the Treasury in London: there are, for example, a few Treasury officials at the IMF/World Bank in Washington DC, and the European Commission. The *Fundamental Expenditure Review* suggested that more Treasury staff should at some point in their career have a spell working abroad and recommended that the Treasury should be ready and willing to finance the required language training to make this feasible.

The *Budget and Public Finances Directorate* has eleven standing teams, as shown in Figure 3.3, shares lead responsibility for the objectives to maintain sound public finances and to keep public expenditure at an affordable level, and also takes lead responsibility for pursuing efficient tax policies and for improving the efficiency of government. It is this directorate that is primarily concerned with co-ordinating and delivering the unified budget, and for setting out new taxation and public expenditure plans. This involves such tasks as producing cash limits consistent with the government's overall spending targets, and monitoring and controlling expenditure against the agreed limits; reviewing plans for future years as part of the information for the current Public Expenditure Survey; keeping under review the systems and procedures to deliver the government's public expenditure objectives; and maintaining the public expenditure database and providing analyses of public spending to Parliament and the public.

The Budget and Public Finances Directorate's lead responsibility for tax policies means that it is the directorate with primary responsibility for preparing the budget and co-ordinating and handling the subsequent Finance Bill. It also has to formulate, including taking into account the views of other interested departments, policy on environmental taxes and vehicle excise duty. Together with the Inland Revenue, Customs and Excise, Department of Social Security, and the Contributions Agency, it keeps the tax system and benefits system under review, in relation to their impact on the economy, and with the intention of bringing into closer alignment the income tax and national insurance contribution systems.

In relation to its responsibility for maintaining a financial control system which delivers continuing improvements in the efficiency of government, the directorate: monitors trends and pressures in central government running costs, and sets limits on departments' running costs (which encourages them to find significant continuing efficiency improvements); follows up the implementation of proposals to achieve greater value for money in the delivery of public services; encourages departments to improve efficiency and to consider privatisation of those parts of central government that do not need to remain in public ownership; implements the government's policy to delegate responsibilities for pay and grading to individual departments, and keeps public and private pay trends under review. In particular, in 1995–96, it was this directorate that was concerned (together with OPS) with implementing pay and grading delegation to all departments by 1 April 1996, involving guidance, support and advice to departments and agencies; promoting the development of best practice management techniques, such as performance measurement and benchmarking in departments and agencies; and encouraging the development of Next Steps principles in departments themselves as well as their agencies.

According to the *Fundamental Expenditure Review*, the new arrangements for this directorate should improve the Treasury's ability to deliver sound public finances – the review team said that they believed

> that one of the contributory factors behind the serious deterioration in the fiscal balance in the early 1990s was the fact that no one group or command in the Treasury was clearly and identifiably responsible for ensuring that the Public Sector Borrowing Requirement came in on track.[38]

It also has the advantage of bringing the Treasury's internal organisation more into line with the new unified budget arrangements, by bringing the tax and public expenditure work of the Treasury much closer together.

The *Spending Directorate* has thirteen standing teams, as shown in Figure 3.3. It shares lead responsibility (with the Budget and Public Finances Directorate) for keeping public expenditure at an affordable level and also has lead responsibility for improving the use of resources and efficiency of markets within the economy. This means that its tasks include examining other departments' financial control systems and individual programmes and projects as necessary, with a view to promoting improved value for money; promoting policies and spending priorities which deliver cost-effectively the government's economic and other objectives; and supporting departments when carrying out their reviews of senior management structures. In terms of public expenditure control, this directorate is concerned with such initiatives as the private finance initiative and the extension of fundamental expenditure reviews to all departments of state. It is also concerned with re-examining the Treasury's detailed controls over other departments, such as the delegated limits for capital projects and approval of transfers within departmental budgets from one expenditure sub-head to another. On the supply side, the directorate is concerned with promoting and developing departmental policies which improve the long-run supply side performance of the economy. The new spending teams identify and address areas of market weakness, facilitate efficient and open markets, and where necessary, sound regulation; and in non-market areas, promote arrangements which use resources efficiently and effectively. The *Fundamental Expenditure Review* specifically recommended that the responsibilities of the Budget and Public Finances Directorate should be kept separate from the responsibilities of the Spending Directorate. This was for three reasons. First, it believed that there would be benefits to the overall control of public expenditure if the final responsibility for advising ministers on what public expenditure target to set was actually separated off from the responsibility for having to identify or agree the detailed savings required to meet this target. Second, the tensions between the Treasury's public expenditure and supply side objectives are best externalised – otherwise the supply side objectives would inevitably be relegated systematically into second place. Third, the review team thought that this arrangement was capable of working in practice, whereas it would have been a serious mistake on simple workload grounds to combine this with the Public Finances Directorate. However, the review also recommended an annual Survey Management Committee to ensure that the two directors actually work together on the Public Expenditure Survey and are kept fully up to date with EDX (the Cabinet Committee which deals with public spending – explained later in this chapter) and the emerging requirements of the Survey.[39]

The *Financial Management, Reporting and Audit Directorate* is directed by the Chief Accountancy Adviser to the Treasury and Head of the Government Accountancy Service, and the directorate has seven standing teams, as shown in Figure 3.3. Its standing teams have the lead responsibility for maintaining a framework for government accounting which makes clear how public sector resources are used. This includes work on the development of an accounting manual for use by departments and others, and work on audit procedures; the application of accruals-based budgeting procedures to the Public Expenditure Survey, planning for capital and in-year control, and considering their application to parliamentary reporting; and also producing a timetable for the implementation of resource accounting and budgeting. The directorate is updating the Treasury manual *Government Accounting*, including its presentation and the possibility of making it available in an electronic format. In addition, it shares, with the Personnel and Support Directorate, lead responsibility for maintaining a professional, well-motivated and outward-looking organisation. In the context of these responsibilities, it scrutinises the Treasury's own budget each year and ensures that the department and each of its directorates have the funds they need to carry out their responsibilities; it manages and controls the Treasury's funds during the year; and it conducts internal audits of the Treasury's expenditure and systems.

The *Financial Regulation and Industry Directorate* has ten standing teams, as shown in Figure 3.3. The directorate currently has the lead responsibility for promoting the greater use of private finance in support of services currently provided by the public sector, and for privatising those parts of the public sector which do not need to remain in public ownership. This involves it in seeking to identify new projects and new areas suitable for privately financed projects and ensuring that lessons and experience from previous projects are applied to future projects.

The present government has been committed to the use of private finance to provide infrastructure and services traditionally regarded as public sector responsibilities. In January 1995 the Chancellor of the Exchequer announced that in future the Treasury would not approve capital projects unless private finance options had been explored; this policy has been developed by the Treasury with guidance on how the policy should be applied. One project in this area announced in 1995 was the redevelopment of the Treasury's buildings in Parliament Street, which would be achieved under the private finance initiative.

On privatisation, this directorate is currently concerned with such responsibilities as selling the remaining holdings of debt in British Telecom and the privatised electricity companies, and deciding how and when to sell its remaining portfolio of shares in privatised companies and BP; working with the Department of Transport on the privatisation of Railtrack; and working with the Department of Trade and Industry on future options for the nuclear industry and on privatisation of Atomic Energy Authority Technology.

The directorate also has lead responsibility for maintaining a regime for the regulation of financial services which preserves a stable financial system, honest markets and the confidence of investors and depositors, while promoting an open, efficient and competitive financial services sector.

In relation to the regulatory system, this involves the directorate working with the Bank of England and the Securities Investment Board to monitor developments at home and abroad in banking and financial services. This involves it in such activities as studying measures to improve the capability to detect, deter and punish financial fraud and market abuse, and improve international regulatory co-operation. It also involves monitoring and assessing the Security Investment Board's discharge of responsibilities transferred to it by the Treasury, overseeing the Stock Exchange as a Competent Authority under the Listing Particulars Directive, considering applications from overseas investment exchanges, and servicing the Financial Services Tribunal. Specific issues currently being addressed include the co-ordination of deregulation, competition policy and utilities' regulation in both the UK and the EU, and the development of UK and EU policies towards industry that enhance long-run economic competitiveness. On procurement policy, the Central Unit on Procurement is developing procurement skills and organisation across departments – through improvements in departmental procurement processes, training workshops and collaborative initiatives.

In addition, the directorate has responsibility for identifying barriers to trade in financial services in overseas markets and advising on how these can be removed. This includes negotiations in Brussels on relevant EU Directives and discussions with overseas regulatory authorities to facilitate multilateral and bilateral financial services access. The directorate also keeps under review the City of London's position as Europe's leading financial centre and advises on measures to strengthen its competitive position.

In 1995 the *Personnel and Support Directorate* had five standing teams, of which two were very small units established to deal with certain projects in the wake of the Fundamental Expenditure Review. The directorate has the lead responsibility for maintaining the quality of the Treasury organisation and ensuring that the department is resourced, staffed and managed to deliver its objectives as effectively and efficiently as possible. Following the Fundamental Expenditure Review, a major programme of work has begun to further these management objectives. For example, the directorate is currently concerned with the Treasury's manpower planning arrangements, and with securing delegation for its own pay and grading arrangements with effect from 1 April 1996. This involves reviewing the skills and expertise needed by Treasury staff in order to decide on the appropriate pay and grading systems for the department; future personnel, appraisal and training arrangements, delegation of some personnel responsibilities to line managers, and improved definition of training needs, particularly in the area of management training. It also includes future accommodation arrangements for the department; improving energy efficiency and environmental initiatives; and all aspects of the Treasury's internal information systems, which includes implementing the plans for the Treasury's New Electronic Office, together with determining future arrangements for IT operational support, and maintaining the Treasury and Cabinet Office in-house library.

As previously indicated, in addition to the standing teams within directorates, where most staff work for most of their time, there are cross directorate, issue-based teams. Two examples from the *Fundamental Expenditure Review* report are in the fields of international work and macroeconomic forecasting. Clearly, there is a lot of international work outside the responsibility of the International Finance Directorate. When promoting UK interests abroad the Director of International Finance has to draw upon support from experts in other directorates (depending on the nature of the issue). Similarly, with the two macroeconomic forecasts that are produced each year by the Macroeconomic Policy and Prospects Directorate, some of the expertise will be drawn from the Budget and Public Finances Directorate. Such cross-directorate activity, according to the report, has the advantage of being a good approach to organisation. In addition, the report asserts that such teams are an important feature of the new approach to Treasury structure and organisation.[40]

Informing Parliament and the public about the government's

economic and financial policies is regarded as the responsibility of all directors, but much of this work on a regular basis revolves around the Treasury's two important regular publications and the other publications which are issued from time to time. The regular publications are the *Financial Statement and Budget Report* (which presents the government's Medium Term Financial Strategy, describes developments in the economy over the previous year, provides a forecast for the first half of the following year, sets out the tax proposals in the budget, summarises the government's spending plans, and gives forecasts for public finances for the year ahead); and the *Departmental Report of the Chancellor of the Exchequer's Departments* (which is one of a series of departmental reports accompanied by a Statistical Supplement to the budget, and covers details of the expenditure for HM Treasury and all the other departments and responsibilities for which the Chancellor is accountable to Parliament). Until recently the Treasury also published two other major publications. These were *The Treasury Bulletin*, which it used to refer to as its flagship publication until it ceased publication in 1993 – it was published three times a year and contained articles to inform public opinion on economic policy issues and the circumstances in which the policies were formed; and *Civil Service Statistics*, which continues to be published, but from the Cabinet Office (as a result of the transfer of functions following the recommendations in the *Fundamental Expenditure Review*) and which presents facts and figures on staffing in the civil service.

THE PUBLIC EXPENDITURE SURVEY (PES)

The public expenditure survey is the key element in the system for medium-term planning and control of public expenditure. It covers the whole of the public sector,[41] brings figures for expenditure in the previous five years up to date and looks ahead for three years. This means that although expenditure for a nine-year period is covered, the effective planning cycle covers a period of three years. In the short term, which means for the coming financial year, the key procedures for planning and control are cash limits, control of the reserve, and the supply estimates. As has been indicated already, the Treasury structure and management system is designed to maintain a continuing focus on government priorities, through the publicised and continuously revised statement of the department's aim, mission and objectives, and also to monitor expenditure to ensure that money is spent as authorised by Parliament. The most important processes are therefore intended to keep spending within the limits stated in the (PES) survey plans by comparing the details of actual expenditure, acquired in the Treasury's computerised Financial Information System (FIS), with the intentions in the plans.

Essentially, then, the PES is the public expenditure planning system by which the government reviews all public expenditure for the three years ahead. This entails all ministers and their departments considering their priorities, the needs of the United Kingdom, and the likely resources to meet those needs. From 1992 the government implemented a number of important changes to the system of public expenditure control, so that it became a more explicitly 'top down' approach. This involved changes at both the management and presentational level and the ministerial level. The new approach was specifically designed to focus more attention on the government's medium-term objective of reducing the share of national income taken by public spending; and it achieves this by settling expenditure totals by dividing up what can be afforded instead of collecting departmental bids first.[42]

At the management and presentational level the government introduced a mechanism, now known as the Control Total,[43] expressed in cash terms. This Control Total differs from previous planning totals because it excludes the main elements of cyclical social security (unemployment benefit and income support for non-pensioners), and debt interest, includes local authority financed expenditure, and excludes privatisation proceeds. The purpose of this new procedure is to include as much public spending as possible, but to reduce the significance of cyclical social security spending. Cyclical social security spending falls when growth in the economy picks up, and therefore had the effect under the previous system of allowing higher than intended spending in other areas, thus obscuring underlying trends. The essential reason for the new approach was therefore to maintain the focus on reducing public sector expenditure as a proportion of the gross domestic product.

At the ministerial level, a particularly important role has been developed for the Cabinet's spending committee, known as EDX. A period of bilateral discussions enables the Chief Secretary to 'set out the field', to get all the figures to fit together, and then to inform EDX at the end of his discussion period, in about June or July. This enables the Cabinet to agree its overall priorities and objectives before the summer parliamentary recess. The Chief Secretary's special responsibility in this process is to put the various options to EDX, keep the score card, and make sure there is good communication between the committee and the Secretaries of State so that informal decisions can be taken.[44] The EDX committee is chaired by the Chancellor, with the Chief Secretary actively involved, and consists of senior ministers who have political insight and responsibility but normally with relatively small programmes of their own, so that their departmental interests are not major issues (in 1995 these included the Deputy Prime Minister, the Home Secretary, and the Leader of the House of Commons). Once the Cabinet has decided on its priorities and the broad outlines of its spending plans, the Chief Secretary and Treasury officials discuss details of individual programmes with the departmental ministers and staffs responsible, in order to agree on the distribution of resources between departments for the following financial year, which begins in April. Ministers from the various departments appear before the committee to argue for their interests. After the size of the total expenditure, together with departmental details, is agreed by EDX for approval by the Cabinet, plans can be developed for the supply estimates. The presentation of supply estimates is the process of getting parliamentary approval for spending specified sums of money for particular purposes. Parliamentary approval for the expenditure of money is then given in the annual Appropriation Act, which fixes the limits to spending by departments. The figures, or votes, in the Appropriation Act then become limits to what can be spent for stated purposes, and if extra provision is required a department has to present a supplementary supply estimate, which also requires Treasury and parliamentary approval.

The Treasury maintains the Financial Information System to monitor departmental expenditure. It acquires its information from departments and from monthly returns from the Paymaster Agency, which controls the government 'bank account'. These details are supplemented by mid-year details from departments showing their own analysis of expenditure in the first half of the financial year, and predictions of end-of-year figures from departments towards the end of the financial year. This information enables the Treasury to continuously monitor public expenditure throughout the year. After the end of the financial year each department accounts for the grant authorised, by sending the Treasury an 'appropriation account' with final details of monies actually spent against each vote. It is this appropriation account, signed personally by the Accounting Officer for the vote, who accepts responsibility for the propriety of the expenditure and the accuracy of the account, which is subsequently audited by the Comptroller and Auditor General and laid before Parliament. When it has been laid before Parliament it becomes subject to the scrutiny of the Public Accounts Committee of the House of Commons, and the

Accounting Officer can be called to give evidence and be examined on details.

PES covers nearly all spending by central government and local authorities. This means that it includes all expenditure by central and local government on providing services, together with grants and subsidies to a wide variety of public sector institutions which would not be able to continue their activities without financial support from public funds (e.g. grants to universities, overseas development aid): it does not, however, involve negotiations on expenditure which is fixed by other bodies such as the UK contribution to the European Community budget (which is subject to separate processes and scrutiny). It also means that once agreement has been reached between the Treasury on the one hand, and departmental ministers on the other, the Treasury has to prepare plans for the budget, for the financial year beginning in the following April, to include proposals for taxation and borrowing to meet the planned and approved expenditure levels. These budget details are then published by the Treasury, as the *Financial Statement and Budget Report*, to accompany the Chancellor's budget statement in the House of Commons in November.

It is important to appreciate that PES operates in terms of cash, not volume. The approved finance therefore in practice determines what can be spent: and the public expenditure system no longer operates, as it did some time ago, on the basis of approving an activity then working out what resources are required to finance it. Consequently, cash limits, once set, cannot be changed unless approved by the Chief Secretary to the Treasury and announced in Parliament. It is therefore not surprising that it is very rare for a cash limit to be exceeded (though cash limits are subject to amendment). It is also not surprising that PES is a planning system on a vast scale, for which the Treasury is responsible, intended to ensure that public expenditure is both properly approved and properly managed.

How this works in practice, with emphasis on ensuring the observance of government priorities on limiting public expenditure, is illustrated by the new approach to planning public expenditure involving a Control Total (see above), adopted since autumn 1992.[45] The measure of expenditure used for setting the public spending objective is known as general government expenditure (GGE). GGE covers not only central government expenditure but also local government spending and central government support for nationalised industries and other public corporations. Until recently government set out to achieve its medium-term public spending goal (i.e. to reduce public spending as a share of national income over time) by focusing on what were known as planning totals, which included only the expenditure of central government directly, together with its support for expenditure by local authorities, nationalised industries and public corporations, and a reserve. Consequently its approach did not encompass those elements of general expenditure which were funded from other sources, such as local authorities' independently raised revenue, though it did include all external finance for public corporations (including their market and overseas borrowing, which required authority from central government).

To ensure that the government's public spending objective is better achieved the new 'top-down' approach, which was introduced from 1993–94, involves setting an annual ceiling (the Control Total), expressed in cash terms, and reflecting an average real growth rate not exceeding 1.5 per cent a year. This gives public expenditure control a more obviously quantifiable objective, but it should be noted that the 1.5 per cent is an absolute upper ceiling, and in practice the Treasury has always sought to get outcomes well below this (so that government has the opportunity to cut taxes as well). The Control Total includes local authority self-financed expenditure, though, as already explained, it excludes both cyclically related social security spending directly related to unemployment and privatisation proceeds. This means that central government will now be influencing and restraining local authority expenditure through varying its financial support for local authorities against other income within their ambit, all within the Control Total. Moreover, the Control Total contains provision for a reserve to provide for such contingencies as unplanned additions to departmental spending or revised estimates of demand-led programmes. Control of the reserve continues another important Treasury power, for expenditure from the reserve has to be authorised by the Treasury, and the reserve (amounting in 1992–93 to £4 billion out of a planning total of £227 billion) is used for increases in expenditure beyond the amounts allocated to programmes. For example, the reserve is used for cash limit increases, usually announced in a written answer to a Parliamentary Question; Parliament's approval for the increase in supply provision is later given by means of a supplementary estimate. The reserve therefore provides a margin for uncertainties which may result from policy changes, new initiatives, contingencies or revised estimates of demand-led programmes. The advantages of the Control Total ceilings are, as with other elements in the present government's approach to public expenditure, to emphasise what government has agreed to be affordable rather than what ministers and departments argue to be desirable, and any elements of conflict are resolved through the Cabinet's EDX Committee.

IN-YEAR CONTROL

Supply estimates are the means by which government obtains authority from Parliament for spending funds in a particular financial year from 1 April to 31 March. The estimates themselves consist of a large number of votes, presented by the Treasury and arranged by the Treasury, for convenience of consideration, into groups called classes. There can be no department without a vote, but departments responsible for a variety of different activities may have a number of different votes; each vote may also be divided into sub-heads. Although departments are individually responsible for their votes they have to work closely at each stage with the Treasury because the Treasury has to ensure that the level of expenditure is affordable, that it is in accordance with the PES, that unexpected needs are provided for, and that money is only spent within approved limits and for the specific purposes approved by Parliament. It is the procedures associated with preparing and presenting the supply estimates that have traditionally given the Treasury such an important role in all aspects of public policy-making. The Treasury is, after all, the government's department for ensuring that its policies for controlling public expenditure are applied in practice.

The main supply estimates are prepared in departments, the final versions being consistent with PES plans,[46] and they are then scrutinised by standing teams in the Spending Directorate, with consultation between the departments and the Treasury during January and early February, when the agreed details are approved by Treasury ministers. After approval, the estimates are then presented to Parliament by the Financial Secretary in March, together with a summary and guide prepared by the Treasury and presented to Parliament by the Chief Secretary. After parliamentary consideration the Appropriation Act, which authorises expenditure, receives the Royal Assent by about the time Parliament rises for the summer recess in late July or early August. However, within this procedure, money can only be spent after it has been approved by Parliament and therefore, to cover the period from the beginning of the financial year in April, departments will have presented, in the previous November, details to the Treasury for sums needed on account, which are approved in mid-December, making cash available for spending from 1 April. About five-twelfths of the previous year's expenditure is made available on account in this way for spending by departments to enable them to continue operating throughout the financial year. In addition, there are three normal opportunities for departments to present supplementary estimates, in the summer, winter and spring. This is necessary to enable departments to cope with unexpected changes in their spending needs. After Treasury scrutiny, the supplementary estimates are presented to Parliament in June, November and February (though they may also, exceptionally, be presented at other times during the year). Consequently, the specialist public expenditure divisions in the Treasury, dealing with the various areas of government business, like the finance divisions in the various departments, are kept busy throughout the year dealing with the various stages of different types of supply estimates. There are also, throughout the year, continuous discussions about the details of provision between departmental finance divisions and officials in the Treasury. In addition, where a department wishes to transfer expenditure between sub-heads within a particular vote, prior approval (virement) has always to be obtained from the relevant officials in the Spending Directorate, acting in these circumstances on behalf of Parliament.

The Treasury therefore has a very important role, exercised by its Spending Directorate, in monitoring departmental expenditure. It maintains, within the Treasury's computer database, a profile of the expenditure of departments, because departments are required to provide details whenever there is a change. It receives, from the Paymaster Agency, details of payments and receipts each month, which are in turn acquired from departments through a procedure known as APEX (Analysis of Public Expenditure). It also receives from departments a mid-year expenditure return, showing the department's own best estimate of expenditure in the first half of the year. In addition, towards the end of the year, it receives forecasts from departments of what they expect their end of year expenditure to be in the context of their provision. After the end of the financial year, each department accounts in detail and against each sub-head, through the Treasury to Parliament, for the amount actually spent. It is these detailed end-of-year accounts that become the focus for examination by the Comptroller and Auditor General and the Public Accounts Committee of the House of Commons.

Much of the work of the Treasury and the departments has, since the introduction of the Financial Management Initiative (FMI) in 1982,[47] been concerned with emphasising the need to achieve what is referred to as value for money. Value for money has been defined by the Treasury as the final social and economic benefit of a policy in relation to cost, though the term is sometimes used as shorthand for the optimum combination of economy, effectiveness, and efficiency.[48] As the FMI is intended to be a total approach to management, covering systems, policies and people, there are no clear limits to the details that may come within Treasury scrutiny. In the last resort, and after all the discussion and advice that may be offered by the Treasury, it is the departmental accounting officer who is answerable for what has happened within his sphere of responsibility; and this applies not only to all details of actual expenditure but also to the wider context of achieving value for money. However, the implications of this accountability are now rather more complex than previously. This is seen, for example, as a result of the creation of agencies. Their chief executives are also accountable, either to their permanent secretaries (where they exist – some agencies are departments in their own right and therefore their chief executives have always been accounting officers) or directly to Parliament; indeed, some chief executives have already appeared, in their personal capacities, to give evidence and be examined by the Public Accounts Committee. Details of the relationship of the Treasury to agencies are considered in the next chapter.

Examples of details of the preparation and presentation of supply estimates are given in the more specialist literature; and the Cabinet Office/Treasury series of pamphlets on Public Expenditure Management is also useful for consultation for this purpose. Important points to note are that Part I of each vote contains an ambit, which is a concise statement of the purpose for which the money will be spent: funds cannot be used for any other purpose, and any change in the wording of the ambit must receive Treasury approval. The ambit appears in a schedule to the Appropriation Act and Parliament authorises specific sums of money to each ambit; this constitutes Parliamentary approval for specific government activities. Part II contains details of the actual expenditure for the most recently completed financial year, together with information about the provision for the current year, and Part III gives details of receipts which are paid directly into the Consolidated Fund (out of which all votes are funded).

Two other concepts important for understanding in-year control are cash limits and running costs. A cash limit is quite simply the maximum amount of cash that can be spent on certain specified services during one financial year; most votes are subject to such limits, and this is stated at the beginning of the introductory note to the vote. It implies that it has been possible to forecast and control reasonably accurately the total expenditure on that vote over a full one-year period, and the cash limit includes any permitted allowance for inflation. An alternative possibility is expenditure that is demand led, where the total expenditure is determined by factors outside government control and is therefore more difficult to predict accurately in advance. Running costs limits relate to a department's expenditure on staff and related expenses such as accommodation and telephones. The purpose of running costs is to set a ceiling on administrative costs while permitting flexibility to managers to vary expenditure on the different elements making up the total running costs. In terms of public expenditure policy, the intention of running costs control is to continue the downward pressure on these costs and encourage the search for greater efficiency. Running costs targets for three years ahead are set in the PES, and they, in turn, are used in determining the running costs limits in the short-term annual estimates.

MONITORING

Financial monitoring is a management tool to achieve control and forecasting of expenditure. As far as central government is concerned, it is important to appreciate that financial monitoring is a continuing process relating to each department, and applied to planned expenditure, current expenditure, and past expenditure. Votes which are subject to cash limits can be monitored most easily because they necessarily involve the intention that cash limits, once set, are not changed during the financial year. However, votes which are demand-led have to be just as carefully monitored, perhaps even more carefully, though the procedure has to be different.

The Treasury maintains its computerised Financial Information System to monitor departmental expenditure. It contains a profile of the expected pattern of expenditure and receipts over the year, which is supplied by departments, agreed by the Treasury, and revised when votes are changed; details of monthly payments and receipts, supplied by Paymaster, who also supplies data four times a month; and departments' mid-year expenditure returns with details of their estimates of expenditure for the whole of a particular year, revised when necessary, as a result of actual experience in the first half of the year. These details are supplemented by mid-year details from departments showing their own analysis of expenditure in the first half of the financial year, and predictions of end-of-year figures from departments towards the end of the financial year. This information enables the Treasury to monitor public expenditure continuously throughout the year. After the end of the financial year each department accounts for the grant authorised, by sending the Treasury an 'appropriation account' with final details of monies actually spent against each vote. It is this appropriation account, signed personally by the Accounting Officer for the vote, who accepts responsibility for the propriety of the expenditure and the accuracy of the account, which is subsequently audited by the Comptroller and Auditor General and laid before Parliament. When it has been laid before Parliament it becomes subject to the scrutiny of the Public Accounts Committee of the House of Commons, and the Accounting Officer can be called to give evidence and be examined on details.

Financial monitoring is, of course, also conducted within each individual department, but the details of departmental procedures do not concern us here. Some of the information required to operate the Treasury's monitoring procedures is also available within departments for managers and budget holders who are responsible for their own operations and for ensuring that they manage within their budget limits. The information is also available, at the departmental level, to monitor the whole range of a department's activities and the effectiveness of its financial planning and control systems. Within the Treasury it is the Spending Directorate that has primary responsibility for these details, and its members work closely with their relevant departments, both in exchanging information and in agreeing action; this becomes especially significant where there is likely to be any excess over previously planned expenditure figures. The monitoring data collected for this purpose is, however, also used by the Treasury's economic planners and forecasters.

In order to operate this monitoring system effectively, departments supply the Treasury with monthly and quarterly information which is then compared with monitoring profiles produced by the Treasury computer. This information is supplemented, in October, by expenditure returns from departments on the first six months of the financial year, and in February with out-turn forecasts (i.e. forecasts of the department's end-of-year figures). However, to minimise the work involved in this continuous process, departments and the Treasury agree early in each financial year on sets of reporting blocks to simplify the number of returns that are provided; and these reporting blocks generally follow the pattern of the sub-heads in each vote. The Treasury then prepares profiles for each reporting block, and the profiles incorporate information about the expenditure patterns throughout the year, so that provision is made for seasonal fluctuations and other factors that are predictably variable. The information in the profiles is of considerable importance to both the departments and the Treasury, because it includes details which are the results of judgments based on the specialist knowledge and expertise in the departments as well as in the Treasury.

From all this information the Treasury then makes certain details publicly available through such opportunities as briefings, press releases, and ministerial speeches. For example, the Treasury provides monthly reports for use within the government service, indicating where divergences are occurring between actual and profiled expenditure, and the overall supply expenditure information acquired is also published in the monthly press notice which gives details of the Public Sector Borrowing Requirement.

END OF YEAR ACCOUNTING

At the end of the financial year, each department accounts for the money it has spent in relation to each vote, including details for each sub-head. This appropriation account, as explained earlier, is the accounting officer's responsibility in terms of both its propriety and accuracy. Once signed, the appropriation account is then audited by the Comptroller and Auditor General (C & AG) and laid before Parliament, together with any observations made by the C & AG.

The C & AG is an officer of the House of Commons, appointed by the Crown following an address from the House of Commons; and the National Audit Office, of which he is the head, has two sets of duties. As Comptroller General he has to ensure that no money is paid out of the Consolidated Fund or the National Loans Fund except for purposes approved by Parliament, and that all monies received by government departments are credited to the Consolidated Fund or the National Loans Fund at the Bank of England. As Auditor General he has to ensure not only that money is only spent as authorised, but also that value for money has been obtained. These responsibilities are wider than they may at first appear because they are concerned, as they always have been since the creation of the C & AG in 1866, with value for money as well as the details in reports of accounts. Consequently, the audits which are undertaken investigate both the management arrangements for achieving economy, efficiency and effectiveness within the departments, and the practical achievement of the specified activities (aims and objectives) according to those criteria.

The C & AG's reports are presented to Parliament and Parliament's work on them is primarily undertaken by the Public Accounts Committee of the House of Commons. This committee of fifteen members of the House of Commons is always chaired by a senior member of the Opposition, often by an ex-Treasury minister, if there is one available. The C & AG and the Treasury Officer of Accounts assist the committee, as witnesses, and the committee examines the appropriation accounts, considers observations from the C & AG, and questions accounting officers from departments who attend as witnesses. It is the duty of the Treasury Officer of Accounts to advise departments about accounting procedures and precedents, and to assist the Public Accounts Committee when there is a justifiable departure from established practice.[49] After the committee has formally reported to Parliament, the details of its report are considered by the department concerned and by the Treasury. Discussions then take place between the Treasury and the department until a reply is agreed between the accounting officer and the Treasury. This is recorded in a Treasury Minute, published as a Command Paper, which is laid before Parliament as the government's response to the Public Accounts Committee's observations. The Public Accounts Committee's reports and the Treasury Minutes then form the basis for a debate in the House of Commons.

THE BUDGET AND THE FINANCE ACT

The budget is the most significant annual parliamentary event for which the Treasury is responsible for advising ministers: it receives a great deal of public and media attention and the debate in the House of Commons takes about a week of parliamentary time. However, the changes in tax rates and details to tighten specific provisions in the tax system are to a large extent the special responsibility of officials in the revenue departments rather than in the Treasury, and some of the implications of these and other relationships with the Treasury are considered later in this chapter. Details of the budget, and of the government's spending plans, are normally considered by the Treasury and Civil Service Committee of the House of Commons which takes evidence from the Chancellor, the Governor of the Bank of England, Treasury officials, and such other experts as it may choose to examine.

Budgetary reform has been a matter of considerable interest in the past fifteen years. After the reforms instituted as a consequence of the 1961 Plowden Report on the Control of Public Expenditure, a gap developed between the announcement of spending and tax proposals. In 1978 the Institute of Fiscal Studies established a committee, under the chairmanship of Lord (William) Armstrong of Sanderstead, a former permanent secretary to the Treasury and Head of the Home

Civil Service, to consider what changes in the analytical framework and presentation of the budget and in parliamentary procedures were required to permit expenditure and revenue plans for the short and medium term to be considered together.[50] The committee's report, which attracted much attention for its critical approach, stimulated debate. In order to overcome some of the difficulties criticised by Armstrong and his colleagues, from 1982 the government introduced the Autumn Statement and, later, made revisions to the form, timing and content of the government's financial reports to Parliament.[51]

Problems arose because, in the past, the sums to be spent by governments and to be raised in revenue were considered at different times – expenditure plans in the autumn, budget proposals in the spring – so that the budget was not an occasion for considering both expenditure and taxation but instead was essentially a tax budget. One of the most important disadvantages of these arrangements was that the system handicapped consideration of a coherent budgetary policy because the budget was a short-term exercise without it being directly related to the long-term implications of expenditure plans. In addition, appraisal in Parliament and outside was limited because of time constraints: the absence of a time interval between the budget proposals and their implementation discouraged changes being made after the proposals were announced. Following the criticisms of the Armstrong Committee on Budgetary Reform there were criticisms in 1982 by the Treasury and Civil Service Committee,[52] and the Government said in reply that it accepted the case for bringing together decisions on public expenditure, tax and borrowing.[53] These were the most important factors in the pre-history of the decision announced by the Chancellor of the Exchequer in 1992 to reform the budgetary timetable.

The new arrangements, operating from 1993, were announced by the Chancellor of the Exchequer in his Budget Speech on 10 March 1992. Consequently, from November 1993 the Chancellor makes one regular Budget Statement to Parliament a year, which covers both the government's tax plans for the year from the following 1 April, and the government's spending plans for the next three years. The Finance Bill, implementing the budget proposals, is now published in January and receives the Royal Assent in May, while work on the next year's budget starts in the summer and continues through the autumn. The Budget Statement is now accompanied by all the details previously contained in the Autumn Statement and the Financial Statement and Budget Report. These amount to a summary of the main budget tax and spending changes; an analysis of departmental spending plans for the next three years; a description of the main tax and National Insurance

Contributions measures and their revenue consequences; a statement of the government's medium-term financial strategy; the short-term economic forecast; detailed material on the likely out-turn for the public finances in the current year, and the revenue forecasts for the year ahead; and information on the cost of tax reliefs. The main estimates for expenditure continue to be formally presented to Parliament in March, relating to spending plans announced in the previous November's budget and effective from 1 April, but the details are already available in the departmental reports, published early in the New Year and in the statistical supplement to the budget. These reforms are likely to help streamline the processes of taxation and expenditure planning and also assist the many other institutions, both within government and outside, that are involved in these procedures. It is some of the relationships with, and influence of, these bodies that are considered next.

RELATIONSHIPS AND INFLUENCES

The evidence presented in this chapter makes it clear that, as Sir Terence Burns has written, the Treasury is at the centre of the formulation and execution of economic policy.[54] Its specific responsibilities are exercised through its directorates, as already explained. The Chancellor influences the economy through his power to set interest rates; he decides (after consulting others) which taxes to levy and what other finances to raise; and he has the power to modify or oppose the spending of other government departments. These opportunities and responsibilities may appear modest as examples of formal power, in comparison with the natural momentum of the economy or in comparison with the powers exercised by central finance ministries of other countries, but they are significant and effective, especially when supported by the influence the Treasury has. Most of the work in raising money for government is done by other departments and agencies (e.g. Inland Revenue, Customs and Excise, Contributions Agency); most of the spending is done by other departments and agencies, especially central government departments and local authorities; the management of the national debt and the foreign exchange reserves is carried out for the Treasury by the Bank of England; and most of the executive functions in ensuring the stability and integrity of the financial system are also handled by such institutions as the Bank of England, the Building Societies Commission and the Securities and Investment Board. The Treasury is therefore left with bringing together the strands of economic policy, co-ordinating it, and representing the economic interests of the government. However, although Sir Terence Burns, Permanent Secretary to the Treasury, has said that 'its position in Government means that it has freedom from pressure groups',[55] this is not strictly correct in the sense in which terms like 'interest' and 'groups' are generally known to students of public policy-making. Indeed, Burns himself drew attention on another occasion to the activity of Treasury officials in dealing with people in No. 10, the Cabinet Office, other government departments, overseas governments and institutions (such as the IMF and World Bank), the Bank of England and other organisations in the City of London, the revenue departments, industrialists, financiers, other managers throughout the public sector, and academics.[56] This is well illustrated by considering some of these relationships, beginning with those in the UK.

Consider, first, the relationship between the Treasury and the Bank of England. The relationship is generally very informal, with senior staff in the Treasury visiting their opposite numbers in the Bank regularly, occasionally for lunch as well as for business. At the time of the Radcliffe Committee on the Working of the Monetary System, in 1958, these contacts were counted, and in a period of three months the Governor and Deputy Governor had over sixty personal discussions with ministers or with officials of the government. Attendance by executive directors, officials and advisers at meetings in Whitehall numbered over 300; in addition, over 400 letters were written by the Bank to Whitehall and over 1,300 telephone conversations took place on policy matters. Moreover, these figures did not take account of the large volume of routine communications (amounting to several thousands) on banking, exchange control and statistical matters.[57] Although these details are now nearly thirty years old, there is plenty of evidence to suggest that the relationship of the Bank of England and the Treasury is much the same; though, with adaptations to accommodate modern technology and recent legislation on particular matters, the details may be rather different.

One example of these changes, and of the more open approach to Treasury work, occurred in the early 1990s. Following the suspension on 16 September 1992 of sterling's membership of the exchange rate mechanism (ERM), the Chancellor of the Exchequer announced that from December 1992 a *Monthly Monetary Report* would be published, following the regular meetings between the Chancellor of the Exchequer and the Governor of the Bank of England. It sets out all the information on which monetary policy judgments are based. Since then, the Bank of England has produced a regular report on progress towards the government's inflation objectives, published in the Bank of

England *Quarterly Bulletin*.[58] Also, since 1994 the Chancellor has regularly published the minutes of the monthly meetings at which he discusses interest rates with the Governor. These minutes are now available six weeks after each meeting and their availability is intended to increase confidence in the anti-inflation policy by increasing the openness with which decisions are taken and making the reasons for particular decisions known.[59]

Another example relates more specifically to interest rates. Since the mid-1970s interest rates have been the main measure to control the level of aggregate nominal demand in the economy, and decisions are made on the basis of a general assessment of monetary conditions; previously they were made primarily on the basis of maintaining a particular exchange rate. In the nineteenth century it was quite clear that decisions on this matter were made by the Bank. In 1917 relations between the Bank and the Treasury were such that Mr Andrew Bonar Law, then Chancellor of the Exchequer, seriously contemplated transferring the government's account to one of the Joint Stock Banks. The account was never, in fact, transferred but Bonar Law's achievement was that he established a principle which was formally fixed when the Bank of England was nationalised.[60] In the period immediately after nationalisation of the Bank, in 1946, the position was quite clear: the Bank had the final responsibility for decisions to change the Bank rate, although the Treasury had the power, under the 1946 Act, to issue directions. In fact, as far as we know, formal directions have never been issued. The Bank always made its decision in the light of what it knew would be acceptable to the Chancellor. This meant that the decision was never a pure decision of the Bank, but a decision of what the Bank felt ought to be done, when it had considered the very important factor of what the Chancellor would accept. The responsibility since the Bank Rate Leak Inquiry of 1957 has been changed. Decisions are now taken by the Chancellor after advice from the Treasury and Bank of England and after consulting the Prime Minister. The focus of responsibility in relation to this particular example of decision-making has therefore changed during the twentieth century, but the degree and intensity of consultation and advice is unlikely to have diminished – even though its direction has changed.

In the 1990s the Treasury acquired responsibility, as a result of transferring functions from the Department of Trade and Industry in 1992, for the regulatory structure over financial services, including the task of negotiating a number of key European directives, designed to facilitate the creation of a single market in financial services.[61] The Treasury's responsibility, however, is essentially a matter of policy and legislation, and of strategic oversight of the system, whereas operational responsibility is for most practical purposes delegated to the Bank of England, the Securities and Investment Board, and the Building Societies Commission (with the DTI being responsible for insurance). Although details are not its responsibility, the Treasury nevertheless has continuous consultation with these institutions, to ensure that the regulatory arrangements are effective and working in practice, and to brief ministers when the supervision arrangements appear to have failed (such as the 1991 collapse of BCCI). The same general principles apply in relation to Treasury borrowing and expertise in tax matters. Although the Treasury borrows money on behalf of the government, the day-to-day operational responsibility for doing this lies with the Bank of England in the bond markets and the Department for National Savings in relation to personal savings; and the specialist tax knowledge is the responsibility of staff in the Inland Revenue and Customs and Excise departments, whose work is closely involved with assessment and collection, and who therefore are the best people to advise on specialist details of taxation.

The Fundamental Expenditure Review suggested ways for the new Finance Regulation and Industry Directorate to reduce its senior management resources (as, indeed, it suggested ways to reduce personnel and responsibilities throughout the Treasury). In the case of this directorate it wondered whether officials working on regulation policy for securities and investment responsibilities could be brought together with officials working on banking responsibilities.[62] This might reduce the senior management resources devoted to this work, simply by passing to other agencies some of the responsibilities currently carried by the Treasury. Such a review may be appropriate because, as with other work within the Treasury, the main reasons for the existing 'demarcations' between the two groups appeared to be that they started off in different departments, and the nature of public or political concern that led to the tasks being undertaken by the Treasury, rather than in any logical allocation of responsibilities on the basis of the Treasury's aim, mission and objectives. Where work is originally allocated, and the precise nature of governmental responsibilities, is often to be found in a particular incident or event giving cause for public concern and government action. Consequently, relationships between the Treasury and other institutions (e.g. Bank of England, Securities and Investments Board, Royal Mint, Stock Exchange) change from time to time in response to the environment within which work proceeds, and there is much to be gained from reviewing responsibilities from time to time to ensure that the internal arrangements are the most appropriate to meet contemporary needs.

Consider, secondly, some of the day-to-day influences of the Treasury over other departments of central government. It has already been explained how, in the nineteenth century, the Treasury acquired some of its important powers by demurring to requests for additional resources. In more recent times other powers have been acquired by the issue of guidance or advice. In the ordinary course of events this often amounts to little more than indications of recommended good practice which are unlikely to be rejected. However, it should be noted that, particularly in financial matters, if such advice and guidance is not followed and the results are unfortunate, the subsequent inquiries by, for example, a parliamentary select committee, may result in serious embarrassment to ministers and/or to officials. It is in this context that advice and guidance in such manuals as *Government Accounting* is seen as being more like instructions than advice for which implementation may be optional. It is this manual which requires departments to consult the Treasury, in advance, on any new proposals outside the categories of delegated authority, and before a paper is circulated to Cabinet or a Cabinet committee, containing any proposal with expenditure implications; it requires departments to provide the Treasury with the information needed to fulfil its responsibilities for the allocation and control of resources, and to consult the Treasury at a formative stage in policy discussions about proposals which could have implications for its responsibilities.[63] These are formidable and comprehensive requirements – but, as has already been said, *Government Accounting* is currently being revised and there is now considerably more emphasis on delegating responsibilities to departments within defined limits. Nevertheless, it is hard to imagine flexibility that gives free rein to departments, simply because of the Treasury's overall strategic responsibilities for all aspects of public finance. This, in turn, ensures that the Treasury has the opportunity to agree in detail the arrangements for delegated authority, including mechanisms for checking on how delegated powers operate in practice and what the arrangements are within departments for the more specific delegation of operational authority. These arrangements, which are intended to ensure that the Treasury effectively achieves its aim, mission and objectives, require a great deal of internal consultation and co-ordination within central government administration and, consequently, considerable scope for non-partisan political activity.

Consider, thirdly, some of the Treasury's contacts in the international context. The United Kingdom's membership of the European

Communities involves substantial flows of both payments and receipts. Indeed, in 1994–95 it was estimated that the UK's net payments would be £2,043 million (the UK being one of the three consistent net contributors, with Germany and France). This compared with a net payment (i.e. after allowing for public sector receipts) in 1993–94 of £1,873 million, and an estimate for 1995–96 of £2,821 million. However, it should be noted that in 1994–95 the UK was expected to have received £3,963 million in public sector receipts from various of the European Community funds (European Regional Development Fund, European Agricultural Guidance and Guarantee Fund, European Social Fund). These payments were received by thirteen government departments.[64] However, the European Communities Act, 1972, ensures that UK contributions to the European General Budget are charged directly on the Consolidated Fund and all receipts by departments are surrendered to the Consolidated Fund. This in turn means that the Treasury has important responsibilities in negotiating both the funding of the UK's obligations and the checking and distribution of receipts (as well as promoting the UK's economic interests in, for example, the discussions on economic and monetary union). As part of these responsibilities, Treasury rules provide procedural details for the application of receipts as appropriations in aid of the relevant vote or votes in the Estimates. Also, in some cases government departments act as agents of an EC body when funds are being allocated to the private sector, or to local authorities; the Treasury then has a role in advising on the responsibilities of departments as agents. For example, arrangements have to be made for noting and monitoring all receipts, reporting transactions to Parliament, and for making them subject to audit by the Comptroller and Auditor General. It also follows that, to ensure the effective co-ordination of policy, departments should consult the Treasury and other departments concerned when they are involved in applications for, or the expenditure of, European funds.[65]

Treasury ministers and their officials spend a great deal of time at European Community meetings, including the monthly meetings of Finance Ministers, and regular meetings such as the Monetary Committee. They maintain a keen interest in the work of the IMF, World Bank, European Bank of Reconstruction and Development, the Paris Club and the Group of Seven meetings (the members of the Group of Seven leading industrial nations, who meet to co-ordinate international co-operation, are the United States, the UK, France, Germany, Italy, Canada and Japan). In relation to all these responsibilities in the international context, as with many responsibilities

within the UK, the Treasury acts by persuasion, advice and encouragement, and it seeks to influence other institutions in ways that
contribute to the achievement of its aim and mission. Similar tactics
may be applied by others, whether they come from industry, commerce
or elsewhere, to influence the Treasury, especially when officials are
preparing advice to ministers or making judgments in accordance with
government policies. This is well illustrated by considering Treasury
responsibilities and activity in relation to parliamentary procedure.

PARLIAMENTARY BUSINESS

All departments of government are responsible for conducting their
ministers' policies and their statutory functions in the most economic,
efficient and effective manner within their financial allocations and
limits. However, each minister, advised by his or her officials, will have
participated in deciding those limits. Ministers will, as far as possible,
have taken advantage of both formal and informal opportunities to
influence Treasury ministers about the national importance of their
department's work and, where appropriate, will also have drawn attention to the importance of their work in the government's programme.
Sometimes, of course, there may also be partisan factors which
become particularly important, especially in relation to general elections, and these, too, will become significant in discussions between
individual ministers. Not all these matters will be undertaken on a
personal and individual basis; there are numerous other opportunities
for political activity in various committees, and ultimately in Cabinet,
but most important of all, in Cabinet committees. This is well illustrated by the fact that in June 1995 the Chancellor of the Exchequer
sat on nine of the Cabinet's sixteen standing committees (the same
number as the Prime Minister), and the Chief Secretary sat on seven
Cabinet committees and on one sub-committee.[66]

In the 1980s, when the Conservative Government was particularly
concerned to reduce public spending and contract the role of the state,
the government set up a small group of ministers, known as the Star
Chamber, and chaired by the then Deputy Prime Minister (Mr
William, now Viscount, Whitelaw), to resolve difficulties that arose
between Treasury officials and officials in departments. Since 1992,
however, this has been replaced on a permanent basis by the Cabinet's
Economic and Domestic Policy (Expenditure) Committee (EDX),
which has the responsibility to consider pressures for greater spending
by some departments within the constraints of available resources. It is
in preparation for the work of this Cabinet sub-committee that the

Chief Secretary discusses, with each spending minister in turn (normally in July), what level of resources should be allocated to their departments within the overall totals agreed. He reports the outcome of these discussions, together with carefully calculated provisions for a reserve to cover unforeseen contingencies, to meetings of the EDX committee in September and October, which then makes proposals to the full Cabinet in October.

The main details of parliamentary procedure in relation to the annual financial cycle are given in Appendix 2, but it should be noted that, as a result of introducing the new unified budget timetable, the Finance Bill receives the Royal Assent in May, and work on the next year's budget begins in the summer and continues through the autumn. Work on some new tax proposals starts as soon as the previous Finance Bill has been enacted. In addition to advice the Chancellor receives from Treasury officials on all aspects of his budget proposals, he also receives views of outside forecasters, some of whom are members of the Panel of Independent Forecasters, and from a large variety of public and private institutions and groups which wish to see their interests advanced or protected. The Treasury also has regular discussions with the Treasury Academic Advisory Panel, which consists of distinguished outside experts in relevant fields. The Chancellor discusses details of the budget with the other Treasury ministers and with senior officials at a residential weekend meeting (in recent years, at Chevening or Dorneywood) which leads to further intensive work within the Treasury on details. Then, as soon as details are settled, instructions are given to Parliamentary Counsel to prepare provisions in the Finance Bill. On Budget Day, the *Financial Statement and Budget Report* (known as the 'Red Book') is published with details of the budget statement and expenditure plans of the various departments and agencies.

The budget, in November, is followed by the Finance Bill, introduced in January, which embodies the budget proposals; all the individual measures are debated in committee or on the floor of the House. Treasury ministers and their officials are heavily involved in the details of this work. However, there are also other parliamentary responsibilities which place heavy demands on Treasury officials. These include debates on Treasury subjects, initiated either by the government or the opposition, and also parliamentary questions, because three-quarters of an hour every four weeks while Parliament is sitting is allocated to deal with questions to Treasury ministers.

In addition to the annual estimates and budget, the Treasury is involved, usually in July, November and February, with presenting supplementary estimates for new proposals or unforeseen require-ments. These estimates give Parliament the opportunity to debate individual spending programmes of the departments, and three days are allotted in each parliamentary year for such debates, on subjects nominated by the departmental parliamentary select committees. One of these select committees, the Treasury Committee (previously the Treasury and Civil Service Committee), has the particular task of considering matters within the responsibility of Treasury ministers. It takes evidence on the budget from the Chancellor of the Exchequer, the Governor of the Bank of England, and Treasury officials, and has special hearings on the government's spending plans.

The Public Accounts Committee scrutinises accounts after they are laid before Parliament at the end of the financial year. It is assisted by the Comptroller and Auditor General and the National Audit Office which scrutinises the accounts to check that money was spent to good effect and on purposes authorised by Parliament. The Committee discusses the reports from the Comptroller and Auditor General, examines the accounting officers from the relevant departments and agencies, and publishes its own reports and recommendations, to which Treasury officials prepare the government's replies. Sometimes Treasury officials also give evidence to the Public Accounts Committee on matters such as financial management in government, or govern-ment purchasing, and in any case the Treasury is always represented at all hearings of the Committee by the Treasury Officer of Accounts (or a deputy) because of its general interest in financial regularity and value for money. There are always debates on the Committee's reports, requiring further participation by Treasury ministers and appropriate briefing by officials.

The Fundamental Expenditure Review paid attention to the new arrangements it proposed for financial reporting to Parliament and drew special attention to co-ordinating the whole range of Treasury contacts with Parliament, its select committees, and the National Audit Office on financial reporting and accounting issues, and the need to maintain a central source of experience and expertise on the rules for government accounting and financial propriety.[67] The new arrangements it proposed stressed the important work of 'developing, maintaining, and agreeing with departments and the relevant parlia-mentary interests, a coherent policy on financial reporting to Parliament, and on providing advice and expertise more generally on central public sector accounting and propriety issues'.[68] The Review queried, in particular, the Treasury's role in the dealings other depart-ments have with the Public Accounts Committee, with a view to keeping this to a minimum.[69] Such recommendations may, indeed, lead to fewer duties for Treasury officials, and therefore to economies, but they may also result in less Treasury influence and consequently, perhaps, to lower Treasury status in the system of government.

The Treasury also has considerable involvement with the select committees, and their sub-committees, concerned with European Community business in both the House of Commons and the House of Lords. These committees usually meet every week when Parliament is in session, to examine EC proposals. Whilst this work is generally a primary concern for officials in the International Directorate, other officials may also be involved when their expertise is appropriate to topics being discussed.

It is therefore not surprising that, because of its work and responsibilities, the Treasury is the focus of much political activity. While most of this activity focuses on ministers, officials have to play their part because they work on behalf of ministers, and it is officials who prepare advice and develop policies. Much of this political activity is internal, within the system of government; it is issue-based rather than ideologically-based; and it is within the environment of this political activity that the Treasury has to ensure that its structure and organisation meet the expectations of its aim, mission and objectives. How this develops and operates in practice is well illustrated by the study, in the next chapter, of the financing and responsibility of Next Steps agencies.

The structure of the Treasury and the details of its organisation and responsibilities are of much greater interest and importance than most basic textbooks indicate. The Treasury remains the key department of Whitehall, but its activities are more in the spheres of influence and persuasion than in the exercise of powers. As Lord Bridges indicated in the 1960s, 'on important financial questions there is constant discussion between the departments and the Treasury . . . and there is a sharing of responsibility';[70] and as Andrew Likierman explained it in the 1980s, referring to public expenditure priorities, 'departments are in a bargaining position' with the Treasury.[71] The department therefore has to be structured and to work in relation to the parliamentary and political environment which exists at any given time, but which may be different at other times. At the ministerial level, the authority of the Treasury depends on the acceptance by other ministers of the views and judgments of the Chancellor of the Exchequer, and this makes it the focus of much political activity by both ministers and officials. Indeed, in terms of the Treasury's duties and organisation the principles are much the same now as when Lord Welby (Permanent

Secretary to the Treasury from 1885 to 1894) referred, in 1879, to the Treasury as 'rather an office of superintendence and appeal than an office of administration'.[72] Welby also spoke of the Treasury as being 'the most political of Departments',[73] because its business leads it to concern itself with every important aspect of government policy. The details given in this chapter indicate the truth of this statement through details of responsibility and practice.

4 The financing and responsibility of Next Steps agencies

There can be no doubt, from what has been said in Chapters 2 and 3 of this book, that the Treasury is the most political of departments. This is evident at the ministerial level because of its key role in the government's programme. Whatever the party in power, the government needs finance to achieve its objectives; taxation is one of the most important interests of citizens in relation to government; and the country's economy is a crucial factor in almost all spheres of international relations. It is therefore not surprising that the work of the Treasury is so important from partisan and ideological perspectives, and it is consequently the focus of much political activity at those levels. However, the Treasury may also be seen as the most political of departments from the perspective of 'closed' politics; that is, the internal politics within the political and administrative system, involving both ministers and officials in aspects of government that rarely get much coverage in the media and where details are rarely the subject of comment, even by the cognoscenti. To illustrate how this works in practice, and how important the role of the Treasury is 'behind the scenes', this chapter concentrates on the role of the Treasury in the creation and monitoring of Next Steps agencies.

The creation of Next Steps agencies to carry out executive functions of government is the most significant administrative reform of the second half of the twentieth century in British central government. It had its immediate origins in the 1988 Report to the Prime Minister from the Efficiency Unit: *Improving Management in Government: The Next Steps*,[1] which made proposals for the government's next steps in modernising and improving the civil service. The House of Commons Select Committee on the Treasury and Civil Service has followed the implementation of the proposals with great interest: there has been enthusiastic and bipartisan support for the reforms, and this has manifested itself most obviously in the proceedings of the Select Committee.

Indeed, the Committee's first report on it said: 'Our concern is that the pace of change should not be too slow, and the extent of change too limited, as long as the consequence of such change is an improved quality of service to Government, Parliament, and society'.[2] The Committee's support has continued in subsequent reports, and in the 1994 Report on *The Role of the Civil Service* it said 'We believe that Next Steps agencies represent a significant improvement in the organisation of Government and that any future Government will want to maintain them in order to implement its objectives for the delivery of services to the public'.[3]

By the beginning of November 1995 there were 109 agencies, plus twenty Customs and Excise executive units and twenty-nine Inland Revenue executive offices working along Next Steps lines, each within the terms of a framework document, and each with its own Chief Executive or head of unit personally accountable for performance.[4] It meant that about 63 per cent of the civil service was working in agencies with a further fifty-five agency candidates and other areas under consideration in the autumn of 1995. The government's intention in the 1994 *Next Steps Review* was that most of the candidates 'should be up and running as agencies by mid-1995', covering around 75 per cent of the civil service.[5] This record easily achieved the government's prediction in its reply to the 1991 report from the Treasury and Civil Service Committee, which had estimated that by April 1992 half the civil service would be in agencies,[6] and was consistent with the Citizen's Charter White Paper, which clearly stated that the Conservative Government's aim was that all the executive activities of government would, as far as practicable, be operating along these lines by the end of 1993.[7] As long ago as November 1991 the government was confidently stating: 'Next Steps now provides the normal framework for carrying out the executive functions of Government'.[8]

THE NEXT STEPS AGENCIES: ORIGINS AND BACKGROUND

The main emphasis in the Next Steps Report was the need for more urgency in the search for better value for money and towards steadily improving services. The terms of reference for the scrutiny team which produced the report were: 'to assess the progress achieved in improving management in the Civil Service', 'to identify what measures have been successful in changing attitudes and practices', 'to identify the institutional, administrative, political and attitudinal obstacles to better management and efficiency that still remain', and 'to report to the Prime Minister on what further measures should be taken'.[9] Its main recommendation was that 'agencies' should be established to carry out the executive functions of government within a policy and resources framework set by a department. It said that some potential agencies may continue within the public service, but others may be more effective outside it. The intention of its recommendations was that officials should be able 'to show real qualities of leadership' because, as the then Prime Minister Mrs Margaret Thatcher said in the House of Commons on 18 February 1988, 'responsibility for the day to day operations of each agency should be delegated direct from the relevant minister to a chief executive'.[10]

The impetus for developing Next Steps agencies owes much to Thatcher's determination to reduce waste and make government more efficient. This was a key feature of her style of government. It was that general approach which motivated her, soon after becoming Prime Minister, to ask Sir Leo Pliatzky, an eminent, recently retired civil servant who had been Second Permanent Secretary in the Treasury, to undertake a critical review of non-departmental government bodies.[11] It was also Thatcher's general approach and determination to make government more efficient, according to an ideology which regarded business values and business methods as the most productive and preferred ideology, that motivated her, in 1979, to set up the Efficiency Unit. This continued as a central theme of the Conservative Government's programme after Thatcher ceased to be Prime Minister. John Major, Thatcher's successor, referred in his Citizen's Charter to Next Steps agencies as 'part of the drive towards more businesslike and decentralised delivery of services'.[12]

The Efficiency Unit was originally created under Sir Derek (now Lord) Rayner, whom Thatcher appointed on a part-time basis as her personal adviser on improving efficiency and eliminating waste in government. In his Efficiency Unit Rayner inaugurated scrutinies of specific areas of government work to propose solutions to problems, achieve savings, and increase effectiveness. These scrutinies quickly became established as a new approach to reviewing aspects of government activity. Scrutinies are intensive exercises focusing on particular areas of work by small teams of staff seconded to undertake them for short periods of time. It was a team of three that carried out the scrutiny that led to the Next Steps Report: Kate Jenkins (then Head of the Efficiency Unit) led the team, with Karen Caines and Andrew Jackson, working under the supervision of Sir Robin Ibbs (Rayner's successor), and helped in certain tasks by other members of the unit. The project followed the regular pattern and constraints of all scrutiny investigations; it was completed within ninety working days, beginning on 3 November 1986 and ending on 20 March 1987.

The Next Steps team's method of working was to interview twenty-one ministers and fifty-two officials; undertake thirteen group discussions with senior officials in different grades; talk with people who had recently left the civil service; visit regional and local offices of departments of government (in Birmingham, Leeds, Manchester, Newcastle, North Fylde and Telford) and RAF Brampton; look at recent major management changes in non-governmental organisations (British Rail, Halifax Building Society, ICI); and meet the Council of Civil Service Unions. It kept closely in touch with developments in the Treasury and Cabinet Office, in particular over progress on personnel management changes and the implementation of the Wilson Report on Budgeting;[13] and examined previous reports on the management of the civil service. The estimated cost of the scrutiny was £50,000. By the time the team had completed its work this scrutiny was one of over three hundred such reviews undertaken since 1979.[14]

In some respects the recommendation for the creation of agencies was very similar to the recommendations in the Fulton Report for more 'accountable management' and for a thorough review of whether large-scale executive operations should be 'hived off' to non-departmental organisations.[15] Indeed, as examples, the Fulton Committee especially mentioned the Royal Mint, air traffic control, and parts of the social services. A decade later the Select Committee on Expenditure recommended a determined drive to introduce accountable units in all areas of executive work and, where possible, in administrative work.[16] The recommendations in the Next Steps Report were not, therefore, entirely new, though the manner in which they were presented was different, involving a certain campaigning style emphasising qualities like value for money, efficiency and effectiveness, and commitment to change. A few quotations from the Report illustrate this well. It said that 'the management of the agency should have as much independence as possible in deciding how objectives are met' (para. 21), 'the head of the agency must be given personal responsibility to achieve the best possible results within it . . . (and) be seen to be accountable for doing so' (para. 22), 'responsibility for performance (should be placed) squarely on the shoulders of the manager of the agency' (para. 23), and 'senior managers must be prepared to show real qualities of leadership, the ability to back their judgement and to take and defend unpopular decisions' (para. 35).

For the purposes of the present discussion it is necessary to emphasise first, the main recommendation, which was for the creation of agencies to carry out the executive functions of government within a policy and resources framework set by a department. Second, the recommendation for a permanent secretary, designated as 'Project Manager' to ensure that the way departments operate is changed 'fundamentally and radically' (para. 4l). Third, the acceptance by the government of the key recommendations, which would, as the Prime Minister told the House of Commons, 'set the direction for further development of management reform in the Civil Service'.[17] Fourth, that responsibility for the management of day-to-day operations of each agency should be delegated to a chief executive who would work within a framework of policy objectives and resources set by the responsible minister, in consultation with the Treasury: 'The Cabinet Secretariat and the expenditure functions of the Treasury will remain and there will still need to be provision at the centre for determining directions, keeping up pressure on departments, and setting standards' (para. 45).

The Prime Minister's announcement, which formed the basis for the subsequent creation of Next Steps agencies, was made in the House of Commons on 18 February 1988. The statement was, in the words of Sir Peter Kemp, 'an implicit act of faith that this approach would bring about greater efficiency and effectiveness in government'.[18] However, it was not an act of faith without accompanying action. When the statement was made the government was already prepared with plans to take quick action to implement the initiative. Soon after the announcement, the Treasury and Civil Service Select Committee made the Next Steps the subject of an inquiry, reporting in July 1988.[19] The Committee was, in general, strongly supportive, drawing particular attention 'to the need to change the culture and attitudes of the civil service',[20] but it recommended that the House of Commons would want to debate the issue of accountability as soon as possible.[21] The evidence it received emphasised the clear lead given by the Prime Minister and other ministers in implementing the initiative, as well as by the Head of the Civil Service and the line managers in the civil service.[22] However, the evidence also revealed Treasury concerns about the development of agencies. As Sir Robin Butler, Head of the Civil Service, put it: 'When the report was being discussed the Treasury were very anxious – and in my view rightly so – that this approach should not weaken the overall controls of public expenditure which are necessary for macro-economic purposes and the control over the pay bill'.[23] The government's reply to the Select Committee reasserted the main aim of the initiative: 'to deliver government services more efficiently and effectively, within available resources, for the benefit of taxpayers, customers and staff'.[24]

Whilst the immediate impetus for the development of agencies is therefore to be found in the Ibbs Report of 1988, this very significant administrative reform owes much to other factors as well. The Ibbs Report was a short document without much analysis and with more assertion than reasoning. Its recommendations were not new, especially as its key proposals had been considered and recommended more than twenty years previously by the Fulton Committee and had also been approvingly referred to from time to time in the intervening years by interested politicians and commentators[25] as well as by the House of Commons Expenditure Committee. The recommendations were acceptable in 1988 because of a combination of factors including: the passage of time and intermittent public discussion of these recommendations over more than twenty years; the evolution of a political climate in which the recommendations were not a matter of sensitive partisan controversy; the forceful and determined attitude of the Prime Minister; and the general acceptability of the ideas within key parts of the administrative system. Moreover, the recommendations were quickly implemented because they required no specific legislation: and this was especially important at a time of legislative pressure. In the British political system, changes in the structure of government departments and arrangements for the civil service can be introduced without the need for prolonged parliamentary discussion. Details for the new agencies, and the implications for other parts of the administrative system, could be worked out fairly quickly, piecemeal, and lessons learned from experience in creating the first agencies could be assimilated quickly for implementing the later creations.

THE FIRST FEW YEARS: THE CURRENT PATTERN OF AGENCIES

A remarkable feature of the development of Next Steps agencies is the speed with which they were set up. The Ibbs Report had, in fact, been presented to the Prime Minister in the spring of 1987, and during the summer detailed proposals were prepared in Whitehall. By October 1987, following the General Election in June, and some four months before the Prime Minister's statement in the House of Commons, ministers were ready to endorse the proposals for the first twelve candidates for agency status. They ranged from the Queen Elizabeth II Conference Centre with a staff of only sixty-five to the Employment Service with a staff of 35,000; and from Her Majesty's Stationery Office with an annual turnover of over £400 million to the National Weights and Measures Laboratory with an annual turnover of little more than £2 million. They also included the Driver and Vehicle Licensing Office, the Passport Office, and Resettlement Units. However, by the end of 1991 there were fifty-seven agencies and thirty Customs and Excise executive units working on Next Steps lines, amounting to nearly 40 per cent of the civil service.[26] The process has by no means slackened since then. Indeed, Sir Peter Kemp told the Treasury and Civil Service Committee in May 1988, that he would be personally sorry if by 1998 three-quarters of the civil service were not working in agencies.[27] In 1991 he was predicting that there would be seventy agencies by July 1992.[28] The intentions of both the politicians directly involved with the creation of agencies, and the members of the Next Steps Project Team has therefore been to maintain the momentum with a determination to achieve the early targets they set themselves. The catchphrase used by Kemp, a catchphrase also used by ministers when reporting developments in publications and in evidence before the Treasury and Civil Service Committee is to emphasise that there are 'more to come'.

Official explanations of these developments have usually emphasised the key elements in creating agencies and then stressed the logical nature of their development from management innovations and reforms introduced since the Conservative Government came to power in 1979. The key elements stress that the aims of agencies are to provide a better quality of service to customers, enhance job satisfaction for the people in the organisation, and achieve better value for money for the taxpayer. In explaining the logical development of Next Steps agencies from earlier innovations and reforms, emphasis is usually placed on the importance of the Financial Management Initiative (FMI).

FMI, like the Next Steps initiative, was a development from a Rayner scrutiny. It drew upon the technique known as MINIS (Management Information System for Ministers), the result of one of the first Rayner scrutinies, which was developed in the Department of the Environment in 1980 but achieved prominence when it was subsequently introduced into the Ministry of Defence by Mr Michael Heseltine. The importance of MINIS was that it showed how a department was organised and who was responsible for each area of activity. It was designed to enable the minister to explore 'who does what, why and what does it cost?' by bringing together information about activities, past performance and future plans for each part of the department.[29]

FMI built upon the experience of MINIS and management accounting and was designed, to quote the words of the White Paper:

To promote in each department an organisation and system in which managers at all levels have:

(a) A clear view of their objectives, and means to assess and, where possible, measure outputs or performance in relation to those objectives;

(b) Well defined responsibility for making the best use of their resources, including a critical scrutiny of output and value for money; and

(c) The information (particularly about costs), the training and the access to expert advice that they need to exercise their responsibilities effectively.[30]

Sometimes, however, the official explanation of the development of Next Steps agencies from the earlier innovations seems more like post-hoc rationalisation because the process may, in fact, have been more a matter of evolution. It does not necessarily seem that it was a further move towards a developmental goal known in advance, though it is fair to add that all these changes were linked by the government's emphasis on efficiency and value for money. The distinctive feature of the Next Steps Report was that it was not focused primarily on management techniques, but was concerned in a more general way with various areas of the executive aspects of government. Moreover, the recommendations in the Next Steps Report may never have been conceived without the Megaw Report on Civil Service Pay, which preceded it in 1982.[31] That report made recommendations for performance-related pay and the introduction of merit scales based on annual reports.

Another factor, at least as important in any explanation of this development, is the role played by Sir Peter Kemp, the Next Steps Project Manager. The Next Steps Report had recommended the appointment of a Project Manager and in February 1988 the Prime Minister told the House of Commons that the government had accepted that recommendation. The person selected for this post was a senior Treasury official who had joined the Ministry of Transport in 1967 as a direct entry principal from the private sector, and was an accountant by training. As Project Manager, he became a Second Permanent Secretary in the Cabinet Office and was also Head of the Office of the Minister for the Civil Service (OMCS); and, as a named individual he became a public figure. Diana Goldsworthy, one of the original members of the Next Steps project team, has written: 'He was known as a creative thinker, as well as a determined negotiator'.[32] Professor Peter Hennessy has referred to 'the appointment of an energetic and almost evangelically open Project Manager in Peter Kemp',[33] and Mr Richard Luce, when Minister for the Civil Service, spoke of Kemp as a man 'who tackles all his work with great energy and is tireless in it'.[34] Kemp himself told the Treasury and Civil Service Committee, when he appeared before it in 1988, that he attended 'with hope and enthusiasm'.[35] He has also referred to the 'risk taking' culture which he hoped to see spread among agency management,[36] and, in answer to another question, said: 'I feel extremely comfortable in this job'.[37]

In addition to a small Next Steps Project Team (initially only three people), to help him plan and co-ordinate the creation of agencies, Kemp set up two other groups. One was the Project Executive, a small working group from the Treasury, the Efficiency Unit, the OMCS, and the Project Team, which met weekly to think through some of the across-the-board issues as they came up, and to make sure that there was agreement about the way that progress was being made. The other was the Project Liaison Group, composed of senior representatives from the main departments, meeting with representatives from the Project Team and the Treasury, to exchange ideas and get endorsement for his proposals.[38] Indeed, there soon became two Project Liaison Groups, one for large departments and one for small departments,[39] but these were later merged again, to form the Inner Project Liaison Group, which continues to meet once a month. Kemp also instituted opportunities for 'friends' (business people, academics and professionals) to comment on the work and participate in conferences and seminars.

One of Kemp's early tasks was to formulate proposals for the special financial arrangements for agencies, which he presented to the Treasury as early as April 1988. From the point of view of the Treasury, agencies may be grouped into two basic categories: those which are funded by charges from customers and those which are supply financed. Some of those funded by charges are designated as trading funds in accordance with the Government Trading Funds Act 1973, which provides a financial framework covering operating costs and receipts, capital expenditure, borrowing and net cash flow. An agency funded on this basis operates like a government-owned company, it is required to earn a prescribed return on current cost assets, has powers to borrow to meet capital expenditure and working capital requirements, and to establish reserves out of surpluses.[40] The 1973 Act has now been amended by the Government Trading Act 1990 (see below, pp. 126–8). An example of a trading fund agency is the Royal Mint, which is a highly successful business. Indeed, whereas the level of profit expected for a public sector business is usually 8 per cent, the current (1993–96) target for the Mint is 14 per cent. Agencies which do not meet the statutory requirements to operate as trading funds are covered by the normal supply procedures, but their expenditure is contained within limits on running costs. Examples are the Contributions Agency, Civil Service College, and Ordnance Survey. In some cases agencies operate on a basis of recovering their costs by charging other government departments or agencies: the Civil Service College is one of these.

Whatever the financial arrangements for particular agencies, their creation and subsequent development have led to a number of anxieties which have been raised by commentators and have also received attention in the proceedings of the Treasury and Civil Service Committee. In the context of this present study, three of the most important matters of concern are briefly explained here. These are the appointment of Chief Executives, the position of staff in relation to other civil servants, and financial and parliamentary accountability. All of these topics have particular relevance to the role of the Treasury.

First, the appointment of Chief Executives. This was a matter considered in 1988 by the Treasury and Civil Service Committee, and it has continued to be interested in the subject because of the possibility that the formation of agencies could provide opportunities for politicians to play a significant role in making appointments to head them. The arrangements, as explained to the Committee in recent years, are that the positions of Chief Executives are normally advertised and the recruitment procedures are the responsibility of the Civil Service Commissioners. The Commissioners always have a place on the selection board, together with someone from the relevant department, often someone from the Treasury, and one or two outsiders. The board ranks the candidates but the minister does not have to accept the board's recommendation – as Kemp told the Treasury and Civil Service Committee: 'After all, it is the Minister making the appointment and not the Commission'.[41] The minister's approval is always necessary, but in the case of the most senior and most sensitive appointments, the Prime Minister is also consulted.[42] The Treasury and Civil Service Committee commented that this seemed to imply a much greater involvement on the part of ministers than before in the appointment of relatively junior staff.[43] In 1990 the Minister for the Civil Service had assured the Committee that the traditional rules on the propriety of appointments would apply to all Chief Executives, but John Garrett MP, a member of the Committee, noted that as these appointments included some at Grade 6 level (i.e. senior principal), they represented involvement by politicians at a lower level of appointment than ever before.[44] Whether they are appointed from internal candidates or from outside through open competition it has been stressed that, for the period of their contracts (and they are all appointed on contracts of only a few years) they are civil servants. Moreover, because the agencies are executive bodies, the minister sets the policy and resources framework within which the Chief Executives operate. As Kemp told the Committee: 'They are operating under discipline and they actually have the choice of doing one of two things. They can buckle down and do what the Minister has asked them to do; or they can resign'.[45]

Second, the position of staff in relation to other civil servants. The position here is not as clear to many observers as it seems to be to senior officials. Sir Robin Ibbs has said that the initial agencies are within government departments,[46] but Garrett thought the creation of agencies was the beginning of the end of a unified civil service which had common conditions of service and established procedures.[47] Sir Angus Fraser raised the question of whether, with the creation of agencies, there will still be a civil service which is a recognisable entity.[48] Mr Richard Luce, then Minister for the Civil Service, argued that the creation of agencies was 'decentralisation' of the service because there would still be common standards including impartiality, equality of opportunity and fair and open recruitment.[49] Sir Robin Butler, however, as Head of the Civil Service, was confident that 'we will retain a unified but not uniform civil service',[50] and this 'rather good way of putting it' (as Butler added) was later repeated by Kemp and Luce and others.[51]

The essence of the confusion is to be found in the difficulty of reconciling such features as flexible pay (often performance-related), diverse conditions of service, devolved responsibility for recruitment, and opportunities for staff to display initiative and enterprise, sometimes appointed on short-term contracts (sometimes outside 'the career service'),[52] with the normal expectations of a bureaucratic system conditioned by ministerial accountability within the British political system. Whilst Kemp, in 1989, asserted that all agency staff would remain civil servants within their department,[53] he also referred to agencies 'breaking loose of the Civil Service completely'[54] and explained the family feeling developing among staff in agencies:

> They do not feel they are in the Civil Service . . . they are more customer oriented and feel they are more vertically oriented

towards the job to be done and to the customers they serve rather than the general concept of the public.[55]

Various Chief Executives have stressed that agency is a state of mind, involving a 'can do' attitude, and that it is about commitment and enthusiasm.[56] However, the Council of Civil Service Unions has pointed out that the creation of agencies also has implications for staff transfers and promotions, which might be difficult if each agency has its own system of pay, grading, conditions of service, and ways of organising work. Moreover, they thought the consequences would include an enormous duplication in the pay and personnel management functions, and asked whether steps were being taken to ensure that the delegation of responsibility and authority was being undertaken in a structured fashion with proper training and resources being made available.[57]

To some extent this position has been clarified by the statement given by the Chancellor of the Exchequer on 24 July 1991. In reply to a written question in the House of Commons, the Chancellor announced the government's intention to introduce more flexible pay regimes for the civil service, both nationally and locally. The Chancellor said he proposed to introduce a closer link between performance and reward for individuals and groups; more delegation to civil service departments and agencies to introduce their own grading structures and do their own pay bargaining; and where these measures were not appropriate, for greater flexibilities within the total overall central pay settlement agreed by the Treasury.[58] By 1 April 1994, twenty-one agencies and the two revenue departments, altogether employing about 60 per cent of the Home Civil Service, had taken delegated responsibility for their own pay and pay-related conditions of service. By April 1996 responsibility for pay and grading of all staff below senior levels had been delegated to departments and agencies.[59] It therefore seems that personnel management approaches that have been and are being introduced into agencies, schools and the national health service are now destined also for the whole civil service.

Third, the question of financial and parliamentary accountability. The Chief Executives of agencies are accountable to both their ministers (whom they often refer to as their customers) and also to Parliament for the economy, efficiency and effectiveness of their agencies. Sometimes Chief Executives also refer to their accountability to the Treasury and their other customers.[60] The Fraser Report drew attention to this matter which, it said, had been raised frequently with its authors. It noted that the relationship between the accounting officer responsibilities of the Chief Executives and the wider responsibilities of the Permanent Secretary as Departmental Accounting Officer had not been properly put to the test in front of the Public Accounts Committee. It added:

> The current text of the Accounting Officer Memorandum appears to give a wider responsibility to the Permanent Secretary for ensuring good management and financial propriety throughout the Department, including the Agency. As a result, central divisions in sponsor Departments felt that they had to carry out their control and monitoring role in a closer and more detailed manner than might otherwise be the case, so as to provide the Permanent Secretary with a reasonable level of assurance, not just on the adequacy of control systems, but also on the activities of the Agency.[61]

It then reported considerable frustration which had been reported to it, over the number of detailed and comparatively trivial management decisions, especially on personnel matters, which had to be referred back to sponsor departments or to the Treasury for approval.[62] It also said that it found a case where an approval for a Chief Executive to spend in excess of his delegated limits for capital expenditure was given by someone in the central finance division three grades his junior.[63]

The Treasury and Civil Service Committee in 1991 found a tendency for the Treasury and OMCS to have detailed rules on management matters for their own requirements, whilst being permissive about the forms in which departments and agencies reported their activities to Parliament and the public.[64] Consequently, this led to questions about the real freedom to operate that was in fact being extended to agencies, and how detailed and rigid the requirements of the Treasury should be. However, as Mr G. H. Phillips, of the Treasury, told the Treasury and Civil Service Committee in 1991, all institutions in the civil service will be linked together with 'certain central bits of "glue" . . . the accountability of Ministers to Parliament, the need for real and tight expenditure control, (and) the need to sustain standards of conduct and probity'.[65] All these are, in one way or another, responsibilities of the Treasury and it is therefore necessary to examine next various facets of the role of the Treasury in relation to Next Steps agencies.

THE ROLE OF THE TREASURY

The Treasury has a number of specific responsibilities in relation to the development of Next Steps agencies. These originate, on the one hand, from its general role as the central department of finance and, on the other hand, from particular responsibilities it has acquired in the creation of agencies. The intention now is to consider the Treasury's overview responsibilities because these set the scene within which the specific details have been worked out. The most important specific elements of Treasury control over Next Steps agencies are discussed later.

As has earlier been explained, the Treasury's fundamental purpose is the planning and control of public expenditure. This means two things. First, that public expenditure in general is consistent with the government's macroeconomic policies and priorities for public expenditure. Second, in detail, it has to ensure that money is spent as Parliament intended and also that it is spent in ways that give good value. It is this fundamental purpose of the Treasury that gives rise to all the elements of detail in the relationships of the Treasury to departments and agencies. In some cases the details are expressed in controls, operational rules, and requirements to send reports to the Treasury; but in many cases the Treasury's roles are more evident in guidance and advice, persuasion and influence.

According to private information obtained by Peter Hennessy, the delay between Prime Minister Thatcher receiving the Next Steps Report from Sir Robin Ibbs, in 1987, and publication in 1988, was caused by the sensitivities and implications of the Report. In Whitehall 'a battle royal ensued in the autumn of 1987 which raged for several months'.[66] This, however, is not surprising. It was not immediately clear how the Treasury's traditional controls over public expenditure would continue when freedom to operate on a more commercial basis was to be given to a large number of executive units in government, and nowhere was this more uncertain than in pay bargaining for the civil service. This was especially important for the Treasury's control of public expenditure because, according to Sir Peter Middleton, then Permanent Secretary to the Treasury, the public sector accounts for about 40 per cent of GDP.[67] The Treasury was understandably anxious to ensure that responsibilities for pay and other powers which might be given to the agencies, with potentially serious economic implications, were maintained as matters of negotiation with the Treasury, and ultimately as matters of Treasury control.[68]

In order to ensure continuing control over public expenditure, the

Treasury spending teams analyse public expenditure bids and output and performance targets in the annual Public Expenditure Survey; they scrutinise estimates, cash limits and running costs totals; and approve major expenditure such as capital investment which is not within a department's delegated authority. In doing this, the Treasury issues rules and guidance through Government Accounting, the Civil Service Management Code, and its guide to setting targets and measuring performance.[69] On pay, which Sir Peter Middleton has said accounts for something like 65 per cent of the running costs of the civil service, the crucial responsibilities, together with the grading of posts and conditions of service, were transferred back to the Treasury in 1981, when the Civil Service Department was abolished. In 1987 the Treasury acquired from the Management and Personnel Office, on its transition to OMCS, further personnel functions, including recruitment policy and the classification of posts. This meant that all personnel management functions which related directly to financial management, manpower and financial conditions of service were back again with the Treasury.[70]

Moreover, the Treasury has a continuing responsibility for financial management and value for money in central government. Value for money is a technique, or general term relating to a group of techniques in public sector management, which achieved prominence soon after the Conservatives were elected in 1979. According to a Royal Institute of Public Administration seminar in 1981, definition of value for money was difficult but a consensus view expected it to revolve around economy (doing things for lower cost), efficiency (doing things right) and effectiveness (doing the right things).[71] This approach, which apparently originates from management consultants and teachers of business studies, seems to have been widely accepted, though it reverses the definitions of efficiency and effectiveness found in the classical literature on management.[72] Value for money became a popular term among politicians in the 1980s; but in the practice of public sector management it became evident, to adopt the words of Sir Ron Dearing, in Treasury insistence on performance measures, performance targets and rigorous testing of performance against them.[73] The Treasury also made its mark in this context by the publication in 1988 of a most valuable pamphlet which built upon its experience in this area: *Policy Evaluation: A Guide for Managers*. Indeed, the glossary in that publication defined value for money in this way: 'Ultimately the final social and economic benefit of a policy in relation to the cost. Sometimes used as shorthand for the optimum combination of economy, effectiveness and efficiency'.[74]

It is because of the Treasury's overall responsibility for the planning and control of public expenditure, and because of its expertise in matters relating to public expenditure, that agencies are not created unless the Treasury is satisfied about the various arrangements and controls relating to them. In particular, the Treasury gives guidance to departments on relevant financial and expenditure issues and their application to departmental responsibilities. The Treasury always asks (as does the OPS) as its initial question, whether the agency approach is the only one in a given context. The possible alternatives that are routinely considered are: abolition, contractorisation, creating a government-owned company, and privatisation. In the early days of the Next Steps initiative the Treasury always ensured that alternatives to agency status were fully considered before an agency was set up.[75] Then, in considering all the aspects within the department's sphere of responsibility, the Treasury brings to bear its background knowledge of the department's expenditure and financial management position, and can offer specialist advice on such matters as accountancy, performance measurement, and target setting.[76] At the end of the agency creation and agency supervision process, it is of particular importance to the Treasury that the new financial systems created to accommodate the new agencies meet the needs of delegated financial responsibility.

It will be evident from this account that, from the Treasury viewpoint, the recommendations in the Next Steps Report had to be related to the various techniques and approaches to public sector management to which the Treasury had itself contributed so much in the 1980s. Indeed, the Next Steps Scrutiny Team which was responsible for the Report was already familiar with these developments and referred to the Wilson review of Multi-Departmental Budgeting, which was printed in 1986. The intention of the Wilson review was

> to encourage the development of budgeting as an effective instrument of expenditure planning and control and as a tool which management can use to improve its resources allocation and to deliver greater economy, efficiency and effectiveness in the accomplishment of its task.[77]

The Wilson review itself was undertaken on scrutiny lines and saw one of the end products of budgeting as line managers being 'tasked with carrying out their activities with the resources allocated so entering into "contracts for performance"'.[78]

After the implementation of the Next Steps initiative was begun, the Treasury was heavily involved, both in ensuring that its overall responsibilities continued in relation to particular agencies, and also in producing information and guidance that would be useful to all agencies. For example, in 1989 it published a White Paper describing the financing and accountability arrangements for Next Steps agencies;[79] it introduced the Government Trading Bill, which, among other things, made provisions to extend the powers to create trading funds; it issued draft guidance (intended to be regularly updated) to departments on setting targets and measuring output and performance; it prepared detailed guidance on agency reports and accounts; it made provisions to increase the range of discretion available to departments, especially in personnel management; and it encouraged departments and agencies to consider tailoring their pay and grading systems to the needs of their businesses.[80] These major changes were all in the same direction as other changes or proposals announced at about the same time: for example, the attention given to delegating more discretion to departments and agencies and the increased emphasis on performance pay and staff grading flexibilities, as announced in the Citizen's Charter and the Chancellor's statement of 24 July 1991.[81]

One facet of the Treasury role that emerged from time to time in its evidence to the Treasury and Civil Service Committee seems directly to result from its general responsibilities as outlined here. As Phillips, of the Treasury, put it in 1990, 'we would see our role very clearly as bearing down and making sure we were in the business of protecting the consumer',[82] 'we want to ensure that these controls are there and money is not being wasted'.[83]

The Treasury's tasks in relation to the Next Steps initiative require its staff to consider two approaches at the same time. One approach is the traditional one of critic, associated with any central department of finance, challenging and seeking out flaws in proposals from departments. The other approach is the constructive one of assisting departments and agencies in the process of delegating responsibilities and functions, and ensuring that the government's intentions (particularly in the 1980s) to encourage flexibility, initiative, and enterprise are put into practice.[84] It is not always easy for the Treasury to achieve a balance between its obligations in these two processes, and this was a matter for comment in the Fraser Report. In particular, it noted concern that, in the process of establishing agencies, 'the centre received additional detailed information about operations which generated demands for yet more information with no clear indication of what purpose it served'.[85] It may sometimes seem that, in terms of popularity in the civil service, the Treasury can never win; though it should be added that, in evidence to the Treasury and Civil Service Committee, representatives of agencies often expressed gratitude for the help and advice they had received from the Treasury.[86] In this context the Treasury has a specially important role at the antenatal stage, when framework documents are being drawn up.

SPECIFIC RESPONSIBILITIES

Framework documents

The Next Steps initiative required departments to review their functions and consider which functions are suitable for agency status. Having taken this initial step, departments were then required to discuss their proposals for agencies with both the Treasury and the OMCS, and to obtain their agreement on the framework document for each agency. The framework document is the basic document for any agency. As Kemp put it on one occasion: it 'governs the thing and has a certain durability';[87] and on another occasion he explained: 'Framework Documents ... are partly mission statements and partly articles of association of a company, partly contracts and partly administrative documents; and partly a bit of all those. But it is a new way of doing things ... '[88] The important points to note are that the framework document sets out an agency's aims and objectives, provides the basis for the agency's relations with its minister, and lays down provisions for its financial and performance accountability to both the minister and to Parliament. It also elaborates certain details so that there is no doubt about the roles and responsibilities of key staff, or about the Chief Executive's freedoms and responsibilities.

At the earliest opportunity the Treasury is therefore involved in the identification and preparation for launch of individual agencies. Once departments have identified potential agencies, they set indicative target dates but the Treasury and OPS are consulted early, even before any public announcement of the target dates, to ensure that the target dates are realistic and sufficiently demanding. The procedure then followed by the Treasury and OMCS (later OPSS, now OPS) has been explained clearly by the Comptroller and Auditor General:

> They look at the appropriateness of the overall policy and resources framework, in particular the performance measures and the arrangements for setting challenging performance targets so as to secure greater efficiency and effectiveness, and for maintaining performance. They also examine proposed delegations on financial, staff and pay matters, and proposed accounting arrangements, in line with their overall responsibilities.[89]

In the final stages of the development of a framework document the departmental minister puts proposals formally to the ministers responsible at the Treasury and OPS.[90]

The framework document therefore sets out the aims and objectives of the agency, the proposed accounting and control arrangements and the respective responsibilities of the minister, the parent department and the Chief Executive. In approving these details the Treasury has to be assured that the parent department has given careful consideration to the extent and implications of delegated authority. Where agencies are given freedoms from central controls these have to be related to prospective improvements in efficiency and effectiveness. It is also necessary for the Treasury to be sure that agencies have developed budgetary and management information systems in accordance with the best public sector practice. Furthermore, agencies are required, and this also is laid down in their framework documents, to provide their responsible minister and Parliament with published annual reports and accounts, 'in accordance with the best commercial practice' and to make these reports publicly available.[91] In addition, the framework document requires the agency to prepare corporate plans which cover three to five years, and also annual plans to be rolled forward as their time comes up. The annual plans have special significance where they are likely to lead to the department bidding for additional public expenditure.[92]

It is the framework document which is intended to establish the contact between the suppliers of a service and the customers. Moreover, as these details are contained in the framework document, they become open to inspection by anyone interested. This approach is indicative of the determination to ensure openness by those responsible for the implementation of the initiative. However, the idea of serving customers in the normal commercial sense of the term is not always strictly appropriate because many operations in the public service are monopolies. This feature was particularly noted in 1990 by the Treasury and Civil Service Committee, which commented:

> Hence the importance of performance indicators set out in agency framework agreements: given the *real* choice between services is not available, replacement mechanisms must be made to work properly. We welcome the assurance by Treasury witnesses that they saw themselves 'very clearly' as in the business of protecting the consumer . . .[93]

Although framework documents are crucial to the individual agencies, their details are not fixtures for all time. They have to be changed when and if their funding status is changed. Furthermore, of course, the aims and objectives of certain agencies may be changed, perhaps in terms of emphasis or even from first principles, when there is a change in government. The late Mr John Smith MP, as Shadow Chancellor of the Exchequer, indicated early in 1991 that a future Labour Government would not attempt to reverse the initiative. He said: 'I do not think there would be merit in a new government seeking to uproot all the plants in the garden, re-arrange their roots, and then, having planted them again, expect them to grow well'.[94] However, in a Parliamentary Debate two weeks later, Dr John Marek said that 'Agencies would be very different under a Labour Government', and John Garrett MP pointed out that 'Agencies are neutral. They can be used by a Labour Government for advancing the conditions of the people and for providing better services to the customer . . .'.[95]

Although the Treasury and the OPS have significant roles to play when framework documents are drawn up, it is important to notice the constitutional significance of these documents. Essentially, a framework document is drawn up between a department and its agency. It should not be seen as being prescribed from the Treasury and the OPS because ultimately, in a constitutional sense, the minister is still accountable to Parliament.[96] In practice, however, it must be difficult for the Treasury and the OPS not to assume a more assertive role than is suggested by the formal requirements which involve them. Not only do the Treasury and the OPS have an already clear perception of the financial arrangements within all departments, they also have specialist knowledge and expertise of the relevant financial procedures and growing experience in the setting up and general supervision of agencies. It is therefore not surprising that their assistance and guidance is appreciated by chief executives, especially in relation to the arrangements and requirements in framework documents.

In evidence to the Treasury and Civil Service Committee, Phillips, of the Treasury, emphasised that once agencies have been set up and have 'been through the framework document, through the responsibilities being laid out, through the agreement for a financial regime, through the development of corporate plans, our involvement directly with agencies will be one in which we step back . . .'.[97] He also said, however, that the normal controls that arise will continue. This means that, after the approval of the framework document, and apart from revisions of it, which will be unavoidable from time to time, the Treasury will still have a number of continuing detailed responsibilities in relation to agencies. These continuing responsibilities are particularly evident in relation to the financial basis for agencies and a variety of aspects of monitoring progress.

Financial regimes

The financial regimes of agencies are considered case by case when they are set up. Agencies are either financed as part of the normal supply procedure or they are given trading fund status in accordance with the Government Trading Funds Act 1973 as amended. However, their status may change over time. This happens, for example, if a supply financed agency becomes eligible and able to operate under the more commercial regime of a self-financing trading fund. Moreover, it may even be possible to see this change of status on a progressive scale, so that an agency may begin by being supply financed, then become a trading fund by building up a pattern of sufficient receipts in respect of goods or services provided, and finally be privatised. This would be consistent with the statement in the Next Steps Report, that an agency 'may be part of government and the public service, or it may be more effective outside it'.[98] This statement is also reflected in the White Paper of 1989, *The Financing and Accountability of Next Steps Agencies.*[99]

Agencies funded as part of the supply procedure (see Chapter 3), as most of them are, may either be resourced through a single departmental vote confined to the agency, or within a wider departmental vote.[100] By this procedure, any receipts from fees or charges for services provided are normally either surrendered to the Consolidated Fund, or are appropriated in aid of the vote. Both current and capital expenditure on running costs are controlled by cash limits in any one year, and these cash limits are an incentive to keep expenditure under control and to achieve economical management.

Within the departmental vote system the general expectations for independence are maintained by provisions to indicate the independent expenditure of the agency. This ensures that the agency accounts appear in a quasi-independent form in the department's Public Expenditure Survey Estimate. The disadvantages of the supply financing procedure are that chief executives are not given sufficient control over their running costs to enable them to feel independent. This, in turn, means that their position in the civil service culture may be little different from their pre-agency position. Early in the creation of agencies it was appreciated that, if they were to achieve the intended degree of flexibility, arrangements had to be developed to ensure that they had an appropriate degree of financial independence.

Under the supply procedure the Treasury has an important role to play at various stages. First, it is involved at the initial stages of the presentation of estimates. Second, however, it is always involved when there is a departmental proposal for virement between the sub-heads of a departmental vote (and if the Treasury does not approve, the department has to present a Supplementary Estimate to get parliamentary approval for any reallocation between sub-heads). According to the 1989 White Paper, the Treasury may be prepared to define in advance the conditions for Treasury support for virement or for Treasury support for a Supplementary Estimate.[101] This may be helpful to both the agency and the Treasury, but it also ensures a continuing and legitimate role for the Treasury in the financing of agencies by the supply procedure. In addition, by an end-year flexibility procedure dating only from 1983, it is sometimes possible, within clearly defined limits, for a department to carry forward underspends, thus enabling greater flexibility in public expenditure in the interests of better value for money.[102]

As a result of the Government Trading Funds Act 1973, it became possible to finance some government activities outside the normal supply procedure, by creating a 'trading fund' for certain specified bodies or other services which consist of or include trading operations or operations in the nature of trading. It was, however, necessary, when creating such a fund, and in order to limit its borrowing, to proceed by a parliamentary affirmative resolution order, and the audited accruals-based accounts had to be presented to Parliament by the Comptroller and Auditor General. There is a note at the end of this chapter on the cash and accruals basis of accounting.

In May 1988 the Treasury and the Next Steps team began work to present proposals to amend the 1973 Government Trading Funds Act, so that the monopoly and statutory services of many agencies could benefit from being financed as trading funds.[103] This led to the announcement on 1 February 1989 by the Chief Secretary to the Treasury that the government intended to amend the 1973 Act to widen the scope for trading fund arrangements.[104] The intention was specifically to add to the range of financial regimes available to agencies, though the wider conditions continued to apply only to bodies which generate receipts for goods or services provided. For example, the new provisions permit a trading fund to be established for an agency whose purpose is internal supply transactions (i.e. providing services for charges paid by other parts of central government). These wider provisions enabled the financial arrangements for the Central Office of Information and the Vehicle Inspectorate (which is directed by statute to provide services and where the fees are fixed by regulation) to be transferred to trading funds. However, it should be noted that the wider provisions are still only *enabling*, and it is the responsibility of the Treasury to make a judgment of suitability before Parliament is presented with an order to create a new trading fund.

Nevertheless, agencies financed as trading funds do not have a completely free hand to operate as private companies would in a commercial context. In December 1991, an internal memorandum to senior managers in Whitehall and its agencies said: 'The fact that a public body can provide a service as well and as cheaply as any outside supplier is not in itself a reason for extending public sector activity'. It also said: 'In general, the presumption is that services should wherever possible be provided by the private sector, with the public sector buying in the services as necessary. This presumption applies in particular where a public body would be competing with the private sector.'[105] This may be interpreted as a discouragement of enterprise in agency officials searching for new sources of income. It may be difficult to reconcile the instructions to operate in a business-like fashion but also not to compete with the private sector.

Furthermore, trading funds do not bring with them opportunities to operate beyond Treasury controls. The 1989 White Paper explained that these controls would concentrate on essential strategic matters. It said the key elements were:

> the external finance limit, which may be positive or negative and which will be the main control. It will be within the departmental expenditure allocation and hence the public expenditure planning total. It will be supplemented by controls on borrowing levels, major capital expenditure, use of reserves, and the distribution of any surpluses – the corporate and business planning process, through which the Government will each year settle the Agency's performance and financial targets.[106]

In fact, however, the 1990 Government Trading Act contains some thirty-six significant references to the Treasury. These range from the necessity for Treasury concurrence before an order may be laid before Parliament; to the requirements for the Treasury to determine the trading fund's external financial limit and the borrowing limits and rates of interest for loans from the parent department to the trading fund; and to the appointment of the fund's accounting officer whose responsibilities are outlined in detail but with considerable flexibility for the Treasury to institute specific detailed requirements about such matters as the information required in the annual report and the manner for presenting the annual statement of accounts. Indeed, the significance of the new provisions in the 1990 Act received appropriate attention in the 1989 White Paper:

> To put beyond doubt the Treasury's powers to ensure that trading fund accounts presented to Parliament are comprehensive in coverage and consistent in form and that they will as necessary reflect changing circumstances, the Government has incorporated in the amending Bill a more explicit power enabling the Treasury to direct their content, methods and principles as well as their form.[107]

Having read such details in the White Paper, legislation, and evidence to the Treasury and Civil Service Committee, the interested observer might wonder at the extent of Treasury controls in circumstances where the increased flexibilities and independence of trading funds are *not* granted. However, in 1991 the government was able to announce that, as a result of the passage of the Government Trading Act 1990, five new trading funds had been set up in that year. It added: 'This enables them to operate their finances as near as possible to the way it is done in the private sector'.[108] By November 1995, twelve agencies, including the Royal Mint (see later), were operating as trading funds and a number of other agencies were working towards trading fund status.[109]

In this, as in other contexts of the government control of quasi-independent bodies, much depends on advice and guidance. Nowhere is this more evident than in the guidance issued by the Treasury on the establishment and operation of trading funds. One of the most interesting items in the guide refers to monitoring arrangements, and stipulates that, as a minimum, trading funds are required to supply parent departments with a monthly or quarterly report, to ensure that the trading fund remains within its external financing limit, together with details of its current expectations of meeting its key targets. In a number of respects it might be said that it is through the monitoring processes that the Treasury responsibilities are maintained on a day-to-day basis.

Monitoring requirements

Each agency is required to prepare each year on a rolling basis a medium-term corporate plan and an annual operating plan containing detailed performance targets for the year immediately ahead.[110] These plans are normally prepared in close co-operation with the parent department and sometimes with the Treasury and the OPS as well.[111]

The preparation and approval of these plans enables the Treasury to be continuously informed of key factors affecting public expenditure and to influence the operation of agencies in terms of efficiency, value for money, and government priorities. These are later compared with the annual reports and annual accounts which agencies are also required to publish in accordance with Treasury guidance.

Within the annual plans, agencies have to state their targets and indicate their procedures for assessing and improving performance. The Treasury, whose reason for involvement originates from the Public Expenditure Survey and its value for money responsibilities, identifies those targets about which it wishes to be consulted, so that it knows how agencies are operating and can also comment on the proposed targets before they are agreed with departments.[112] Moreover, as a general rule, targets have so far been set on the basis of at least a minimum 1.5 per cent per annum reduction for 'efficiency savings',[113] though it is unclear whether this general rule is expected to be applied into the indefinite future. The success of an agency is then measured by the extent to which it meets its targets and improves its service to customers;[114] and the Treasury, OPS and other departments use this information for their overall evaluation of the initiative.[115] The assessments are later published in the annual reviews: there were six up to the end of 1995. One feature of the 1994 annual review was the announcement that, for its year, 275 quality of service targets were set and 214 were met or bettered; 137 financial performance targets were set and 109 were met or bettered, and 147 efficiency targets were set and 127 were met or bettered. In the 1995 review the presentation of these details was different and made valid comparison difficult; however, the review said that in 1994–95 1,400 key performance targets were set and 83 per cent were met.[116]

How this works in practice, and how it affects the attitudes of staff, has been explained by Mr Ron Oliver, of the Vehicle Inspectorate Executive Agency:

> That we have over-achieved the targets does not mean that they were soft targets. I think what it means is that Executive Agency, as a concept, works. We were set very tight targets; we believed, in-year, this last financial year, that we would not achieve our target. As management, we were very concerned and we went to great lengths, we discussed it with our staff and we told them that unless we took fairly drastic measures to look at our costs, look at our efficiency, find ways of improving our organisation, we would not meet our target and that we would be seen as a major 'fail', in

terms of us as a business, in which we want to be seen as successful, so we did take steps within-year to tighten up even further and that was at a time, as I said, of very adverse business conditions. The problem is that we are talking, when we are talking about these targets, of relatively small percentages and even with our fairly sophisticated management system, finance and information system, it is difficult to forecast the actual out-turn. As it is, we have come in with a better performance and that better performance is a mixture of forecasting inaccuracy, we are lucky if we can forecast within half a per cent, and staff who, because of the Agency, are determined to succeed and have actually produced better efficiencies than we would have expected, see that as good news rather than a threat.[117]

The Treasury has invested considerable effort in assisting to identify suitable targets and relating them to agency corporate plans and has produced a paper of guidance for this purpose. An early issue of this Treasury guidance on target setting, which was made available to the Treasury and Civil Service Committee in 1991,[118] accepted variations in the usage of concepts and terminology. Later, in November 1991, following a recommendation from the Committee, the government stated that a consistent use of terminology for target setting would be a desirable element in the openness and accountability which Next Steps seeks to promote. Consequently, the Treasury published, in 1992, a revised version of 'Executive Agencies: A Guide to Setting Targets and Measuring Performance', which contains a glossary of terminology.

It is important to note that the guide to setting targets, intended for officials advising ministers on targets to be set 'externally' for agencies, is not mandatory and recognises that flexibility will be appropriate from agency to agency. It encourages the sequence to be followed: objectives, output and performance measures, and then targets. It indicates that targets will usually fall under one or more of the headings: (a) financial performance, which means the corporate financial performance of the agency; (b) output (suitable only for certain types of agency); (c) quality of service; and (d) efficiency. It says that targets should be published before the start of the financial year, for example, through a Parliamentary Answer. It also explains the main concepts and terms used in dealing with measures, indicators and targets, and provides examples to illustrate how to calculate various indices.

To supplement the specified and published targets, agencies have also developed customer service programmes. For example, the

Treasury and Civil Service Committee was told in 1990 that the Laboratory of the Government Chemist had initiated a Total Quality (Customer Service) programme so that all staff understood the importance of constantly improving the quality of service to customers.[119] In 1990 Mr Richard Luce, then Minister for the Civil Service, told the Committee that great enthusiasm for the agencies was indicated by the fact that thirty-one out of thirty-three agencies had surveyed their customers.[120]

In order to assist departments and agencies in preparing agency annual reports and accounts to meet 'the minimum standard in form and content', the Treasury has issued two sets of guidance, containing checklists of the contents expected. This guidance says that annual reports should contain:

- the essential background which a reader might reasonably require to understand the report and accounts e.g. the main aims of the Agency and an outline of its principal activities;
- a summary of the agreed corporate strategy and the Agency's business prospects, including any significant changes in policy, activities planned for the future;
- a review of the main activities over the past financial year, including a statement on any significant changes in policy, activities or the Framework Document during the year;
- a statement, prominently displayed, on the achievement of objectives and published key performance targets (financial and non-financial) over the past year. Key performance targets should include unit cost or other efficiency and quality of service targets. Actual and planned/budgeted values should be shown and explanations of significant variances;
- a summary of the actual outcome of the key performance indicators over the past 5 years (as an annex);
- a table of the past and current key performance targets;
- for the reporting year the names of: the key staff/Management Board (if there is one); any non-employee members of management or advisory boards; the Auditors.[121]

Agency accounts should contain:

- a foreword: more details to supplement the basic information in the foreword may be included in the annual report;
- an operating/income and expenditure statement;
- a balance sheet or a statement of the assets and liabilities (where appropriate);

- a cash flow reconciliation statement i.e. a flow of funds (sources and applications) statement;
- notes to the accounts: these should include a statement of performance against key corporate financial targets and information on the remuneration of the chief executive and higher paid employees.[122]

Another area where Treasury monitoring is apparent concerns the appointment, pay, and grading of staff. The position here was summarised by the Comptroller and Auditor General in 1989:

> The delegation of responsibility to Agencies for staff matters such as complements, recruitment, and promotion is to be determined by parent departments and the Treasury having regard to such factors as the size of the Agency and its in-house experience and expertise in such matters.[123]

In practice, pay arrangements in the civil service have become more flexible in recent years, incorporating opportunities for performance pay and local pay additions, so in this sphere the creation of agencies has taken advantage of existing opportunities and, where appropriate, developed them further. When new flexibilities are desired, the Treasury has to be satisfied that the changes are clearly related to prospective improvements in efficiency and effectiveness.[124] All agreements with staff for the introduction and extension of pay linked to performance require Treasury agreement.[125]

The arrangements for recruiting staff in departments as well as agencies were changed fundamentally from 1 April 1991. This change has enabled departments and agencies to recruit all their own staff below Grade 7 (principal); appointments to Grade 7 and above, and to the 'fast stream' remain the responsibility of the Civil Service Commissioners. This means that departments and agencies can, within specified rules, which are subject to 'light handed, economical and systems based'[126] monitoring by the Commissioners, choose whether to do their own recruiting or contract the work to private companies, including Recruitment and Assessment Services. Recruitment and Assessment Services was the agency developed out of part of the Civil Service Commission. On 30 September 1996 it was sold to Capita Group plc.[127]

Her Majesty's Stationery Office made particular advances in its arrangements for staff flexibility, by introducing 'a tailor-made scheme specifically for HMSO staff',[128] though in doing so it was required to satisfy the Treasury that its job evaluation system was compatible with, and correlated to, civil service grading standards.[129] A further element of Treasury involvement with the management of HMSO, which was responsible to Treasury ministers, was that the new arrangements there involved the appointment of a Board of Directors which included up to three non-executive directors appointed by Treasury ministers on the recommendation of the HMSO Chief Executive. It is not known how far this Treasury participation at board level contributed to the changes in the HMSO pay and grading system, but HMSO was often referred to as the leading agency for introducing a completely new pay and grading system.[130] In 1995 it was announced that the government intended to appoint financial advisers to consider urgently the future of HMSO, with a view to privatisation, providing satisfactory arrangements could be made for the future provision of services to Parliament. On 30 September 1996 it was sold to the National Publishing Group.[131]

Recruitment policy, questions of pay, pay negotiations and industrial relations are all continuing matters for which the Treasury retains overall responsibility. This is important because, as Mr C. W. Kelly, of the Pay Group in the Treasury, said in 1990: 'There is clearly a risk that people will see flexibility as actually meaning higher pay. You will not be surprised to hear that that is not what we mean'.[132] Moreover, with the creation of agencies, and the delegation of functions from departments to them, the Treasury keeps the level of senior posts in departments under regular review, to ensure that the implications of the delegation are taken into account.[133]

Despite the cautious approach in some of the Treasury statements about delegated pay and grading systems and their need to deliver 'demonstrable and preferably measurable improvements in value for money, including improved recruitment and retention where necessary',[134] the Treasury has announced significant progress in the development of agency group incentive schemes (and these were before the Chancellor's statement, outlined above, of 24 July 1991). By 18 June 1991, eleven bonus schemes had been approved, and seven were up and running.[135] In April 1991 it produced a useful internal publication outlining forty selected flexibilities in the field of personnel management, pay and allowances available to departments and agencies, although, as the document makes clear, all the flexibilities must be exercised within the constraints of agreed running costs, or other financial disciplines. The document is brief but it set out in a user-friendly manner key points about each of the flexibilities, conditions that go with them, general comments, and the name of the contact person in the Treasury for further information and advice.[136]

Furthermore, the Treasury is continuing to develop and approve further flexibilities in pay schemes and, in particular, the special performance-related pay arrangements for chief executives. With all these schemes the Treasury has to ensure that they are set up on a sensible basis that is robust, that they measure up well against Treasury guidelines to ensure that the cash is available to pay for new schemes, and that, at the end of the day, there are appropriate benefits for taxpayers as well as staff.[137]

In addition to the general monitoring arrangements by the Treasury in connection with targets, annual reports and accounts, and the appointment and financing of staff, other forms of monitoring may apply from time to time for specific purposes. For example, the Vehicle Inspectorate Executive Agency achieved agreement from the Treasury to a lease car scheme;[138] certain specific financial information is required every month from the Employment Service Executive Agency;[139] and the Employment Service Executive Agency has to negotiate directly with the Treasury on capital bids for new buildings, computer systems, and things like that. Indeed, many agencies are likely to be constrained by monitoring requirements in specific areas even though, as Sir Peter Middleton has said, it is a matter more of making Treasury views known than of exercising a veto.[140] The way this works in practice is, however, best illustrated by considering the cases of three agencies: the Civil Service College, the Contributions Agency, and the Royal Mint.

EXAMPLES OF AGENCIES

The Civil Service College

The Civil Service College is part of the Cabinet Office (Office of Public Service). It was founded in 1970[141] following a recommendation in the Fulton Report that a college should be created to help bring about a more professional civil service, and it became an executive agency on 6 June 1989. At the time of writing (1995) it reports to the Chancellor of the Duchy of Lancaster who is also Minister for Public Service. Its latest framework document, revised to be effective from 26 June 1995, states that its purpose is to develop managerial and professional skills among civil servants and promote best practice in government, both in management and in key professional areas.[142] This statement of purpose is supplemented by other general statements about the nature and purpose of the College, both in the framework document and elsewhere. For example, in the Foreword to the framework document, the Chancellor of the Duchy of Lancaster said that agency status has enhanced the College's 'ability to deliver . . . training more efficiently and effectively, by providing it with a sharper, more businesslike framework in which to operate', and 'From 1995–96 the College will be required fully to recover its costs by revenue from its operations, in fair competition from others. In addition, we are considering the College's suitability for Trading Fund status'.[143] In Chapter 2 of the framework document the College's general statement of purpose is elaborated by saying that the College provides management training for civil servants, particularly those at, or aspiring to, relatively senior positions; specialist training in key professional areas or at advanced levels; and related consultancy and research.

The College's framework document was particularly well regarded when the agency was launched. Mr Peter Jones, then Secretary of the Council of Civil Service Unions, thought it was the best one to emerge in the early years because it gave more freedom to the Chief Executive than had been laid down in comparable documents for other agencies;[144] and Mr T. R. H. Luce, of the Treasury, said he thought the document was 'very highly suited to its function of determining the relationship between the College and their (sic) sponsor department and the objectives of the College itself'.[145]

The framework document makes it clear that 'College staff are civil servants, subject to Civil Service conditions of service';[146] the College will 'deliver the agreed Strategic and Business Plans in fair competition with others without tying departments to the use of the College';[147] and the College is 'required to cover its full costs from income on an accruals basis', with performance against targets being reported quarterly to the Minister.[148] The Chief Executive is directly responsible to the Minister for the efficient organisation, direction and management of the College, and the Accounting Officer of the Office of Public Service has appointed him as the Accounting Officer for the agency.

This means that the Chancellor of the Duchy of Lancaster is accountable to Parliament for the College as part of the Office of Public Service. With advice from OPS, the Chancellor of the Duchy determines the role which the College plays in supporting OPS policies, appoints the Chief Executive, approves the College Strategic Plan and the Annual Business Plan, sets the annual performance targets of the College, and receives from the Chief Executive the annual report and accounts. Although the College has, in the past, received a central payment towards its costs, from 1995–96 it is required fully to recover its costs by revenue from its operations.[149]

The College's accounts show that in 1994–95 it earned £18.5 million from courses and consultancy and also received the last of its annual central payments from OPS, of £700,000. However, it should be noted that in recent years it has benefited from considerable capital investment: for example, in the three years ending in 1992–93 capital investment at the College amounted to nearly £12.5 million.[150] As a result of this investment it pays depreciation on its accrual accounts for its non-property assets and additional rent to Property Holdings; in 1992–93 this included rent for Sunningdale Park which was estimated at around £1 million a year.[151] The College is subject to net running cost control on the OPS Vote, and on 11 November 1994 the Treasury issued a direction in accordance with the Exchequer and Audit Act 1921, which laid down the requirements for the form and presentation of the annual accounts.

The College's Strategic Plan covers a five-year period, is normally produced every three years, and is reviewed annually. The Strategic Plan 1991–95 identifies the College's primary market as being 'those who are looking for the frameworks, motivation and skills to enable them better to lead and manage the process of service delivery and organisational development in government'.[152] The Strategic Plan's financial perspective explains that the College is required to set, and justify, an annual cost per student day target, which is subject to approval by both the Minister and the Treasury.[153] The more detailed Annual Business Plan, which is confidential to the College, gives details of the number and types of courses and students, manpower and accommodation arrangements, capital investment, pricing policy, performance targets, financial forecast and such other information as the OPS may require.[154]

The Principal presents annually to the Minister of Public Service a *Report and Accounts*; this is published and copies are deposited in the library of the House of Commons.[155] The College is internally audited each year and is also subject to audit by the Comptroller and Auditor General. Indicators of efficiency and quality of provision are published in the *Report and Accounts* and the details are reported quarterly to OPS. Annual targets for improving value for money are agreed with OPS Ministers and the Treasury.[156] The OPS approves (and seeks any necessary approval for) capital expenditure: on land and buildings, on maintenance and minor new works, and on items or projects estimated to cost more than £100,000.[157] The College has authority to develop pay arrangements, including performance pay, 'within existing flexibilities', and 'other arrangements, subject to Treasury approval, where these are necessary for the purposes of its

Strategic and Business Plans'.[158] The full details of financial delegations and personnel management delegations were also listed in annexes to the original framework document.

According to the then Principal, Mr Roger Jackling, when the College was launched as an agency it acquired a clearer definition of its role, and the market in which it operated and its priorities, and the Principal and College Management Board acquired additional managerial discretion to run the business, and also quantitative and qualitative targets for which they became directly accountable. He thought the greater flexibility in financial and personnel management matters, acquired when agency status was conferred, would help the College to make best use of staffing and other resources.[159]

The College's first Annual Report as an agency proudly announced that it had met its financial objectives, exceeded its plans for the overall volume of student days delivered, and exceeded its target for the number of students at Grade 7 and above who attended the College.[160] There were two reasons for these good results. One was improvements in utilisation of the College's premises; the other was a significant increase in the training provided by College staff but away from College premises, in departments. The College was particularly pleased that it achieved a good score on its course evaluation indicator – which asks students to assess on a scale of 1 to 6 how far a course succeeded in meeting its objectives. On the evaluation indicator the College achieved an average rating of 77.8 per cent (of students marking boxes 1 or 2 out of 6) against a target of 76 per cent and this compared with an achievement of 75 per cent in 1988–89 against a target of at least 70 per cent. By 1994–95 it had achieved 81 per cent against its target of 80 per cent.

Since becoming an agency in 1989 the image of the College and the attitudes of its staff have changed, with more emphasis on high quality publicity. For example, the annual report is now much more attractively designed, as is the Prospectus of Courses (by 1995 this was a weighty volume of over 350 pages, A4 size).

A new value for money indicator was introduced in 1990. This is based on a four-part questionnaire to students covering quality of training, accommodation, catering and support services. Also in 1990, a new computerised Management Information System (MS), written by Oracle Corporation, was introduced to provide a relational database with access to it across the College, to enhance both the efficiency of internal procedures and service to customers. At the same time, the College's accounting systems were developed, in accordance with the Treasury Guidelines on Memorandum Trading Accounts, to meet the requirements of the full accruals accounting basis approved by the Treasury. This includes details of fixed assets and debtor control.[161] Along with all these changes the College introduced a new visual identity colour scheme, typefaces and a logo with the strapline: 'Management in Government' underneath the College name.

In March 1991 the College invited a specialist firm to undertake a survey of attitudes and values of all members of staff, and found a high commitment to customer service and a high 'appetite for change'.[162] However, there were fewer student days than the target because private sector firms, in competition with the College, cut their prices as the recession gathered pace and because the Ministry of Defence imposed a moratorium on spending (the MoD is one of the College's largest customers, providing income of over £2 million in 1990–91). Again, there was an increase in training delivered outside College premises. The College had initial discussions with a range of consultancy firms to prepare a major study of the pay and grading of its teaching staff. The College also used a specialist market research company to undertake a telephone interview survey of civil servants to assess their attitudes to the College. This aspect of performance indicator assessment has been developed further, so that, for example, since 1990 the College has been tracking customer assessments at twenty-six service points to identify areas for improvement. The College also developed and consolidated its new visual identity with colour schemes, fabric and carpet designs and with a new generation of literature using innovative cover designs.

The 1994–95 *Report and Accounts* was even more confident and optimistic than its predecessors. During that year more than 30,000 people attended College programmes; UK courses were not only being run in the College premises at Sunningdale Park, Ascot, and at Belgrave Road, London, but also in Scotland and Sheffield, in customers' premises and in hotels; and overseas there were courses in Hungary and South Africa. In 1993 the College reported to the Treasury and Civil Service Select Committee an impressive list of over twenty private sector customers (including Barclays Bank, Leeds Permanent Building Society, Vickers PLC and Wimpey Group Services Ltd).[163] It offered a wide variety of courses (over 500 titles were listed in 1995) including courses for efficiency planning, priority-based cost management, benchmarking, business process engineering, and the private finance initiative. It also reported with great pleasure that, as part of a consortium (with Cranfield University and Manchester Business School) it had been chosen to provide a Public Sector MBA, starting in July 1996.

By 1992 the nature of the College's activity was clearly stated by the Principal as comparable to a business and management school. The College's emphasis was increasingly on training and specifically running courses to meet the needs of its customers. It operated according to the guidelines and advice not only from its then parent department OMCS, but also from the Treasury. Moreover, its activities tended to be evaluated according to measurable criteria. Jackling clearly focused on its key characteristics as a business when he emphasised the advantages of agency status for the College, in terms of defining its role and market; and a few years later Marianne Neville-Rolfe explained in a radio interview with David Walker that 'Principal' was only half her title. She said: 'the old-fashioned title of Principal related to being a teaching institution, while the new title of Chief Executive relates to running a business'.[164] The role of the Treasury is also clearly evident in all the ways outlined earlier in this chapter. However, in case it may be thought from this brief and selective account that the College did not know what its role was in earlier years, before it had a framework document, strategic and business plans, the College should also be seen in a historical perspective.

The First Annual Report by the Principal (1970–71) outlined the task of the College as 'to seek to unite scholarship and practice by the determination and application of methods of analysis relevant to the work and problems of the Civil Service'.[165] Moreover, he referred to the College's research programme which, he said, 'will be valuable in our teaching, meet the needs of the departments and foster the development of the social sciences'.[166] In the Principal's Second Annual Report he went further and said the College had 'to earn the respect of . . . the academic community'.[167] In that same report he announced the College's complement of research staff: one Research Officer and six Assistant Research Officers (including one vacancy). Even in its earlier years the College, according to its first Principal, was in constant communication with the departments 'who are our customers' and invited the views of students.[168] The early years therefore saw the College, as, indeed, it was envisaged by the Fulton Committee, as a specialist institution of learning;[169] and Sir William Armstrong, Head of the Civil Service at that time, hoped that it would become the focus for research and studies in public administration, organisation and government.[170] Twenty years later the College may be seen more as a commercial institution of specialist training. Published references to research now associate it more narrowly with consultancy and training.[171] It is not surprising, therefore, that the 1993–94 Annual Report said that 'The College does not currently undertake any pure research. The research and development that we engage in underpin the training and consultancy services that we provide to our customers'.[172] In the 1994–95 *Report*, the Principal acknowledged that the debate over the College as an academic institution versus the College as a practitioner training centre beset its early growth, but he then added: 'The debate was never completely resolved but the practical relevance of the College's courses has become a major selling point and the lack of independent research at the College has been mourned by only a few'.[173] During 1994–95 the College had an income from consultancy amounting to some £600,000, and consultancy contracts had been won by the College in the UK and abroad – for example, for management development in the States of Jersey and for supporting public sector reform for the government of Namibia. He then said: 'Our continuing role in Hungary has won great acclaim from the government there and we have been significantly involved with several other important reform projects in Ukraine, Columbia, Indonesia, the Czech Republic and South Africa'.[174]

In October 1993, following a 'prior options' review, and considerable coverage in the press[175] that the Treasury had plans to privatise the College, it was announced that the College would continue to be an executive agency within government for a further four-year term. Towards the end of 1995 ministers decided to re-open the question of the College's status by announcing a review to assess the scope for greater private sector involvement.

In its early years the Civil Service College was much more like a university college than a business school, and nowhere is this more evident than in the proposals then discussed for research and publications of College staff. The change in emphasis, with the conferral of agency status, to more businesslike approaches and customer orientation, may be more easily measurable and more amenable to Treasury controls and guidelines, but it is also associated with a change in emphasis for the purpose of the College, reflecting a change in the culture within it and surrounding it.

The Contributions Agency

The Contributions Agency is responsible for all operational aspects of the National Insurance Contributions Scheme. The income generated contributes to the cost of the National Health Service and also finances such contributory benefits as retirement pensions, unemployment and invalidity benefits. The agency, which was created on 2 April 1991, is part of the Department of Social Security (DSS); and its headquarters and large-scale central operations are at Longbenton, Newcastle-upon-Tyne. Its framework document states that its purposes are to ensure compliance with the law in respect of national insurance contributions, maintain individual national insurance records, and provide an effective and efficient service to the DSS, other government departments, the business community and members of the public.[176]

Before 1990 the collection of national insurance contributions was managed, within the DSS, alongside benefits work, and staff in local offices engaged in benefits work and contributions work were interchangeable. However, in 1990, following a feasibility study, contributions work was given a separate management structure in a Contributions Unit, with dedicated line management but within the DSS Central Office, Newcastle-upon-Tyne. The Contributions Agency is therefore a development from the interim structure of the Contributions Unit. Under the new structure, contributions staff in DSS local offices have been organised into areas and divisions separate from the comparable structure of the Benefits Agency. The key feature of the new structure is its focus on becoming a dynamic, target-driven organisation.[177] To implement this focus the agency emphasises value for money and has developed a business management process with a refined Management Information System. On 2 August 1991 the Contributions Agency issued a Contributors' Charter and an Employers' Charter. It was the first public body to publish such charters following the publication, the day before, of the White Paper *The Citizen's Charter*.[178] These charters outline service standards that contributors and employers can expect from the agency and they cover such topics as courtesy, information and assistance, fairness, and what to do if dissatisfied.

The agency uses the services of the Inland Revenue to collect most national insurance contributions through PAYE: in 1993–94 national insurance contributions amounted to £38 billion, in respect of some 33 million contributors.[179] The agency also provides information from about 63 million individual contributions records in response to a total of over 10 million inquiries per year, relating to benefits or contributions matters.[180] The framework document states that the Chief Executive, from 1995 Mrs Faith Boardman, has full authority for managing the agency and for its day-to-day operations. She ensures that staff are assessed against agreed performance targets and, as Agency Accounting Officer, she is responsible to the Departmental Accounting Officer for all internal consultancy, review and audit arrangements.[181]

Each year the Chief Executive prepares and submits to the Secretary of State for Social Security an annual Business Plan and a review of the strategy covering the longer-term plans for the organisation and performance of the agency.[182] The agency's strategy and future requirements are, however, specified in co-ordination with the annual Public Expenditure Survey, because funding for the agency is obtained through the normal supply process within the DSS vote. The funding requirement for the agency is now over £236.5 million, plus £3.5 million capital costs. The agency's Business Plan sets out such details as: key performance targets set by the Secretary of State; the agency's general priorities; strategies to achieve the agency's objectives and to improve performance; the agency's work programme, patterns of expenditure, and manpower requirements; and proposed initiatives to improve performance. The business targets include completing the work programme within the budget of £240 million, achieving a 10 per cent increase in the collection of contribution arrears, clearing 99 per cent of benefit inquiries in two working days to 98 per cent accuracy, and answering 95 per cent of employer, contributor and personal pension inquiries within ten working days. Milestones listed in the 1995–96 Business Plan include awarding a private finance contract for the replacement national insurance recording system and completing the market testing of the agency's personnel, training and typing work.[183] The Chief Executive provides regular reports to the Permanent Secretary for monitoring the agency's performance in meeting its objectives and targets.[184]

Each year the Chief Executive produces the agency's Annual Report and Accounts, in accordance with Treasury and National Audit Office requirements.[185] The Annual Report and Accounts are submitted to the Secretary of State, who lays them before Parliament; they are published and placed in the libraries of both Houses of Parliament. The first Report and Accounts were published in October 1992, but in subsequent years they have been made available before the parliamentary summer recess. The agency operates within gross running costs control; work undertaken by the agency for approved customers outside the DSS is paid for on a repayment basis. The agency now produces accounts on an accruals basis and has an appropriate management system to review its performance and expenditure against specified targets and budgets.

The Chief Executive is supported by a Management Board, consisting of the second tier officials – the directors of planning, personnel, finance and facilities management, central operations, and compliance and education – together with a non-executive member from outside the civil service with extensive experience of the electricity industry. She has a variety of delegated powers including: authority to authorise capital projects up to certain limits (currently £1 million for Information Technology (IT) projects and £3.75 million for non-IT projects); power to vire from running costs into capital or other non-running cost sub-heads, subject to Treasury approval; power to switch expenditure between running cost budgets (such as consultancy to salary); authority to carry forward agreed amounts of underspent running costs and underspent capital within specified limits; and power to reinvest in the agency's business any proportion of efficiency savings agreed with the Secretary of State and, where appropriate, the Treasury.[186] The Permanent Secretary consults the Treasury as appropriate about the agency's financial management flexibilities. The Agency's accounts are audited internally in accordance with the provisions of the Government Internal Audit Manual, issued by the Treasury to provide direction, advice and information on internal audit; they are also subject to audit by the Comptroller and Auditor General.[187]

The framework document states that the (now 8,600) Contributions Agency staff (9,500 in 1995) are civil servants and the agency has established its own Whitley structure.[188] The Chief Executive has authority to grade posts up to and including Grade 7, subject to Treasury grading standards and civil service regulations. Because the agency maintains close links with the other DSS agencies (Benefits, Child Support, War Pensions, Resettlement, and Information Technology) staff continue to enjoy the advantages of career development within the DSS. The agency has developed its own pay arrangements within the flexibilities of agreements reached nationally between the Treasury and the civil service unions. The Chief Executive already has authority to introduce an efficiency related bonus scheme and may also, in consultation with the Treasury, review existing arrangements with the aim of ensuring that they meet the operational and business objectives of the agency. The agency has introduced its own performance pay system based on annual performance appraisal. The agency is also having discussions with the Treasury about introducing a new pay and grading review to link pay with jobs performed rather than grade, aimed at strengthening its increasingly performance-based culture.[189] In addition, the agency 'has delegated authority from the Permanent Secretary to develop new working patterns/arrangements or alter existing arrangements, to meet the needs of its business, subject to Treasury approval of any new schemes which would involve variation of national terms and conditions'.[190]

According to the first Chief Executive, Ann Chant, the advantages of the agency structure are that the agency has greater flexibilities and clearer accountability than the previous arrangements, and discrete business objectives that sharpen the commitment and initiatives of staff and management. She explained to the freelance journalist Helen Pickles that the work of the agency is not economically viable, but it is a public service.[191] Although there may be some prospects of privatising the agency's support services, it is difficult to imagine how the core business could be privatised, because of confidentiality, the necessity to carry out benefit and pension related inquiries, however specific, and its sheer scale. Although there are more opportunities for management flexibility in this type of agency, compared with the work being done by a government department, it is not yet clear why these opportunities for flexibility could not have been introduced into the Contributions Unit. However, they weren't. It seems that agency status and the changes associated with it have brought a new attitude to accountability, less anonymity for its management and staff, and opportunities to develop new services for employers, businesses and self-employed national insurance contributors. The agency has good relations with staff in its parent department but has direct contact with the Treasury on such matters as the introduction of personnel flexibilities and funding for Information Technology; and it has encountered no problems with these relationships.

The Royal Mint

The Royal Mint became an agency on 1 April 1990. However, it has a history which can be traced back for over 1,100 years.[192] It is a department of central government but is managed as a commercial enterprise and has, since 1 April 1975, been operating as a trading fund under the Government Trading Funds Act 1973. This Act lays upon the minister responsible (in this case the Chancellor of the Exchequer) the duty:

(a) to manage the funded operations so that the revenue of the fund . . . is not less than sufficient, taking one year with another, to meet outgoings which are properly chargeable to the revenue account; and

(b) to achieve such further objectives as the Treasury may from time to time, by minute laid before the House of Commons, indicate as having been determined by the responsible Minister (with Treasury concurrence) to be desirable of achievement. [193]

In practice this means that, because the Mint is operating as a trading fund it receives advice and its objectives are determined in consultation with the Treasury, but the Treasury pays for the Mint's services just like any other customer (a contract for supplying United Kingdom circulating coins from 1 April 1995 to 31 March 2000 was signed in March 1995),[194] and the surpluses achieved by the Mint accrue to the Consolidated Fund as dividends. However, because the Mint is a department in its own right, and its Chief Executive is the departmental accounting officer, the relationship of the Mint to its sponsoring department, the Treasury, avoids the problems noted by the Fraser Report involving accountability to a sponsoring departmental accounting officer.

The Mint, which competes with private sector commercial organisations and the mints of many foreign governments, is a very successful commercial enterprise. It is located in Llantrisant, in South Wales, where it occupies a 30-acre site, currently employs nearly 1,000 people, and has the capacity to produce over 70 million coins a week. Its primary responsibility is to provide United Kingdom coinage, but, on average, it exports two-thirds of its annual production of 15,000 tonnes of coins to over 100 countries. It also manufactures a variety of uncirculated quality coins, military and civil decorations and medals, and royal and official seals.

The Chancellor of the Exchequer is Master of the Mint, but the Deputy Master, who is appointed by the Chancellor, with the agreement of the Prime Minister, following open competitive recruitment, exercises all management and operating responsibilities.[195] He is the Chief Executive, Accounting Officer, and Chairman of the Mint's Board of Directors. As the Mint is a government department, all its staff are civil servants and their conditions of service are laid down in the normal way by Treasury and OPS regulations and guidance. The selection of coin designs for the United Kingdom is, however, referred to the Royal Mint Advisory Committee on the Design of Coins, Medals, Seals and Decorations, which meets at Buckingham Palace, under the Presidency of HRH the Duke of Edinburgh, and includes people who are prominent in the arts and public life.[196]

The Mint has a large variety of customers including clearing banks in the United Kingdom, the purchasers of medals and seals, coin collectors and numerous foreign governments – for example, orders for coins in 1994–95 were received from seventy-four countries.[197] It has a fully fledged marketing department (with a staff of forty) for Collector Coin, which uses all normal methods of advertising and promotion. This department runs Coin Clubs with over 150,000 members in the

United Kingdom and 75,000 members in the USA, a quarterly newsletter, and specific mailings for collector coins and medals. A particularly successful commercial development is that the Mint provides coins and medals in special packaging to organisations to use as business incentives.[198]

Before it became an agency, when alternatives were being considered, the most likely alternatives were that the Mint could have been privatised or become a company wholly owned by the government: this was in view of the Mint's long standing and very successful commercial operations. However, the agency position, with the Mint continuing as a government department, was chosen because of the Mint's long history, connections with the Bank of England and Royal Family, and the need to maintain without question its security and integrity for its important export business. Furthermore, transfer to company status would have required legislation, with public debate that could have had adverse commercial effects. In 1994, following a review of the Mint's performance and status, it was announced that ministers had decided to retain the Mint as an agency under government ownership.[199]

The Mint's framework document was first issued in 1990, when the Mint became an agency. Like those of other agencies, this document is available on request, and it indicates clearly the close relations between the Mint and the Treasury. For example, it is the Treasury which decides what provision should be made in the Estimates for United Kingdom coinage, though the Mint decides on a day-to-day basis how closely to meet the demands of the banks for coinage. The Treasury selects, for examination annually, up to three investment projects in excess of £150,000 included in the Corporate Plan, and also looks at a sample of the Mint's post-implementation reviews to see whether they have achieved their objectives. Any money in the Mint's fund which appears not to be immediately required for funded operations is invested in such Government Securities as the Treasury may approve. Like other framework documents, the Mint's is to be reviewed by the Mint and its sponsoring department (the Treasury) no less frequently than every three years.[200]

The Mint has prepared, and updates each year, a four-year Corporate Plan, which it discusses with Treasury officials and which is approved by Treasury ministers. This plan, which for commercial reasons is confidential to the Mint, includes such details as the objectives for each market sector, forecast sales and profit performance, forecast manpower requirements, and forecast consolidated operating statements, balance sheets, and funds and resources statements. The financial consequences of implementing any significant extra activities or investment not provided for in the Corporate Plan are always discussed with the Treasury, and such activities are not undertaken unless approved by the responsible minister. The Mint's Annual Business Plan, which is also confidential to the Mint, contains details of commercially sensitive targets and performance indicators approved by the Treasury.

However, the preparation of the corporate and business plans does not involve close cooperation with the Treasury, unlike most other agencies, because the Mint is a department in its own right, and OPS is never involved. These plans are self-generating with wide participation within the Mint, and they are part of a disciplined and sophisticated planning process. For example, the planning process requires a thorough review, once a year, of the main and subsidiary strategies that underlie the Mint's operations, and of the lessons that have most recently been learned. Second, it is a vehicle for securing ministerial agreement to plans for the business and to performance targets (there is not normally any other ministerial involvement). Third, it produces a working document, used for day-to-day management purposes to convey information within the Mint about its business.

In accordance with the Government Trading Funds Act 1973, the Treasury approves the form of the accounts and may require additional data to be provided for the information of Parliament. The 1994–95 report and accounts showed that sales turnover reached £106.5 million, including 66 per cent overseas sales, and the Mint paid £15 million to the Consolidated Fund as a dividend. In that year the Mint was particularly successful in obtaining orders for overseas circulating coins, winning over 90 per cent of the business for which it tendered. Its key target for 1990–93 was 12.5 per cent average current return on assets, but from 1993 the three-year financial target had been increased to 14 per cent return on assets. The Mint's accounts are internally audited and it is also subject to audit by the National Audit Office.

Although the Mint has been operating as a trading fund since 1975, the Deputy Master has said that the Mint was well prepared in 1990 'to seize the opportunities of progressively greater freedom to manage its affairs in accordance with best private sector practice'. It marked its change of status, on becoming an agency, by adopting a new Corporate Identity in blue, white and silver, which reflects the Mint's 'unique combination of long tradition and modern commercial orientation'.[201] The 1990–91 report noted that agency status had created 'an awareness and concern about possible consequences for the change and there has been a reawakening of interest in the Whitley system'.[202] In 1991 it also said that, as an agency, it had 'moved closer to a revised pay and grading structure for senior managers and has been able to recognise the performance of its staff through a recently established profit sharing scheme'.[203] The details of this scheme, discussed with the unions and agreed with them, was approved by the Treasury. In 1995 the Mint received delegated authority to conduct its own pay negotiations for all categories of employee and it introduced a new scheme for paying and grading non-industrial staff to meet its own requirements. These staff are now recruited to posts, not grades, and there are seven pay bands. Comparable arrangements for industrial staff were being developed in consultation with the relevant trade unions in 1995.[204]

COMMENTS

The creation of Next Steps agencies in the past five years is consistent with the government's general approach to public sector management. This approach is clearly reflected in two of the government's policy statements of 1991: *The Citizen's Charter*[205] and *Competing for Quality*.[206] The Prime Minister said that he wanted *The Citizen's Charter* to be one of the central themes of public life in the 1990s. Key themes in the Charter include more privatisation, wider competition, and more performance-related pay. The government's record since 1979 has already been strong in implementing these themes. For example, it has privatised forty-six major businesses, accounting for about two-thirds of the former state sector of industry.[207] The government introduced compulsory competitive tendering for local authorities and is looking urgently at ways of extending competition further.[208] In the civil service, performance-related pay now applies to most staff, and in the agencies, many chief executives are on short-term performance-related contracts and their pay is directly related to performance.[209] In *The Citizen's Charter* the government said that it wants to extend these applications to involve more delegation on decisions on pay, more rewards for performance and penalties for failure, and greater delegation and flexibility in the civil service.[210]

The *Competing for Quality* White Paper states the general beliefs behind these policies and sets out how competition will be expanded in the public sector. It asserts that competition is good for users of public services and for the economy as a whole, that the need for effective competition applies across public services, and that competition is the best guarantee of quality and value for money.[211] It also makes two other important statements. First, in advocating a new, more business-like approach to public sector management, it says:

> The defects of the old approach have been widely recognised: excessively long lines of management with blurred responsibility and accountability; lack of incentives to initiative and innovation; a culture that was more often concerned with procedures than performance. As a result, public services will increasingly move to a culture where relationships are contractual rather than bureaucratic.[212]

Second, it states that: 'The best of public sector management now rank alongside the best of private sector management'.[213] The intention is therefore to replace some of the most important traditional features of public service with more business-like and, wherever possible, commercial approaches. The implication is that, in its record for being business-like and commercial, the public service has been inferior to private sector management. It might, however, be argued that the British public service, much admired elsewhere for its ethos and high standards, had not previously set out to be business-like and commercial, if those terms relate to the narrow provision of services that are commercially viable.

The main achievement of this general philosophy, which includes the creation of executive agencies is, consequently, to change the culture of British public administration. As has already been explained, the creation of agencies as an administrative reform was achieved because of a combination of factors in the political and administrative environment, at a time of almost unprecedented ideological stability resulting from Conservative successes in three successive general elections. Within some of the agencies where the change in culture has been most evident, agency status became the catalyst for change. For example, in the Vehicle Inspectorate, the first executive agency, this has included the creation of a corporate identity; the encouragement of teamwork by the introduction of a performance bonus scheme based on efficiency savings made by the Inspectorate as a whole; a new attitude to customer service; structural change with increased delegation of functions; new methods of communication and decision-making; and a new approach to emphasising the targets of the organisation. From being created as the first executive agency in 1988, the Vehicle Inspectorate became, in April 1991, the first agency to be awarded trading fund status. The Inspectorate's major customer is the Secretary of State for Transport, who requires it to carry out statutory testing of vehicles (e.g. goods vehicles and public service

vehicles) and enforce roadworthiness legislation. This
customer–contractor attitude is a major change in the public sector,
about which even the first Next Steps Project Manager had certain
reservations. He told the Public Accounts Committee in 1989:

> The customer can be the immediate member of the public you are
> dealing with, the customer can be seen as being the Minister who is
> in charge of the organisation, the customer can be seen as
> Parliament representing the public as a whole. The word 'customer'
> is a very dangerous and difficult word to use in the context of
> public service.[214]

However, ministers sometimes seem quite happy to think of themselves as customers, although this is surprising in the context of the
British system of government. For example, Mr William Waldegrave,
when Chancellor of the Duchy of Lancaster, said: 'We are the
purchasers and if we don't get the service we want, we will have to
look elsewhere'.[215] The customer–contractor relationship is probably
the most important change introduced into the public service by
creating agencies. It is a main feature of their approach to management and, as Kemp said in 1989: 'We are actually seriously trying to
alter how Government does things'.[216] Once the customer–contractor
relationship is introduced, other changes follow. Again, the Vehicle
Inspectorate provides a good example. According to a report by the
Comptroller and Auditor General, the culture in the Inspectorate has
been changed significantly from one that encouraged minimisation of
risk and costs to one that emphasises maximisation of effectiveness
and value for money.[217]

The Treasury, with its responsibility for the control of public expenditure, is without doubt the most important part of central
government for implementing the government's general approach to
public sector management. When the Next Steps Report became available, recommending the creation of agencies, the Chancellor and
Treasury officials were not at all sympathetic, primarily because of the
potential lack of control over public expenditure. However, the main
responsibilities of the Treasury in this initiative were agreed, and these
responsibilities have been explained above. There are, however, two
other factors which are also important in this context. One is the background of the first Project Manager: it was valuable for the Treasury
and for the Project Team that Kemp already knew the Treasury officials and that they knew him. Indeed, according to Dennis Bird, the
Treasury had urged the choice of one of their own, and were delighted
when the post went to Peter Kemp.[218] Before his appointment as

Project Manager, Kemp spent about three months in the Treasury, as deputy secretary, working on public expenditure; before that he worked for five years in the Treasury on pay and management; and before that he had various jobs in the Treasury, going back to 1973.[219] However, it should also be noted that Kemp was made redundant in 1992, after most of the agencies had been set up, and replaced by a new Project Manager, Mr Richard Mottram.

The other factor that has not so far been mentioned may be generally summarised as influence, persuasion and advice. These are in addition to specific Treasury responsibilities relating to framework documents, strategic plans, business plans, and annual reports and accounts. Good examples of the Treasury's more general influence and persuasion are to be found in official manuals for operating practice. Some of the provisions of the Civil Service Management Code are well known; they include rules applicable to a wide variety of circumstances but also advice on good personnel management practice. Less well known are the details in Government Accounting. This is the guide on accounting and financial procedures for the use of government departments. It includes statements on the principles of government accounting and explanations of important features of central government financing, and also details of numerous 'requirements' and 'rules', as well as matters of 'guidance', 'advice' and 'encouragement'.[220] It also contains a number of general statements of the catch-all type. Three examples illustrate this well: 'departments should ensure that the Treasury and Cabinet Office (OMCS) are provided with all the information needed to fulfil their responsibilities';[221] 'The Treasury must be consulted specifically on any proposal outside ... delegated categories';[222] and requirements for Accounting Officers to co-operate with the 'Treasury by, for example, providing information about succession plans, development and training'.[223]

What all this amounts to is that, whilst numerous provisions exist for agencies to exercise discretion and flexibility in management, their managerial freedoms and commercial aspirations are kept firmly within bounds.[224] Indeed, there is evidence to suggest that these bounds are in some cases restricting. With the creation of agencies it might even be argued that the Treasury now has more control over public expenditure than it had previously. A recent report on the relationship between the Department of Transport and its agencies saw no justification or need for the Treasury to continue to be involved in the agreement of corporate or business plans, for it to be involved in the approval of targets or fee levels, or for it to be involved in monitoring.[225] In view of all the opportunities for control and influence, it is not surprising that Mr Ron Oliver, Chief Executive of the Vehicle Inspectorate, told the Treasury and Civil Service Committee in 1991: 'we do not have significantly greater freedoms'.[226] Moreover, it could well be that, with staff mobility and duplication of some delegated functions, there could be a loss of economy of effort and, after further experience has been acquired, there may be some reversal of certain freedoms publicised as being associated with agency status, and a return to more management responsibility being exercised by ministers and departments. Departments have, themselves, changed since the creation of agencies. With some of the additional flexibilities and delegated powers announced in the Chancellor's statement of 24 July 1991 and in the Civil Service Order in Council 1991, it is possible that some departments now have as much independence as agencies in personnel management.

Two further difficulties nevertheless remain. One difficulty arises from the variety of institutions that are now agencies, ranging from commercially viable enterprises to units for which it is difficult to produce cogent arguments for their transfer to agency status. Because agencies have been created by executive decisions and without legislation, there is no clear and authoritative definition of what an agency is. The other difficulty arises from the meaning of other key terms associated with the new approach to public sector management. For example, it is not entirely clear what operating on a more business-like basis means when public services are not paid for directly by consumers and instead are funded through the supply procedure; it is not clear in all contexts how performance pay will operate successfully where services are monopolies; and it is not clear how annual cost savings of 1.5 per cent per year can be applied indefinitely without affecting efficiency and effectiveness. All of these issues are now within the scope of the special responsibilities of the Treasury.

The creation and monitoring of agencies provides insights into the 'closed' politics mentioned at the beginning of this chapter. Indeed, Nigel Lawson, Chancellor of the Exchequer from 1983 to 1989, has offered some valuable comments on this in his autobiography. He has recorded that Ibbs believed 'that the route to efficiency in the public sector was to mimic the private sector as closely as possible' and he was always sympathetic to complaints of spending departments that they could do a better job if the Treasury ceased to deny them the resources to do their job properly. Lawson was keen on privatisation and the discipline of the market place, but he recognised that it was not relevant where public services were provided free at the point of use, so that a price mechanism did not operate. That was why, he said, 'Treasury control was essential. The alternative was no financial discipline at all.'[227]

When Ibbs presented his report recommending the creation of Next Steps agencies, it was clear to Lawson that insufficient attention had been given to the two questions of parliamentary accountability and maintaining effective control of the agencies' expenditure (in which Ibbs had no interest). The battle that followed between the Treasury, led by Sir Peter Middleton, then its Permanent Secretary, and 10 Downing Street, represented by Sir Robin Butler as Cabinet Secretary, resulted in a concordat. This included an understanding that agency status would always be seen as second best to privatisation, and that agencies would be set stiff financial targets which would be agreed with the Treasury and monitored by the Treasury. Lawson added that 'the public interest was further secured by the appointment of a senior Treasury official, Peter Kemp, as the manager of the "Next Steps" project'.[228] Lawson commented that agency status reversed some of the negative effects on civil service morale of the economies of the early 1980s, by giving the staff a sense of ownership, and might make privatisation less difficult. The main result seems to have been that the Treasury was able, at least to some extent, to ensure that responsibilities were built into the creation of agencies to preserve the Treasury's role in relation to public expenditure implications. Matters of parliamentary accountability remain unresolved.[229]

NOTE ON THE CASH AND ACCRUALS BASES OF ACCOUNTING

Source: HM Treasury, *Trading Accounts: A Guide for Government Departments and Non-Departmental Public Bodies*, HMSO, 1989.

Accounts prepared on a cash (receipts and payments) basis simply record all receipts and payments occurring within the period of account. Capital expenditure (e.g. cost of purchasing fixed assets) is treated no differently from current expenditure (e.g. cost of employing staff). No account is taken, or adjustment made, in a receipts and payments account for changes in the value of stocks, debtors or creditors. Cash accounting may be suitable where a body has few fixed assets (such as land and buildings, plant and machinery, and motor vehicles) and few stocks in hand and where its operations do not materially involve the giving or taking of credit. The receipts and payments account is normally supplemented by a statement of balances rather than a formal balance sheet.

In contrast to the cash-based method of accounting, the accruals (income and expenditure) approach records revenues and costs as they are earned and incurred, not as money is received or paid. For example, a sale is recorded when the body has the right to demand payment from the customer, and a purchase is recorded when the liability to pay has arisen. In addition, the cost (or value) of fixed assets is charged against income as depreciation over the estimated useful lives of the assets.

The aim of the income and expenditure account (which may also be referred to as the profit and loss account or the operating account) is to match the cost (or value) of resources consumed in a financial period with the income earned in that period, with a view to disclosing a surplus or loss for the period. In addition to the income and expenditure account, the year-end financial statements include a balance sheet and a statement of source and application of funds. A balance sheet is a statement of the assets and liabilities as at the end of the financial period, and a statement of source and application of funds shows the sources from which funds have flowed into the business during the financial period, the ways in which they have been used, and the resultant impact on working capital balances.

5   Reflections

Some thirty-five years ago, when he wrote his book *Anatomy of Britain*, Anthony Sampson described the Treasury building, which, he had been assured by a messenger, contains a thousand rooms and nine miles of corridors, as 'the central citadel of Whitehall'. He added: 'If anyone were to wish to bring the British administration to a halt, it is on this building, rather than on parliament opposite, that he should drop his bomb'.[1] The last few years of the twentieth century have brought significant changes in various aspects of the British system of government, but the changes have been at least as significant for the Treasury as they have for any other department. As this book was being completed the government's private finance initiative (PFI) was having its effect on the very building in which the Treasury is housed: the Treasury is expected to vacate the building in 1998 and reoccupy part of it in 2001.[2]

As Sampson observed when writing about the Treasury, its building has special prestige (which, he entertainingly suggested, was indicated by the presence of window boxes with flowers), and it is not surprising that the sale of the building attracted comments and criticisms. However, for present purposes the sale indicates the significance of change in contemporary public administration and how quickly it can be implemented. Such changes now make stability and continuity, as reflected in the past writings of Sampson and others, including distinguished scholars, look rather dated. For example, Sir Ivor Jennings' book on the Cabinet,[3] first published in 1936, held an important position as a standard work on its subject for over thirty years, but it now seems rather odd that his chapter on 'Treasury Control' should begin with control of the civil service – though it was the Treasury's most important function when Jennings was writing. Since then, the Civil Service Department has been created and abolished,[4] and most modern textbooks would probably give pride of place, when dealing with central responsibilities for the civil service, not to the Treasury but to the Cabinet Office (Office of Public Service).

Other very important changes have also recently been announced within the ambit of the responsibilities of the Chancellor of the Exchequer. Two are mentioned here, for illustrative purposes, partly because they are so significant, but also because they should encourage readers to look out for other announcements as they are made. One of these is the proposal to sell the Paymaster Agency, a department of government in its own right, accountable to the Chancellor of the Exchequer. Paymaster is responsible for paying about 1.6 million public service pensions every year, with a value of more than £8.7 billion, and for other pensions administration services for government departments. It also provides banking-type services for some 1,400 public service organisations which, in 1995, involved payments of some £800 million. Paymaster was founded in 1836, became a Next Steps agency in 1993, and was subject to a 'prior options' review in 1995 (all agencies are now subject to such reviews – further details are explained in the 1994 White Paper on the Civil Service).[5] The government announced its intention to privatise the agency on 15 July 1996; and it was stated in September 1996 that the sale should be completed by the end of March 1997.[6]

The other important change concerns National Savings. National Savings became an executive agency on 1 July 1996, reporting to the Chancellor of the Exchequer. Its task is to raise funds for the government by selling savings products and schemes to the public; these schemes include Premium Savings Bonds, National Savings Certificates and Pensioners Bonds.[7] As the National Savings agency will also be subject to a 'prior options' review it seems possible that it, too, may soon be a candidate for privatisation.

Students of public policy-making, particularly when studying public policy-making in liberal democracies, must nearly always be students of change. They must not only be aware of the changes in institutional structures, and in the legal perspectives and constraints on what departments of government do, they must also be students of the sources of powers and the requirements for the exercise of legitimate power. In addition, they must make every possible effort to keep up to date with what the contemporary arrangements and procedures are, and develop evaluation and critical skills to be able to assess stated intentions and the continuously changing provisions to achieve them. This is no easy task and it is therefore prudent to be somewhat tentative about formulating reflections that in other contexts might have the misleading security and significance often associated with 'conclusions'.

Lord Bridges chose 'Reflections' as the title for the concluding chapter of his book *The Treasury*,[8] and it is with reservations that Bridges' title has been borrowed for the last chapter of this book. Like Bridges' volume, the purpose of this book has been to describe Treasury duties and organisation as they exist today, and to show how they have developed over the years. In addition, an attempt has been made to provide introductory insights into the policy-making role of this most important and prestigious department in British central government. The reservations about offering tentative conclusions must therefore reflect all the uncertainties generally associated with policy-making studies, which include: caution to allow for the changes that are continuously introduced in all aspects of the world of practical affairs; caution about accepting as complete and authoritative what may be only partial or preliminary views of very recent events; and caution about evaluating what is most important when a somewhat different approach or viewpoint, perhaps offered as early as tomorrow, may require a more or less fundamental re-evaluation. Moreover, Bridges had the great advantages of his personal qualities and skills, he worked in the Treasury for most of his working life, and there can be no substitute for the mature reflections of such an experienced and distinguished Treasury official.

Bridges, in taking what he called 'a backward look', drew particular attention to two changes which took place during his years at the Treasury. The first of these was the decision that permanent secretaries should be the accounting officers of their departments, thereby ensuring that 'the responsibility for policy, and for the financial consequences of that policy, went hand in hand'. Bridges accepted that that might appear 'an obvious essential in any sound organisation', but he assured his readers that it was one of the biggest changes in his experience.[9] In recent times this point has a rather different significance. Permanent secretaries are, of course, still the accounting officers for their departments, but most central government operations are now undertaken by the 125 Next Steps agencies which employ over 354,000 civil servants, some 72 per cent of the total of those working in the Home Civil Service.[10] This has given rise to much debate about accountability for the executive work of agencies. Ministers, it is sometimes said, are responsible for policy, and agencies (and their chief executives, who are their accounting officers), are responsible for operations. Troubles arise when there is by no means a definite division between the two. As with policy and administration (or management), what may be deemed a policy matter in one context may be an operational matter in another context; much depends on a variety of criteria, among which one of the most important is the position of the assessor in making the distinction. This was particularly well illustrated by the Learmont Inquiry, which reviewed Prison Service Security in England and Wales, and the escape from Parkhurst Prison on 3 January 1995.[11]

The second change to which Bridges drew particular attention when taking his 'backward look' was 'Warren Fisher's determination to weld the Civil Service into a single effective organisation, conscious of its unity, and his insistence on closer, more cordial relations between those serving in different departments'.[12] Bridges went on to say that Fisher was one of the civil servants who contributed most to the development of the Treasury – his work and influence set going the changes which led to the Treasury having (certainly at the time Bridges wrote) predominant responsibility for the *management* of the civil service. That position has without doubt changed fundamentally in the last few years, as readers of this book will be only too aware. However, three points, in particular, are worth making about this. The first point concerns the present state of the civil service. Second, the continuing role of the Treasury as the pre-eminent department of government is considered. Third, there is the question of the Treasury's exercise of power and influence.

First, some comments on the present state of the civil service. It is, clearly, a very different civil service from the days of either Fisher or Bridges. Indeed, it has been argued that, as a unified civil service, it no longer exists. It has been re-defined;[13] there is now devolved authority to departments and agencies for recruitment (and, furthermore, with the sale in 1996 of the Recruitment and Assessment Services agency, there is no longer even a successor agency to the Civil Service Commission, which was abolished in 1991); and as for staff grading, pay, and conditions of service, there is not very much left to identify as characteristics that the civil service has in common.[14] Furthermore, staff work in units which, far from displaying a team spirit with a common civil service ethos, compete with each other, issue contracts to each other, and, in so doing, charge what are thought to be 'commercial' rates for their services. The 1994 White Paper on the Civil Service quoted Sir Robin Butler's key principles of the civil service, which he said were: 'integrity, impartiality, objectivity, selection and promotion on merit and accountability through Ministers to Parliament'.[15] Where these general characteristics relate to good management practice they are by no means features peculiar to the civil service; they similarly apply to good management practice elsewhere. Even with the so-called principle of accountability through ministers to Parliament, it should be noted that agency chief executives are now, apparently, accountable to Parliament and the people for operational matters for which ministers do not accept responsibility. Consequently it may be said that now there is no unified civil service but numerous separate public services.

Second, it might be thought that the present role of the Cabinet Office, with the management responsibilities of the Office of Public Service, and the increasing devolution of authority to departments, has meant a decline in the status of the Treasury. There is no evidence for any such decline in status, even though the Treasury no longer has the management responsibilities it previously had. When Bridges was writing he confidently asserted that the Treasury was the central department of government. Moreover, when discussing the possibility of the management of the civil service being taken out of the Treasury and given to a separate department he made it quite clear that in his opinion that would be a false step, weakening both the management and the financial functions. He added: 'You cannot have two centres'.[16] Since then, much of the management of the civil service was allocated to the Civil Service Department and, in more recent years, to a sub-department within the Cabinet Office. Nevertheless, the Treasury still maintains its key role.[17] This is for at least two reasons. Treasury staff are almost as much an elite as they ever were. Partly, this is because so many of the best new recruits to the civil service continue to express a preference to work there – this is still the general impression one gets from candidates during the selection procedure. This helps to maintain the self-confidence often associated with an elite. Peter Hennessy put this well when he said it was a 'surprisingly self-confident department'.[18] Good people choose to work there because its work is known to be important, and it is thought that even secondment to the Treasury is generally advantageous in career terms; but the attractions are not merely career advancement and the attractions of being part of an elite. As has already been explained, the Treasury has key financial responsibilities in government, the control of money brings power, and the details of Treasury work bring knowledge of a variety of aspects of the work of other government departments.

Third, it should be noted, as it has throughout this book, that power being exercised by the Treasury should not be seen as a sort of naked authoritarianism; the way the Treasury works – and has to work, it must be recognised – is much more subtle than that. Much is achieved by persuasion and influence. Chapter 2 showed how this was done in the past, particularly when the Treasury demurred; Chapter 3 indicated how, during the public expenditure survey, the Treasury acquires knowledge of a whole range of activities in other departments. Knowledge on this scale and also with depth of detail is important, and maintaining a stable macroeconomic environment is part of its mission, with objectives that include keeping public expenditure to a level that is affordable, stated in its current aim, mission and objectives. Therefore the present relationship of the Treasury and its officials when dealing with other departments is achieved through a combination of rules and procedures (e.g. in the way the Treasury is involved in setting targets for Next Steps agencies) but also through the influence and persuasion of an apparently self-confident elite staff dealing with officials elsewhere who have a wary respect for Treasury staff. Generally there is frequent contact between officials in the Treasury and the officials they deal with in other departments; this is important for understanding how the Treasury works. Sometimes there may be tensions associated with this relationship, but if tensions occur little is said to reveal details outside the administrative system. For example, market testing, the initiative that came from the *Competing for Quality* White Paper, published in 1991, originated from the Treasury, and seems to be founded on the belief that the introduction of competition is the preferred approach to reducing costs. This approach differs from the creation of agencies, an approach that did not originate in the Treasury, and which seems to be based on the belief that the way to reduce costs is by setting rigorous targets. It is, perhaps, not surprising that there has been speculation about controversy associated with these two approaches; and perhaps also associated with the departure of Sir Peter Kemp from his position as Next Steps Project Manager in 1992.[19] Peter Hennessy has reported that after the Next Steps Report was agreed 'A battle royal ensued in the autumn of 1987 which raged for several months'.[20] This is confirmed by the details given in Lawson's autobiography. Without knowing the full story there is plenty of evidence to indicate Treasury activity in the 'closed' politics of the administrative system (as mentioned in Chapter 4).

This study of the Treasury began by drawing attention to the importance of the Treasury (by whatever name it may be called) in all systems of government. Government has to have financial resources to enable it to undertake its obligations, but the way the Treasury developed in Britain, with its special and peculiar significance in the context of a largely unwritten constitution, is unique: much power in British government is exercised and accepted without the need for legislation, often to the great surprise of foreigners. Sophisticated arrangements developed for ensuring accountability, not only within the Treasury organisation, but also through using the Treasury to authorise and control the work of other departments within government. However, by 1668 the Treasury was recognised as the office with responsibility for all financial questions.

Once it achieved its pre-eminent position in relation to all governmental expenditure, it also acquired a special relationship with the House of Commons. Money, it became established, had to be granted for clearly defined purposes and its expenditure limited within time constraints. From these early principles it was a short step to ensuring that expenditure was properly planned; and also that the expenditure and activities of the various departments of government were co-ordinated. Demands for economy were exerted by Parliament, and the Treasury in turn exerted its demands on the departments; the Treasury became the medium by which, in effect, Parliament exercised control over government expenditure; the power of the purse brought with it a voice in all decisions of policy and administration.

Again, it was a short step, though a step which took some time to be taken, from financial control to the position where the Treasury acquired responsibility for recruitment of staff and for their conditions of service. Nevertheless, the step was taken by the middle of the nineteenth century, when it was recognised that the Treasury was 'the central office for the revision of the public establishments'.

Consequently, by the late nineteenth century, the Treasury acquired a rich fund of knowledge and experience, not only about financial matters, but about what was going on throughout the system of government. The Treasury attracted the best candidates from the civil service recruitment competitions, and sent some of its best men to other departments; this, in turn, facilitated good communication and co-operation, and reinforced the role and status of the Treasury throughout the system of government.

By the first half of the twentieth century the Treasury had acquired a distinctive status in the governmental process, and its staff acquired attitudes of superiority and control within a unified civil service which the Treasury itself had had a very significant role in creating. However, its by then distinguished status had been achieved piecemeal, in an unplanned fashion, over hundreds of years: it had achieved a distinctive position in relation to Parliament, commanding responsibilities over public expenditure, and responsibilities over civil service personnel management. It was never an important department in terms of its administrative responsibilities, it was essentially a department of control and supervision.

Its status was greatly enhanced under Sir Warren Fisher. In the period immediately after the end of the First World War the civil service became a unified service and the Treasury under his leadership became its central department. Fisher emphasised the importance of teamwork and co-operation within the service, played a major role in staff appointments and promotions, and publicly expressed the standards he expected of himself and others. Bridges continued as a worthy, though not direct, successor in these respects to Fisher, so that by the middle of the twentieth century the unity of the civil service was accepted as a commonplace. It was the institutional leadership of this unified service that then became one of the prime functions of the Treasury.

After the Second World War, the Treasury enhanced its control and influence over the national economy; it pioneered a new style of management involving the development of new management techniques; and it acquired a somewhat miscellaneous collection of new functions which were allocated within the ambit of Treasury responsibilities because there was no obvious alternative department to which they could conveniently be added.

The Plowden Report of 1961 was a watershed. It marked the end of the post-war period and the beginning of a new period of professional management. A regularised system was developed for the control of public expenditure, with the Treasury re-directing its energies into controlling both the policy and programme stages. To achieve this, the internal structure of the Treasury was reorganised. Later, some of its functions were re-allocated to the Department of Economic Affairs and the Civil Service Department. However, these changes also introduced uncertainty within the Treasury and criticism from outside. The Treasury had been left with a primarily advisory role, to the Chancellor of the Exchequer, and its loss of key responsibilities meant that both its controlling role and its influence role were reduced. Some of its most important responsibilities in relation to the civil service were allocated to the Cabinet Office (in fact to a sub-department within it, which, over a period of time, changed its name from MPO to OMCS, to OPSS, then to OPS).

The Treasury today is still the key department of government, but it is a department that has had its organisation and functions reformed and refocused in the mid-1990s. The latest review has been the result of the 1994 FER exercise, as explained in Chapter 3. This most important review has left the Treasury with a sharpened focus on its work which revolves around the public expenditure survey. It now aims to be a department with a strategic role within the system of government; its size has again contracted (with fewer staff, and other savings through information technology within the Treasury and elsewhere in the system of government), and a greatly clarified statement of its aims and objectives. The way it is structured has also been revised, with an attempt to build on its collegial ethos, to develop relatively flexible teams of staff working on designated management tasks. Control of other departments is now less over matters of detail and more over financial management and control systems.

These recent major changes are to a large extent the result of the policies of a government which has been in power for an extended period of years, and it is a government which has been able to make an impact that would have been difficult in a shorter period of office. The changes have clearly been designed to be the most suitable for carrying out other government policies (for example, for implementing the private finance initiative, market testing, and privatisation policies). The new institutional structure and approaches to management are also consistent with modern approaches to management practice, which emphasise outputs, not inputs. The overall impression any reader may be expected to gain from Chapter 3 of this book is that the modern Treasury has been reviewed to produce a leaner, sleeker organisation, better organised to implement policies intended to achieve improved value for money and to raise questions about the role of the state at the present time.

The modern Treasury is without doubt at the centre of the formulation and execution of government economic policy. For example, it effectively sets interest rates, it decides which taxes to levy and when and how other finance should be raised, and it has powers to veto the spending of other government departments. Nevertheless, much of this responsibility is still exercised, as it has been for many years, by persuasion and influence.

However, major questions remain for the future. The Treasury has an enhanced role as the main financial channel between the United Kingdom and the European Communities, because the Treasury negotiates on behalf of the UK, and it checks and distributes funds from the EC. Meanwhile, the numerous new agencies that have been created (as explained in Chapter 4), and the wider devolved authority given to departments of government and their agencies, have effectively marked the end of the British civil service as a unified service. Reliance is being placed on the Treasury giving advice and guidance on good practice (e.g. through *Government Accounting*) and on the importance of effective consultation and co-ordination. These changes in institutional structures and approaches to management in government have been introduced as a result of government policies, but it should be noted that they have largely received support from the opposition political parties, and a change in the party of government is unlikely to result in reversals of the changes. Nevertheless, there is likely to be scope for reviewing the review in a few years' time. What has happened in fact is that the core responsibilities of the Treasury (as at present conceived) have been analysed and revised but the personnel management responsibilities, and more specifically the ones of lesser status, that have always been accorded less prestige in the civil service, are now within the Office of Public Service. Perhaps that Office is already undergoing its own FER; but whether or not it is, there is likely to be growing concern about the present and future condition of those aspects of government which were previously Treasury responsibilities. Has the passage of time reduced their importance? What would Fisher and Bridges say if they could be asked to act as a sort of Northcote-Trevelyan inquiry at the turn of the century?

In some respects the Treasury continues with the responsibilities it has had for hundreds of years, though they are subject to change and the emphasis on particular priorities in government is altered from time to time. Its responsibilities in serving its ministers and parliament in matters relating to public spending continue. It is the department that leads in terms of good practice in the accounting and control of public resources. It influences other departments by having a broader perspective which sharpens their economic and financial calculations. It is the department that raises questions about what is in the taxpayer's interest – and this is an especially important contribution to public policy-making in its widest context because the Treasury has to ensure that the enthusiasms of other departments for their various policies are optimised and balanced.

In other respects, any understanding of such historical continuity has to be tempered with an appreciation of recent change. The Treasury's responsibilities for overseeing public expenditure, if not for actually managing and/or controlling it in detail, now have a different emphasis. Perhaps this reflects a general understanding that good practice exists in the private sector as well as in the public sector, and also that professional standards and expectations in an increasingly specialised world have a part to play in ensuring that good practice continues without the necessity of measures for control in detail. However, the emphasis on fashionable approaches to management has resulted in the Treasury losing some of its special status, which depended on its emphasis on high standards in *public* policy-making.

The Treasury still has a crucial part to play in the system of government, through ensuring that the government's aims and objectives are upheld and implemented; but it has lost the professional responsibilities it began to acquire in the nineteenth century in relation to the civil service. The strong links between these two spheres – on the one hand, the focus on the highest standards of control over public expenditure, with all its implications; and on the other hand, the focus on account-ability through ministers to parliament – formed the bedrock on which the ethos of the civil service was built. No sensible person would suggest that keeping accurate accounts, emphasising the achievement of value for money, and ensuring proper accountability for manage-ment decisions (whatever meaning may be given to such broad expressions) should not receive high priority. What is missing, or at least is weak and understated, in the contemporary context, is the links between those matters and the ethos of public service associated with accountability through ministers to parliament. When these are sepa-rated, as they have been between the Treasury and the Cabinet Office, and between the Treasury and the departments and their agencies, the Treasury is in danger of becoming little more than a department with a major concern for accounting methods and the control of public expenditure. No doubt these high standards and good practice in financial management are as important in government as in all large organisations. However, good public policy-making in the context of a liberal democracy, especially one with the unique system of govern-ment in the United Kingdom, may require much more emphasis on the implications of the word *public*. It must never be forgotten that policy-making in government is for the benefit of the public.

Appendix 1
Glossary of terms*

Accounting Officer An officer appointed, normally by the Treasury, in compliance with Section 22 of the Exchequer and Audit Department Act, 1866, to sign the Appropriation Accounts and any other accounts within his responsibility. By virtue of that duty, he has the further duty of being the principal witness on behalf of the department before the Committee of Public Accounts to deal with questions arising from those accounts and from the Comptroller and Auditor General's reports to Parliament under the National Audit Act, 1983.

Ambit (of a vote) The description in Part I of a Supply Estimate, or a Supplementary Supply Estimate, which describes and limits the purposes for which provision is made. The Ambit appears in a schedule to the Appropriation Act and Parliament authorises specific sums of money to each Ambit.

Appropriation Account An end-of-year account of money voted by Parliament which compares the Supply Estimate with actual payments made and receipts brought to account, and explains any substantial differences. An Appropriation Account is prepared for each Vote.

Appropriations in aid Receipts which, with the authority of Parliament, are used to finance some of the gross expenditure on a Vote, thus reducing the amount to be issued from the Consolidated Fund.

Capital expenditure Expenditure on new construction, land, extensions of and alterations to existing buildings and the purchase of any other fixed assets (e.g. machinery and plant) including vehicles having an expected working life of more than one year. Also includes expenditure on stocks and grants and lending for capital purposes.

---

* Source: Supply Estimates, 1995–96, for the Year Ending 31 March 1996, Summary and Guide, Cm 2775, HMSO, 1995, pp. 42–44.

Cash limit   The limit on the net amount of cash that can be spent on certain specified services during one financial year. The limit will usually be equal to the amount of cash limited provision within a vote but will be lower than this when agreement has been reached to reduce provision, for example, to offset an increase elsewhere.

Class   A group of Estimates covering a department or departments included within a specific departmental report.

Consolidated Fund   The Exchequer account into which are paid gross tax revenues, less repayments, and all other Exchequer receipts not specifically directed elsewhere. Issues from the Fund are made to meet expenditure shown in Supply Estimates.

Consolidated Fund extra receipts   Receipts related to expenditure in the Supply Estimates which Parliament has not authorised to be used as appropriations in aid.

Contingencies Fund   A fund which can be used for urgent expenditure in anticipation of provision by Parliament becoming available. It is limited to 2 per cent of the previous year's total authorised Supply provision. Drawings on this fund must be repaid when Parliament has voted the additional sums required.

Control Total   The aggregate of the elements of public expenditure which the government plans and controls to achieve its wider objective for general government expenditure.

Economic classification   An analysis of public sector accounting transactions according to their economic character. It is based on the classification used by the Central Statistical Office for compiling the accounts of national income and expenditure.

Estimate Day   A day set aside by Parliament for the debate of Main or Supplementary Supply Estimates.

Executive Agencies   In February 1988, the Prime Minister announced that the government had accepted the main recommendations of the report by the Efficiency Unit entitled 'Improving Management in Government: the Next Steps'. To the greatest extent practicable, the executive functions of government, as distinct from policy advice, would be carried out by clearly designated units, referred to as Agencies. The main aim of the Next Steps initiative is to deliver services more efficiently and effectively within available resources, for the benefit of tax payers, customers and staff.

Financial year The year from 1 April to 31 March of the next.

Grant Money voted (i.e. granted) by Parliament to meet the services shown in Supply Estimates. Also used in individual sub-heads of Supply Estimates to describe an unrequited payment to an individual or body in the private or public sector. See also 'Grant in Aid' and 'Subsidy'.

Grant in Aid A grant from voted monies to a particular organisation or body where any unexpected balances of the sums issued during the financial year will not be liable for surrender to the Consolidated Fund.

Main Estimate See 'Supply Estimate'.

National Audit Office This office carries out the audit of every Appropriation Account other than its own.

Net sub-head A net sub-head is created when receipts are offset against expenditure in a specific sub-head, rather than appropriated in aid of the Vote as a whole. In most cases the receipts equal the expenditure and only a token £1,000 is shown to be voted.

Outturn Actual expenditure.

Reserve The public expenditure Control Total includes a Reserve which provides a margin for uncertainties and is intended to cover any future additions to departmental spending, whether these result from policy changes, new initiatives, contingencies or revised estimates of demand-led programmes.

Revised Estimate See 'Supply Estimate'.

Running costs Running costs are the gross costs of administration of central government, including the pay and accruing superannuation liability costs of civil servants together with associated general administrative expenditure including the costs of accommodation, travel, training, etc.

Section A group of sub-heads in the same Vote. Sections provide a means of summarising an Estimate if, for example, it covers more than one area of public expenditure and provides a link to the departmental report.

Sub-head Expenditure within a Vote which is separately identified in the Supply Estimate and Appropriation Account.

Subsidy   A grant (i.e. an unrequited payment) to a producer or trader which is deemed to benefit the consumer by reducing the selling price of the product or service. See also 'Grant'.

Supplementary Estimate   See 'Supply Estimate'.

Supply Estimate   A statement presented to the House of Commons of the estimated expenditure of a department during a financial year, asking for the necessary funds to be voted.

Token sub-head   See 'Net sub-head'.

Token Vote   In some cases receipts of a kind that could be appropriated in aid of the Vote are expected on a scale equal to or greater than the expected gross expenditure. In these circumstances, sufficient of the expected receipts are shown as appropriations in aid to leave only a nominal balance, usually £1,000, to be voted as Supply. Part III of the Estimate shows the balance of the receipts expected which are payable to the Consolidated Fund as extra receipts (see above). In addition a Supplementary Estimate for a token sum may be presented, for example to transfer some existing provision to a new service in the same Vote.

Vote   An individual Supply Estimate.

Vote on account   Money granted by Parliament to carry on public services from 1 April until the passing of the Appropriation Act, which authorises the issue of the full amount required for the whole year.

Appendix 2
Parliamentary procedure*

Parliament's consideration of the Supply Estimates is part of its Supply procedure, by which Parliament approves Government's requests for funds. In outline the process can be seen in six steps:

1 the Government requests certain funds;
2 to support each request, information is provided about what the money will be spent on and who will be responsible for ensuring it will be spent properly;
3 Parliament considers these requests, investigates some more fully and debates a few of them;
4 if Parliament votes in favour of the requests it passes an Act to make the cash available;
5 to help enhance its control, Parliament gives legislative force to the Ambits of the Estimates which specify the purposes for which the money may be spent; and
6 after expenditure has been incurred, it is audited and accounted for to check that the amounts and purposes approved have not been exceeded.

This process extends over a period of more than two years, starting before the financial year in which expenditure is to be incurred and ending almost twelve months after that year has ended. At any one time Parliament may be considering expenditure that relates to more than one financial year. Furthermore, a single document or procedure may cover more than one step for expenditure which relates to a single financial year. For example, the Estimates cover both the first step (a request for money) and some of the second (supporting information).

* Source: Supply Estimates 1995–96, for the Year Ending 31 March 1996, Summary and Guide, Cm 2775, HMSO, 1995, pp. 22–24

Supply procedure   Under long-established constitutional practice, it is for the Crown (the Government) to demand money, the House of Commons to grant it and the House of Lords to assent to the grant.

Parliament gives statutory authority for funds to be drawn from the Consolidated Fund (the Government's general bank account at the Bank of England) to meet most expenditure by government departments and certain related bodies by Acts of Parliament known as Consolidated Fund Acts and by an annual Appropriation Act. Parliamentary procedure leading to the passing of these Acts is known as 'Supply procedure'. Funds are made available under the Acts only for a specified financial year.

Main Estimates   The process begins with the presentation by the Treasury to Parliament of Main Supply Estimates containing a request for funds for the coming financial year. The aim is to present the Main Estimates before the end of March each year.

Presentation to Parliament does not authorise government departments to spend the sums requested. Part I of each Estimate forms the basis of a Supply Resolution which is normally voted on by MPs in the House of Commons before the end of July. A Consolidated Fund (Appropriation) Bill is then brought in and passed before Parliament rises for the summer recess.

Appropriation Act   The resulting Appropriation Act authorises departments to spend up to the amount requested in the Main Supply Estimates and in any Summer Supplementaries (see below). It not only gives parliamentary authority for the total sums requested to be issued from the Consolidated Fund but also limits the way in which this money can be spent by prescribing how the overall sum is to be appropriated to particular Estimates in order to finance specified services. It also appropriates to individual Estimates sums provided under the Consolidated Fund Acts passed since the previous Appropriation Act.

Revised Estimates   Revised Estimates affecting some expenditure may be presented to replace the original ones before the Supply Resolution is voted on. They normally reduce the provision sought in the original Estimate or vary the way in which it is to be spent.

Votes on Account   Parliament does not normally approve the Main Estimates until around the end of July or early August, so funds for early months of the financial year are provided by a system of Votes on Account. These are normally presented to Parliament in the previous November, along with the Winter Supplementary Estimates (see below). In general they seek, for the coming financial year, 45 per cent of the amounts authorised to date in the current year.

Supplementary Estimates The Government may decide to ask Parliament for additional money during the year. Supplementary Supply Estimates, where necessary, are usually presented in June (Summer), November (Winter) and February (Spring). Following any Estimates Day debates, and the vote on the necessary Supply Resolution, formal statutory authority for extra funds is provided by the Appropriation Act in the case of the Summer Supplementaries, and by separate Consolidated Fund Acts in the case of the Winter and Spring Supplementaries. The Winter Consolidated Fund Act also covers the vote on Account. Exceptionally, as necessary, Supplementaries may be presented at other times.

Contingencies Fund There is also a Contingencies Fund which can be used to finance urgent expenditure, in anticipation of Parliamentary approval of Estimates. Total advances outstanding at any one time must not exceed 2 per cent of the previous year's total Estimates provision. Drawings on this fund are repaid when Parliament has voted the additional money.

Accounts and audit Supply Estimates are based on a cash accounting system for payments and receipts. The provision for expenditure reflects the amounts expected to be paid in the year. No provision is made for commitments entered into but not yet matured.

After the end of the financial year an Appropriation Account is prepared for each Estimate which, after being certified by the Comptroller and Auditor General (and reported on where necessary), is laid before the House of Commons in the autumn following the end of the financial year to which it relates.

The accounting and audit arrangements for some expenditure including grants in aid, and certain subscriptions to international organisations are different from those for most expenditure. These exceptions are indicated by a common set of symbols used in all Estimates.

Under the National Audit Act 1983 the Comptroller and Auditor General also carries out value for money studies of departments' expenditure. The Public Accounts Committee's examination of departments in these studies substantially enhances the accountability provided through the Appropriation Accounts.

Excess Votes If expenditure on any Vote exceeds the funds available, and it is too late to seek a Supplementary Estimate, the excess will appear in the department's Appropriation Accounts and will be reported on to the Public Accounts Committee by the Comptroller and Auditor General. Subject to that report, the necessary provision is sought in an Excess Vote. A Statement of Excesses is presented to Parliament by the Treasury, usually in February of the following year at the same time as Spring Supplementary Estimates. Funds are then voted in March (i.e. eleven months after the end of the financial year to which they relate).

Parliamentary debate Parliament's consideration of individual Estimates is primarily a task for departmentally related Select Committees, which examine the expenditure of particular departments. A Committee may decide to examine individual Main or Supplementary Estimates, ask their department for more information about some aspects and examine ministers and officials about particular areas of expenditure. A Committee's conclusions often take the form of a Report which is printed by the House.

The House of Commons has an opportunity to debate, and vote on, individual Estimates on three Estimates Days in each Parliamentary Session. When this happens the debate is generally informed by a Report from the relevant Select Committee. The time available in Estimates Days is allocated on the advice of the Liaison Committee, whose membership includes the Chairmen of the Departmental Select Committees. In addition, the government may make some extra time available for debates on special Supplementary Estimates.

Proceedings on Consolidated Fund Bills are formal, i.e. not open to debate.

Parliamentary timetable Under Standing Orders of the House of Commons, seven clear days must elapse between the presentation of an Estimate and the vote on the related Supply Resolution. The government aims to leave at least 14 days between presentation and the vote, and to give Select Committees advanced proof copies of Supplementaries ahead of presentation, although this may not always be possible. In practice, some 5–7 weeks are usually available for Select Committees to examine Supplementaries on the three main occasions when they are presented; this period is necessarily shorter if there are any late revisions and for any special Supplementaries.

Parliament's consideration of Estimates is therefore generally concentrated in three periods:

1 March–July for Main Estimates and June–July for Summer

Supplementaries, including any Estimates Day debates, followed by the Appropriation Act;

2 November–December for Winter Supplementaries and any associated debates, followed by a Consolidated Fund Bill; and

3 February–March for Spring Supplementaries and any associated debates, also followed by a Consolidated Fund Bill.

Consolidated Fund standing services   Parliament has passed statutes that authorise certain expenditure to be charged directly to the Consolidated Fund and not be subject to the annual Supply procedure. These 'Consolidated Fund standing services' include payments to the National Loans Fund to service the National Debt, payments to the Northern Ireland Consolidated Fund of a share of UK tax revenues, most payments to the European Communities, Her Majesty's civil list and the salaries and pensions of some people who hold offices which are constitutionally independent of the Executive, such as the Speaker of the House of Commons, the Comptroller and Auditor General, United Kingdom members of the European Parliament and the judiciary.

Notes

GENERAL EDITOR'S INTRODUCTION

1 J. A. Chandler, *Public Policy-Making for Local Government*, Croom Helm, 1988.
2 John M. Pfiffner and Robert V. Presthus, *Public Administration*, The Ronald Press Company, 1935 (1960 edn), p. 367.
3 Ministry of Reconstruction, *Report of the Machinery of Government Committee*, Cd 9230, HMSO, 1918, p. 17.
4 Luther Gulick 'Notes on the Theory of Organisation', in Luther Gulick and L. Urwick, *Papers on the Science of Administration*, Institute of Public Administration, New York, 1937. The complete list of activities represented by the mnemonic are: planning, organising, staffing, directing, co-ordinating, reporting, and budgeting.
5 Colin Thain and Maurice Wright, *The Treasury and Whitehall, the planning and control of public expenditure, 1976–1993*, Clarendon Press, 1995.
6 Lord Bridges, *The Treasury*, George Allen and Unwin, 1964.

1 THE TREASURY IN PUBLIC POLICY-MAKING

1 See, for example, Brian W. Hogwood, 'Public Policy', *Public Administration*, 1995, Vol. 73, pp. 59–73; and R. A. W. Rhodes, 'The Institutional Approach', in David Marsh and Gerry Stoker (eds) *Theory and Methods in Political Science*, Macmillan, 1995, pp. 42–57.
2 For a succinct explanation of this term see R. A. W. Rhodes, 'The Institutional Approach'.
3 PRO/CAB 134/308, 3 June 1949.
4 PRO/CAB 134/309, Note by Bridges, 7 December 1950.
5 R. A. W. Rhodes, 'The Institutional Approach', p. 48.
6 David Easton, *The Political System, An Inquiry into the State of Political Science*, Alfred A. Knopf, 1953, Ch. 6. See also R. A. W. Rhodes, 'The Institutional Approach', p. 48.
7 PRO/T222/678, minute by Woods, 29 July 1994.
8 Samuel Brittan, *The Treasury Under the Tories 1951–1964*, Secker and Warburg and Penguin, 1964; *Steering the Economy, the Role of the Treasury*, Secker and Warburg, 1969, and Penguin, 1971 (revised edn).

9 Hugh Heclo and Aaron Wildavsky, *The Private Government of Public Money: Community and Policy within British Politics*, Macmillan, 1974.
10 *Ibid.*, p. xxi.
11 For some of the difficulties encountered at that time, see Richard A. Chapman, 'Decision Making Revisited', *Public Administration*, 1990, Vol. 68, pp. 353–67.
12 Hugh Heclo and Aaron Wildavsky, *The Private Government of Public Money*, p. xi.
13 *Ibid.*, pp. xxi–xxii.
14 Colin Thain and Maurice Wright, *The Treasury and Whitehall: the planning and control of public expenditure, 1976–1993*, Clarendon Press, 1995, p. v.
15 *Ibid.*, p. 5.
16 Richard A. Chapman, *Decision Making: A Case Study of the Decision to Raise the Bank Rate in September 1957*, Routledge and Kegan Paul, 1968.
17 Maurice Wright, *Treasury Control of the Civil Service 1854–1874*, Clarendon Press, 1969.
18 Colin Thain and Maurice Wright, *The Treasury and Whitehall*.

2 HISTORY: FROM EARLIEST TIMES TO THE PRESENT DAY

1 R. E. Welby 'Duties and organisation of the Treasury of the United Kingdom', 1879, reprinted in Edward Bridges, *The Treasury*, Allen and Unwin, 1964, pp. 222–26.
2 Quoted in Bridges, *The Treasury*, p. 41.
3 Treasury and Civil Service Committee, Eighth Report, 1987–88, *Civil Service Management Reform: The Next Steps*, HC 494 II, HMSO, 1988, Q 335 and 371.
4 Henry Roseveare, *The Treasury: The Evolution of a British Institution*, Allen Lane, The Penguin Press, 1969, p. 20.
5 Sir Thomas W. Heath, *The Treasury*, G. P. Putnam's Sons Ltd, 1927, p. 21.
6 Roseveare, *The Treasury*, p. 58.
7 Heath, *The Treasury*, pp. 137–38.
8 Henry Roseveare, *The Treasury 1660–1870: the foundations of control*, Allen & Unwin, 1973, Introduction.
9 Heath, *The Treasury*, p. 138 and Bridges, *The Treasury*, pp. 18–19.
10 See Roseveare, *The Treasury*, pp. 81–82. These orders are reprinted in Henry Roseveare, *The Treasury 1660–1870: the foundations of control*, pp. 113–15.
11 Roseveare, *The Treasury*, p. 80.
12 Bridges, *The Treasury*, p. 23.
13 Roseveare, *The Treasury*, p. 68.
14 Heath, *The Treasury*, p. 10.
15 Roseveare, *The Treasury*, pp. 100–1.
16 *Ibid.*, p. 110.
17 Bridges, *The Treasury*, p. 67.

18 Roseveare, *The Treasury*, p. 114.
19 Bridges, *The Treasury*, p. 25.
20 Quoted by Roseveare, *The Treasury*, p. 136.
21 Roseveare, *The Treasury*, pp. 215 and 138.
22 An extract from this Act is reprinted in Roseveare, *The Treasury, 1660–1870: the foundations of control*, p. 171.
23 Maurice Wright, *Treasury Control of the Civil Service 1854–1874*, Clarendon Press, 1969, p. 1.
24 Quoted by Roseveare, *The Treasury*, p. 141.
25 Roseveare, *The Treasury*, pp. 154–64.
26 Wright, *Treasury Control*, p. xix.
27 Richard A. Chapman, *The Higher Civil Service in Britain*, Constable, 1970, Ch. 2. See also *Reports of Committees of Inquiry into Public Offices and Papers Connected Therewith*, HMSO 1854.
28 Treasury Minute dated 12 April 1853, reprinted in Chapman, *The Higher Civil Service in Britain*, pp. 155–57.
29 *Ibid.*
30 Quoted in Edward Hughes, 'Civil Service Reform 1853–55', *Public Administration*, 1954, Vol. 32, pp. 17–51.
31 The Northcote-Trevelyan Report has been reprinted a number of times, including in *Public Administration*, 1954, Vol. 32, and as an Appendix to the Report of the Fulton Committee: *The Civil Service, Vol. I, Report of the Committee 1966–68*, Cmnd 3638, HMSO, 1968.
32 K. C. Wheare, *The Civil Service in the Constitution*, Athlone Press, 1954, pp. 7 and 10.
33 Chapman, *The Higher Civil Service in Britain*, pp. 30–31. See also Edward Hughes 'Civil Service Reform 1853–55', *Public Administration*, 1954, Vol. 32, p. 38.
34 Roseveare, *The Treasury*, p. 172. See also Maurice Wright, *Treasury Control*, p. 68.
35 Edward Hughes, 'Civil Service Reform 1853–55', *Public Administration*, 1954, Vol. 32, pp. 46–47.
36 Roseveare, *The Treasury*, p. 181.
37 78 HL Deb., 4s., Col. 32 (30 January 1900). See also Roseveare, *The Treasury*, p. 183.
38 Quoted in Roseveare, *The Treasury*, p. 184.
39 Roseveare, *The Treasury*, pp. 185–92.
40 *Ibid.*, p. 198.
41 *Ibid.*, p. 219. See also *The Diary of Sir Edward Walter Hamilton 1885–1896*, Dudley W. R. Bahlman (ed.), University of Hull Press, 1993.
42 Wright, *Treasury Control*, p. 3.
43 *Ibid.*, p. 198.
44 *Ibid.*, p. 205.
45 *Ibid.*, p. 204.
46 *Ibid.*, pp. 363–66.
47 Hamilton Lowe, 21 September 1869, PRO, Hamilton Semi-official Correspondence, iv, quoted by Wright, *Treasury Control*, p. 41.
48 Roseveare, *The Treasury*, pp. 210–11 and 227.
49 Bridges, *The Treasury*, pp. 108–9.
50 Wright, *Treasury Control*, p. 309.

51 Roseveare, *The Treasury*, p. 185.
52 Bridges, *The Treasury*, p. 29.
53 *Ibid.*, p. 160.
54 Ministry of Reconstruction, *Report of the Machinery of Government Committee*, Cd 9230, HMSO, 1918.
55 Roseveare, *The Treasury*, p. 244.
56 See Richard A. Chapman and J. R. Greenaway, *The Dynamics of Administrative Reform*, Croom Helm, 1980, pp. 73–100.
57 PRO/CAB 21/72, quoted in Chapman and Greenaway, *The Dynamics of Administrative Reform*, p. 74.
58 V. R. Markham, *Return Passage*, Oxford University Press, 1953, p. 147, quoted by Hans Daalder, *Cabinet Reform in Britain 1914–63*, Oxford University Press, 1964, p. 277; Margaret I. Cole (ed.), *Beatrice Webb's Diaries 1912–24*, Longman, 1952, p. 83.
59 See, for example, Haldane Centenary Essays, *Public Administration 1957*, Vol. 35, pp. 217–65; Charles H. Wilson, *Haldane and the Machinery of Government*, the twenty-fourth Haldane Memorial Lecture, delivered at Birkbeck College, London, 5 December 1956.
60 Haldane Report, Part II, para. 2, p. 17.
61 Haldane Report, Part II, para. 4, p. 18.
62 Haldane Report, Part II, para. 12, pp. 18–19.
63 Haldane Report, Part II, para. 15, p. 19.
64 Haldane Report, Part II, para. 7, p. 18.
65 Haldane Report, Part II, para. 16, p. 20.
66 Haldane Report, Part II, para. 20, p. 21.
67 Haldane Report, Part II, para. 22, p. 21.
68 PRO/CAB 134/308, Memorandum by HM Treasury, 27 June 1949.
69 Chapman and Greenaway, *The Dynamics of Administrative Reform*, p. 84.
70 Rosamund M. Thomas, *The British Philosophy of Administration: A Comparison of British and American Ideas 1900–1939*, Longman, 1978, p. 195.
71 Lord Bridges, *The Treasury*, p. 175.
72 Wright, *Treasury Control*, pp. 39–40.
73 *Ibid.*, pp. 40–41.
74 *Ibid.*, pp. 88, 97.
75 Sir H. P. Hamilton, 'Sir Warren Fisher and the Public Service', *Public Administration*, Vol. 29, 1951, p. 38.
76 Treasury File, T.110.
77 *The Sunday Times*, 3 October 1948.
78 Sir H. P. Hamilton, 'Sir Warren Fisher and the Public Service', *Public Administration*, Vol. 29, 1951, pp. 3–38.
79 Eunan O'Halpin, *Head of the Civil Service: A Study of Sir Warren Fisher*, Routledge, 1989.
80 PRO/T199/351 and PRO/T222/504.
81 *First and Second Reports from the Committee of Public Accounts, together with the proceedings of the Committee, Minutes of Evidence, Appendices and Index, Session 1935–36*, HC 45, 144, HMSO, 1936, Q 4443.
82 *Ibid.*
83 *Public Accounts Committee, 1936, Q 4607; Royal Commission on the Civil*

Service (1929–30), Minutes of Evidence, HMSO, 1930, Q 18787, 18887 and p. 1270.

84 *Public Accounts Committee*, 1936, Q 4607.
85 *Royal Commission on the Civil Service (1929–30)*, Q 18787.
86 *Public Accounts Committee*, 1936, Q 4578.
87 Bridges, *The Treasury*, p. 173.
88 *Royal Commission on the Civil Service (1929–30)*, p. 1267, para. 4.
89 Sir H. P. Hamilton, 'Sir Warren Fisher and the Public Service', *Public Administration*, Vol. 29, 1951, p. 14.
90 *Royal Commission on the Civil Service (1929–30)*, p. 1267, para. 5.
91 *Ibid.*, Q 18693.
92 *Report of the Board of Enquiry appointed by the Prime Minister to investigate certain statements affecting Civil Servants*, Cmd 3037, HMSO, 1928.
93 *Ibid.*, para. 54.
94 *Ibid.*, para. 59.
95 *Royal Commission on the Civil Service (1929–30)*, p. 1268, para. 12.
96 *Public Accounts Committee*, (1936) Q 4483.
97 *Ibid.*, Q 4542.
98 Eunan O'Halpin, *Head of the Civil Service*, p. 62.
99 Sir H. P. Hamilton, 'Sir Warren Fisher and the Public Service', *Public Administration*, Vol. 29, 1951, p. 38.
100 Bridges, *The Treasury*, pp. 117–18.
101 Richard A. Chapman and J. R. Greenaway, *The Dynamics of Administrative Reform*, Ch. 4.
102 L. D. White, *Whitley Councils in the British Civil Service: A study in Conciliation and Arbitration*, Chicago, University of Chicago Press, 1933; Henry Parris, *Staff Relations in the Civil Service: Fifty Years of Whitleyism*, Allen and Unwin, 1973; Richard A. Chapman and J. R. Greenaway, *The Dynamics of Administration Reform*.
103 Bridges, *The Treasury*, pp. 110–11.
104 *Report of the Committee on the Training of Civil Servants*, Cmd 6525, HMSO, 1944.
105 Richard A. Chapman and J. R. Greenaway, *The Dynamics of Administration Reform*, Ch. 3.
106 Heath, *The Treasury*, London and New York, Putnams, 1927, p. 122, and Roseveare, *The Treasury*, p. 246.
107 PRO/T162/965/50877/1.
108 Roseveare, *The Treasury*, pp. 237–9.
109 *Ibid.*, pp. 269, 286.
110 *Ibid.*, p. 271.
111 PRO/T273/309.
112 446 HC Deb., 5s., Col. 1467 (2 February 1948).
113 446 HC Deb., 5s., Col. 1466 (2 February 1948).
114 Sir Ivor Jennings, *Cabinet Government*, Cambridge University Press, 1959, p. 326.
115 Sir Edward Bridges, *Treasury Control*, The Athlone Press, 1950.
116 *Sixth Report from the Select Committee on Estimates, Session 1957–8, Treasury Control of Expenditure*, HC 254-I, HMSO, 1958.
117 *Control of Public Expenditure*, Cmnd 1432, HMSO, 1961.
118 Sir Richard Clarke, *Public Expenditure, Management and Control*,

Macmillan, 1978; Samuel Brittan, *Steering the Economy*, Penguin Books, 1971.

119 Sir Richard Clarke, *Public Expenditure, Management and Control*, Ch. 2.

120 Sir Richard Clarke, *New Trends in Government*, HMSO, 1971.

121 *The Reorganisation of Central Government*, Cmnd 4506, HMSO, 1970.

122 Clarke, *Public Expenditure, Management and Control*, p. 36.

123 Bridges, *The Treasury*, p. 141.

124 Roseveare, *The Treasury*, p. 300.

125 Clarke, *New Trends in Government*, p. 66.

126 Bridges, *The Treasury*, pp. 141–4.

127 Samuel Brittain, *The Treasury Under the Tories, 1951–1964*, Penguin Books, 1964; see also Roseveare, *The Treasury*, p. 333.

128 Thomas Balogh, 'The Apotheosis of the Dilettante', in Hugh Thomas (ed.) *The Establishment*, Anthony Blond, 1959.

129 Brian Chapman, *British Government Observed*, Allen and Unwin, 1963.

130 *The Administrators, the Reform of the Civil Service*, Fabian Tract 355, The Fabian Society, 1964.

131 *Whitehall and Beyond, Jo Grimond, Enoch Powell and Harold Wilson: Three Conversations with Norman Hunt, with a Comment by Lord Bridges*, BBC, 1964.

132 *Sixth Report from the Estimates Committee, together with the Minutes of the Evidence taken before Sub-Committee E, Session 1964–65: Recruitment to the Civil Service*, HC 308, HMSO, 1965.

133 *The Civil Service Vol. I, Report of the Committee, 1966–68*, Cmnd 3638, HMSO, 1968. See also Richard A. Chapman (ed.), *The Role of Commissions in Policy-Making*, Allen and Unwin, 1973, and G. K. Fry, *Reforming the Civil Service: The Fulton Committee on the British Home Civil Service 1966–1968*, Edinburgh University Press, 1993.

134 See Tom Lester, 'The Unmaking of Mintech', *Management Today*, November 1973, pp. 91–3, 198, 200, 204.

135 Harold Wilson, *The Labour Government 1964–70*, Penguin Books, 1974, p. 24.

136 *Royal Commission on the Civil Service*, Cd 6210, HMSO, 1912.

137 *Final Report of the Committee Appointed to Inquire into the Organisation and Staffing of Government Offices*, Cmd 62, HMSO, 1919, paras. 15, 18.

138 *Royal Commission on the Civil Service, Minutes of Evidence*, HMSO, 1930, Q 18735.

139 Bridges, *The Treasury*, p. 203.

140 *Sixteenth Report from the Select Committee on National Expenditure, Session 1941–42, Organisation and Control of the Civil Service*, HC 120, HMSO, 1942.

141 *Fifth Report from the Estimates Committee, together with the Minutes of Evidence taken before Sub-Committee C, Session 1963–64: Treasury Control of Establishments*, HC 228, HMSO, 1964. See also Nevil Johnson, *Parliament and Expenditure: The Estimates Committee 1945–65*, Allen and Unwin, 1966, Ch. 3.

142 P. J. Grigg, *Prejudice and Judgment*, Jonathan Cape, 1948, p. 36.

143 Bridges, *The Treasury*, p. 158.

144 *Fulton Report*, para. 246.

145 *Fulton Report*, para. 21.

146 *Fulton Report*, paras 250, 251.
147 *Fulton Report*, para. 253.
148 *Fulton Report*, para. 261.
149 *Fulton Report*, para. 266.
150 *Civil Service Department/Treasury Study Team Report. The Integration of HM Treasury and the Civil Service Department*, Annex 1, para. 48.
151 *Developments on Fulton*, National Whitley Council, 1969: *Fulton – A Framework for the Future (1970)*, National Whitley Council, 1971; and *Fulton – The Reshaping of the Civil Service during 1970*, National Whitley Council, 1971.
152 *Civil Service Statistics*, Civil Service Department, 1981.
153 *Eleventh Report from the Expenditure Committee, Session 1976–77, The Civil Service*, HC 535, Q 1817.
154 *Ibid.*, para. 75.
155 *Ibid.*, para. 81.
156 *Ibid.*, para. 88.
157 *First Report from the Treasury and Civil Service Committee, Session 1980–81, The Future of the Civil Service Department*, HC 54, HMSO, 1980.
158 *The Independent*, 23 July 1992.
159 *First Report from the Treasury and Civil Service Committee, Session 1980–81, The Future of the Civil Service*, HC 54, HMSO, 1980, Q 777.
160 For further details of the history of the CSD, see Richard A. Chapman, 'The Rise and Fall of the CSD', *Policy and Politics*, Vol. 11, No. 1, 1983, pp. 41–63.
161 *Control of Public Expenditure*, Cmnd 1432, HMSO, 1961, paras. 44, 90.
162 *Plowden Report*, para. 36.
163 W. J. M. Mackenzie, 'The Plowden Report: a translation', *The Guardian*, 25 May 1963.
164 Richard A. Chapman and J. R. Greenaway, *The Dynamics of Administrative Reform*, Ch. 4.
165 John Greenwood and David Wilson, *Public Administration in Britain Today*, Unwin Hyman, 1989, p. 128.
166 *Efficiency and Effectiveness*, Cmnd 8616, HMSO, 1982, App. 3.
167 *Peat Marwick Financial Management in the Public Sector: A Review 1979–84*, Peat, Marwick, Mitchell & Co., London, 1984.
168 Richard A. Chapman, 'Concepts and Issues in Public Sector Reform: the Experience of the United Kingdom in the 1980s', *Public Policy and Administration*, Vol. 6, No. 2, 1991, pp. 1–19.
169 Roseveare, *The Treasury*, p. 20.
170 Roseveare, *The Treasury*, Ch. 3.
171 Sir Edward Bridges, *Treasury Control*.

3 STRUCTURE AND ORGANISATION

1 *Budgetary Reform*, Cm 1867, HMSO, 1992. See especially para. 13.
2 *The Civil Service, Continuity and Change*, Cm 2627, HMSO, 1994.
3 HM Treasury, *Fundamental Review of Running Costs, A report to the*

Chancellor of the Exchequer by Sir Colin Southgate and Others, HM Treasury, 1994.

4   HM Treasury, *Departmental Report of the Chancellor of the Exchequer's Departments and Net Payments to European Community Institutions: The Government's Expenditure Plans 1993–94 to 1995–96*, Cm 2217, HMSO, 1993, para. 1.6.

5   HM Treasury, *Departmental Report of the Chancellor of the Exchequer's Departments and Net Payments to European Community Institutions: The Government's Expenditure Plans 1994–95 to 1996–97*, Cm 2517, HMSO, 1994, p. 4.

6   HM Treasury, *Departmental Report of the Chancellor of the Exchequer's Smaller Departments, Net Payments to European Community Institutions: The Government's Expenditure Plans 1995–96 to 1997–98*, Cm 2817, HMSO, 1995, pp. 2–3.

7   HM Treasury, *Chancellor of the Exchequer's Smaller Departments*, Cm 2817, p. 21.

8   *Ibid.*

9   HM Treasury, *Her Majesty's Treasury,* undated pamphlet issued to general readers and new recruits to the Treasury staff.

10 HM Treasury, *Chancellor of the Exchequer's Smaller Departments*, Cm 2817.

11 *Ibid.*, p. 1.

12 *Civil Service Yearbook*, HMSO, 1995.

13 HM Treasury, *Chancellor of the Exchequer's Smaller Departments*, Cm 2817, p. 3.

14 *Ibid.*, p. 2.

15 HM Treasury, *Fundamental Review of Running Costs*, para. 1.8.

16 *Ibid.*, para. 1.4.

17 *Ibid.*, para. 1.10.

18 *Ibid.*, para. 9.14.

19 *Ibid.*, pp. 35–6.

20 *Ibid.*, para. 3.2.

21 *Ibid.*, para. 2.8.

22 *Ibid.*, para. 3.9.

23 *Ibid.*, para. 4.11.

24 *Ibid.*, para. 4A.15.

25 *Ibid.*, Ch. 6.

26 *Ibid.*, para. 5.5

27 *Ibid.*, para. 5.15.

28 *Ibid.*, para. 6.16.

29 *Ibid.*, para. 6.23.

30 *Ibid.*, para. 6.30.

31 HM Treasury, *Chancellor of the Exchequer's Smaller Departments*, Cm 2817, Ch. 1 , para. A3.

32 HM Treasury, *Improving the Treasury; Initial Decisions on the Fundamental Expenditure Review of Running Costs*, 1994.

33 HM Treasury, *Chancellor of the Exchequer's Smaller Departments*, Cm 2817, Ch. 1, para. C8.

34 *Ibid.*, Ch. 1, para. C13.

35 HM Treasury, *Fundamental Review of Running Costs*, para. 16.1.

36 *Ibid.*, para. 15.13.
37 *Ibid.*, para. 7.7.
38 *Ibid.*, pp. 88–9.
39 *Ibid.*, pp. 111–12.
40 *Ibid.*, pp. 56–7.
41 Details in this section are derived mainly from the Cabinet Office/HM Treasury set of six booklets, *Public Expenditure Management*, HMSO, 1989.
42 HC Deb., 6s., Vol. 214, Col. 380 (18 November 1992).
43 HM Treasury, *Financial Statement and Budget Report 1995–96*, HMSO, 1994.
44 See House of Commons, Treasury and Civil Service Select Committee, First Report, Session 1992–93, *The 1992 Autumn Statement and the Conduct of Economic Policy, together with the Proceedings of the Committee, Minutes of Evidence and Appendices*, HC 201, HMSO, 1993, Q369.
45 'A new approach to controlling public expenditure', *Treasury Bulletin*, Vol. 3(3), 1992, pp. 11–17.
46 Cabinet Office/HM Treasury, *Public Expenditure Management: 1. Public Expenditure Survey*, HMSO, 1989.
47 *Efficiency and Effectiveness*, Cmnd 8616, HMSO, 1982, App. 3.
48 HM Treasury, *Policy Evaluation: A Guide for Managers*, HMSO, 1988, p. 34.
49 Lord Bridges, *The Treasury*, George Allen and Unwin, 1964, p. 49.
50 *Budgetary Reform in the UK, Report of a Committee chaired by Lord Armstrong of Sanderstead*, Oxford University Press for the Institute of Fiscal Studies, 1980.
51 *Budgetary Reform*, Cm 1867, HMSO, 1992, para. 7.
52 *Sixth Report from the Treasury and Civil Service Committee, Session 1981–82, Budgetary Reform*, HC 137, HMSO, 1982.
53 *Second Special Report from the Treasury and Civil Service Committee, Session 1981–82, Budgetary Reform: Observations by HM Treasury on the Sixth Report from the Committee, Session 1981–82*, HC 521, HMSO, 1982.
54 Sir Terence Burns, 'Some reflections on the Treasury' in S. Holly (ed.), *Money, Inflation and Employment, Essays in Honour of James Ball*, Edward Elgar, 1994.
55 Sir Terence Burns, 'Change and the Treasury', a lecture at the University of Durham, 27 April 1994.
56 Sir Terence Burns, 'Some reflections on the Treasury'.
57 Quoted in Richard A. Chapman, *Decision-making*, Routledge and Kegan Paul, 1968.
58 HM Treasury, 'Recent developments in UK economic policy', *Treasury Bulletin*, Vol. 3(3), 1992, pp. 1–6.
59 Announced by the Chancellor of the Exchequer, 13 April 1994. See *The Independent*, 14 April 1994.
60 Robert Blake, *The Unknown Prime Minister*, Eyre and Spottiswoode, 1955, Ch. 22.
61 Sir Terence Burns, 'Some reflections on the Treasury'.
62 *Fundamental Review of Running Costs*, para. 12.27.

63 HM Treasury, *Government Accounting*, HMSO, 1989, Ch. 5.
64 HM Treasury, *Chancellor of the Exchequer's Smaller Departments*, Cm 2817.
65 *Government Accounting*, Ch. 4.
66 Colin Thain, *Treasury Power and Failure: Economic Policy, Whitehall and the UK's Decline*, Working Paper 08/95, Centre for Research in Economics and Law, University of Ulster, 1995.
67 *Fundamental Review of Running Costs*, Ch. 11.
68 *Ibid.*, para. 11.10.
69 *Ibid.*, para. 11.12.
70 Lord Bridges, *The Treasury*, p. 40.
71 Andrew Likierman, *Public Expenditure, Who Really Controls it and How*, Penguin Books, 1988.
72 See Lord Bridges, *The Treasury*, Appendix V, pp. 222.
73 *Ibid.*, p. 41.

4 THE FINANCING AND RESPONSIBILITY OF NEXT STEPS AGENCIES

1 Efficiency Unit, *Improving Management in Government: The Next Steps*, *Report to the Prime Minister*, HMSO, 1988.
2 Treasury and Civil Service Committee, Eighth Report, Session 1987–88, *Civil Service Management Reform: the Next Steps, Vol. I, together with the Proceedings of the Committee*, HC 494 – I, HMSO, 1988, para. 10.
3 Treasury and Civil Service Committee, Fifth Report, Session 1993–94, *The Role of the Civil Service*, Vol. 1, HC 27–1, 1994, para. 168.
4 Cabinet Office, *Next Steps: Briefing Note*, 1 July 1994, Cabinet Office (OPSS), 1994.
5 *The Next Steps Agencies: Review 1993*, Cm 2430, HMSO, 1993. See also, Cabinet Office, *Next Steps Briefing Note*, 1 July 1994, Cabinet Office (OPSS), 1994; and *Next Steps: Moving On*, Cabinet Office, 1994.
6 *The Next Steps Initiative: The Government reply to the Seventh Report from the Treasury and Civil Service Committee, Session 1990–91*, HC 496, Cm 1761, HMSO, 1991.
7 *The Citizen's Charter: Raising the Standard*, Cm 1599, HMSO, 1991, p. 36.
8 *The Next Steps Initiative: The Government reply*, Cm 1761, 1991, p. 1.
9 *The Next Steps, Report*, Annex C.
10 127 HC Deb., 6s., Col. 1149 (18 February 1988).
11 *Report on Non-Departmental Public Bodies*, Cmnd 7797, HMSO, 1980.
12 *The Citizen's Charter*, p. 36.
13 *Multi-Departmental Review of Budgeting: Executive Summary*, HM Treasury, 1986.
14 *The Next Steps, Report*, Annex C.
15 *The Civil Service, Vol. I, Report of the Committee, 1966–68*, Cmnd 3638, HMSO, 1968, Ch. 5.
16 Expenditure Committee, Eleventh Report, Session 1976–77, *The Civil Service, Vol. I – Report*, HC 535 – I, HMSO, 1977, para. 94.

17 127 HC Deb., 6s., Col. 1149 (18 February 1988).
18 E. P. Kemp, 'The "Next Steps" Project: Efficiency and Effectiveness in the UK Civil Service', in T. P. Hardiman and Michael Mulreaney (eds) *Efficiency and Effectiveness in the Public Domain*, Dublin: Institute of Public Administration, 1991.
19 Treasury and Civil Service Committee, Eighth Report, Session 1987–88, *Civil Service Management Reform*, HC 494 – I.
20 *Ibid.*, para. 18.
21 *Ibid.*, para. 51.
22 *Ibid.*, Q. 110.
23 *Ibid.*, Q. 256.
24 *Civil Service Management Reform: The Next Steps, The Government reply to the Eighth Report from the Treasury and Civil Service Committee, Session 1987–88*, HC 494 – I, Cm 524, HMSO, 1988.
25 For example, John Garrett and Robert Sheldon, *Administrative Reform: the Next Steps*, (Fabian Tract 426), Fabian Society, 1973.
26 *Improving Management in Government: the Next Steps Agencies: Review 1991*, Cm 1760, HMSO, 1991.
27 Treasury and Civil Service Committee, Eighth Report, Session 1987–88, *Civil Service Management Reform*, HC 494 – I, Q. 23, 24.
28 *The Next Steps Initiative: The Government Reply*, Cm 1761, 1991, p. 1.
29 *Efficiency and Effectiveness in the Civil Service: Government Observations on the Third Report from the Treasury and Civil Service Committee*, Cmnd 8616, HMSO, 1982, para. 27.
30 *Ibid.*, App. 3.
31 *Report of an Inquiry into the principles and the system by which the remuneration of the non-industrial Civil Service should be determined* (Chairman, Sir John Megaw), Cmnd 8590, HMSO, 1982.
32 Diana Goldsworthy, *Setting up Next Steps*, HMSO, 1991, p. 12.
33 Dr Peter Hennessy, 'Appendix 1', in Treasury and Civil Service Committee, Eighth Report, Session 1989–90, *Progress in the Next Steps Initiative, together with the Proceedings of the Committee, Minutes of Evidence and Appendices*, HC 481, HMSO, 1990, p. 60.
34 Treasury and Civil Service Committee, Fifth Report, Session 1988–89, *Developments in the Next Steps Programme, together with the Proceedings of the Committee, Minutes of Evidence and Appendices*, HC 348, HMSO, 1989, Q. 317.
35 *Ibid.*, Q. 1.
36 Peter Kemp, *The Next Steps: A Review of the Agency Concept*, London: Royal Institute of Public Administration/Arthur Young, p. 13. Quoted in Treasury and Civil Service Committee, Fifth Report, Session 1988–89, *Developments in the Next Steps Programme*, HC 348, para. 41.
37 Treasury and Civil Service Committee, Eighth Report, Session 1987–88, *Civil Service Management Reform*, HC 494 – II, Q. 69.
38 Diana Goldsworthy, *Setting up Next Steps*, pp. 20–22.
39 Report by the Comptroller and Auditor General, *The Next Steps Initiative*, 410, HMSO, 1989, App. 2, para. 7.
40 Goldsworthy, *Setting up Next Steps*, pp. 30–31. See also the Royal Mint, Annual Reports.

41 Treasury and Civil Service Committee, Eighth Report, Session 1989–90, *Progress in the Next Steps Initiative*, HC 481, Q. 21.

42 Treasury and Civil Service Committee, Eighth Report, Session 1987–88, *Civil Service Management Reform*, HC 494 – II, Q. 267; and Treasury and Civil Service Committee, Eighth Report, 1989–90, *Progress in the Next Steps Initiative*, HC 481, Q. 23.

43 Treasury and Civil Service Committee, Eighth Report, 1989–90, *Progress in the Next Steps Initiative*, HC 481, para. 33.

44 Treasury and Civil Service Committee, Eighth Report, Session 1989–90, *Progress in the Next Steps Initiative*, HC 481, Q. 165.

45 Treasury and Civil Service Committee, Seventh Report, Session 1990–91, *The Next Steps Initiative, Report, together with the Proceedings of the Committee, Minutes of Evidence and Appendices*, HC 496, HMSO, 1991, Q. 435.

46 Treasury and Civil Service Committee, Eighth Report, Session 1987–88, *Civil Service Management Reform*, HC 494 – II, Q. 114.

47 John Garrett, 'Memorandum', in Treasury and Civil Service Committee, Eighth Report, Session 1987–88, *Civil Service Management Reform*, HC 494 – II, p. 50.

48 Sir Angus Fraser, 'Foreword', in Efficiency Unit, *Making the Most of Next Steps: The Management of Ministers' Departments and their Executive Agencies, Report to the Prime Minister*, HMSO, 1991.

49 Treasury and Civil Service Committee, Fifth Report, Session 1988–89, *Developments in the Next Steps Programme*, HC 348, Q. 320.

50 *Ibid.*, Q. 320.

51 For example, Treasury and Civil Service Committee, Eighth Report, Session 1989–90, *Progress in the Next Steps Initiative*, HC 481, Memorandum by Peter Kemp, para. 3(d); Q. 145.

52 Treasury and Civil Service Committee, Fifth Report, Session 1988–89, *Developments in the Next Steps Programme*, HC 348, para. 31.

53 *Ibid.*, para. 56.

54 *Ibid.*, Q. 11.

55 Treasury and Civil Service Committee, Seventh Report, Session 1990–91, *The Next Steps Initiative*, HC 496, Q. 326.

56 Treasury and Civil Service Committee, Fifth Report, Session 1988–89, *Developments in the Next Steps Programme*, HC 348, Q. 89, 97, 140.

57 Treasury and Civil Service Committee, Seventh Report, Session 1990–91, *The Next Steps Initiative*, HC 496, App. 3.

58 195 HC Deb., 6s., Col. 604–5 (24 July 1991).

59 *Next Steps Review, 1994*, Cm 2950, HMSO, 1994, p. iii.

60 For example, Treasury and Civil Service Committee, Fifth Report, Session 1988–89, *Developments in the Next Steps Programme*, HC 348, Oral evidence of Mr Ron Oliver, Vehicle Inspectorate Executive Agency.

61 Efficiency Unit, *Making the Most of Next Steps: The Management of Ministers' Departments and their Executive Agencies, Report to the Prime Minister*, HMSO, 1991, para. 3.15.

62 *Ibid.*, para. 3.19.

63 *Ibid.*, para. 3.7.

64 Treasury and Civil Service Committee, Seventh Report, Session 1990–91, *The Next Steps Initiative*, HC 496, para. 21.

65 *Ibid.*, Q. 393.
66 Peter Hennessy, *Whitehall*, Secker and Warburg, 1989, p. 618.
67 Treasury and Civil Service Committee, Eighth Report, Session 1987–88, *Civil Service Management Reform*, HC 494 – II, Q. 383.
68 *Ibid.*, Q. 256.
69 *Ibid.*; 'Memorandum submitted by HM Treasury', Annex, para. 1, p. 70. See also *Executive Agencies: A Guide to Setting Targets and Measuring Performance*, HMSO, 1970.
70 Statutory instruments: 1981 No. 1670, The Transfer of Functions (Minister for the Civil Service and Treasury) Order 1981; 1987 No. 2039, The Transfer of Functions (Minister for the Civil Service and Treasury) Order 1987.
71 Royal Institute of Public Administration, *Value for Money Audits; Proceedings of a Seminar*, RIPA, 1982.
72 For example, Chester I. Barnard, *The Functions of the Executive*, Harvard University Press, 1938, pp. 60–61. See also Richard A. Chapman 'Strategies for Reducing Government Activities', in Gerald E. Caiden and Heinrich Siedentopf (eds) *Administrative Reform Strategies*, D. C. Heath 1982, pp. 59–69.
73 Treasury and Civil Service Committee, Eighth Report, Session 1987–88, *Civil Service Management Reform*, HC 494 – II, Memorandum by Sir Ronald Dearing, p. 90.
74 HM Treasury, *Policy Evaluation: A Guide for Managers*, HMSO, 1988.
75 Treasury and Civil Service Committee, Eighth Report, Session 1989–90, *Progress in the Next Steps Initiative*, HC 481, Memorandum submitted by HM Treasury, p. 23.
76 Treasury and Civil Service Committee, Fifth Report, Session 1988–89, *Developments in the Next Steps Programme*, HC 348, Memorandum submitted by HM Treasury, p. 51.
77 HM Treasury, *Multi-Departmental Review of Budgeting: Executive Summary*, HM Treasury, 1986, para. 1.1.
78 *Ibid.*, para. 1.4.
79 HM Treasury, *The Financing and Accountability of Next Steps Agencies*, Cm 914, HMSO, 1989.
80 Treasury and Civil Service Committee, Eighth Report, Session 1989–90, *Progress in the Next Steps Initiative*, HC 481, Memorandum submitted by HM Treasury, p. 23.
81 *The Citizen's Charter*; and 195 HC Deb., 6s., Col. 604–5 (24 July 1991).
82 Treasury and Civil Service Committee, Eighth Report, Session 1989–90, *Progress in the Next Steps Initiative*, HC 481, Q. 71.
83 *Ibid.*, Q. 82.
84 Treasury and Civil Service Committee, Eighth Report, Session 1987–88, *Civil Service Management Reform*, HC 494 – II, Q. 326.
85 Efficiency Unit, *Making the Most of Next Steps*, para. 3.20.
86 For example, Mr Ron Oliver, Vehicle Inspectorate Executive Agency, Q. 115 and Dr Paul Freeman, HMSO, Q. 138, in Treasury and Civil Service Committee, Fifth Report, Session, 1988–89, *Developments in the Next Steps Programme*, HC 348.
87 Treasury and Civil Service Committee, Eighth Report, Session 1989–90, *Progress in the Next Steps Initiative*, HC 481, Q. 24.

88 Treasury and Civil Service Committee, Seventh Report, 1990–91, *The Next Steps Initiative*, HC 496, Q. 423.
89 Report by the Comptroller and Auditor General, *The Next Steps Initiative*, 410, HMSO, 1989, para. 20.
90 Treasury and Civil Service Committee, Fifth Report, Session 1988–89, *Developments in the Next Steps Programme*, HC 348, para. 6.
91 Report by the Comptroller and Auditor General *The Next Steps Initiative*, 410, HMSO, 1989, App. 2.
92 Treasury and Civil Service Committee, Eighth Report, Session 1989–90, *Progress in the Next Steps Initiative*, HC 481, Q. 25.
93 *Ibid.*, para. 54.
94 Quoted in Treasury and Civil Service Committee, Seventh Report, Session 1990–91, *The Next Steps Initiative*, HC 496, p. ix.
95 191 HC Deb., 6s., Cols. 679 and 691 (20 May 1991).
96 See evidence of Mr T. H. R. Luce in Treasury and Civil Service Committee, Fifth Report, Session 1988–89, *Developments in the Next Steps Programme*, HC 348.
97 Treasury and Civil Service Committee, Fifth Report, Session 1988–89, *Developments in the Next Steps Programme*, HC 348, Q. 258.
98 Efficiency Unit, *Improving Management in Government*, para. 19.
99 HM Treasury, *The Financing and Accountability of Next Steps Agencies*, Cm 914, para. 2.6.
100 Report by the Comptroller and Auditor General, *The Next Steps Initiative*, 410, para. 47.
101 HM Treasury, *The Financing and Control of Next Steps Agencies*, Cm 914, para. 3.14.
102 *Ibid.*, para. 3.18.
103 Goldsworthy, *Setting Up Next Steps*, p. 31.
104 HM Treasury, *The Financing and Accountability of Next Steps Agencies*, Cm 914, Ch. 4.
105 *The Independent*, 27 December 1991.
106 HM Treasury, *The Financing and Accountability of Next Steps Agencies*, Cm 914, para. 4.20.
107 *Ibid.*, para. 5.11.
108 *Improving Management in Government: The Next Steps Agencies: Review 1991*, Cm 1760, HMSO, 1991, p. 6.
109 *Next Steps, Briefing Note, 1 November 1995*.
110 Report of the Comptroller and Auditor General, *The Next Steps Initiative*, 410, para. 26.
111 Goldsworthy, *Setting Up Next Steps*, p. 30.
112 Treasury and Civil Service Committee, Seventh Report, Session 1990–91, *The Next Steps Initiative*, HC 496, Q. 401.
113 'Further Memorandum submitted by the Council of Civil Service Unions', in Treasury and Civil Service Committee, Seventh Report, Session 1990–91, *The Next Steps Initiative*, HC 496, para. 132.
114 Treasury and Civil Service Committee, Fifth Report, Session 1988–89, *Developments in the Next Steps Programme*, HC 348, para. 54.
115 Memorandum submitted by HM Treasury, in Treasury and Civil Service Committee, Fifth Report, Session 1988–89, *Developments in the Next Steps Programme*, HC 348.

116 *Next Steps: Agencies in Government Review 1994*, Cm 2750, HMSO, 199 ₹, pp. vi–viii; *Next Steps: Agencies in Government Review 1995*, Cm 3164, HMSO, 1996, p. v.
117 Treasury and Civil Service Committee, Seventh Report, Session 1990–91, *The Next Steps Initiative*, HC 496, Q. 68.
118 'Appendix to the Memorandum submitted by HM Treasury: Executive Agencies – Setting Targets and Measuring Performance: A Guide', in Treasury and Civil Service Committee, Seventh Report, Session 1990–91, *The Next Steps Initiative*, HC 496.
119 Treasury and Civil Service Committee, Eighth Report, Session 1989–90, *Progress in the Next Steps Initiative*, HC 481, Evidence, p. 8.
120 *Ibid.*, Q. 142.
121 'Appendix to the Memorandum submitted by HM Treasury: Annual Reports and Accounts', in Treasury and Civil Service Committee, Seventh Report, Session 1990–91, *The Next Steps Initiative*, HC 496.
122 *Ibid.*
123 Report of the Comptroller and Auditor General, *The Next Steps Initiative*, 410, para. 35.
124 *Ibid.*, para. 39.
125 *Ibid.*, para. 62.
126 *Civil Service Commissioners' Report 1990–91*, Office of the Civil Service Commissioners, 1991, p. 3. See also Richard A. Chapman, 'New Arrangements for Recruitment to the British Civil Service: Cause for Concern', *Public Policy and Administration*, 1991, Vol. 6, No. 3, pp. 1–6.
127 *Next Steps Briefing Note, October 1996.* See also House of Lords, Select Committee on the Public Service, Session 1995–96, First Report, *The Government's Proposals for the Privatisation of Recruitment and Assessment Services (RAS), with evidence*, HL 109, HMSO, 1996; and HL Deb., 6s., Vol. 574, Cols 1530–1575 (25 July 1996).
128 Treasury and Civil Service Committee, Fifth Report, Session 1988–89, *Developments in the Next Steps Programme*, HC 348, Q. 11.
129 *Ibid.*, 'Supplementary Memorandum by HMSO'.
130 Treasury and Civil Service Committee, Seventh Report, Session 1990–91, *The Next Steps Initiative*, HC 496, para. 28.
131 *Next Steps Briefing Note*, October 1996.
132 Treasury and Civil Service Committee, Eighth Report, Session 1989–90, *Progress in the Next Steps Initiative*, HC 481, Q. 72.
133 *Ibid.*, 'Supplementary evidence submitted by HM Treasury', p. 103.
134 See 'The Government Reply to the Treasury and Civil Service Committee Report on the 1991 Budget', quoted in Treasury and Civil Service Committee, Eighth Report, Session 1990–91, *The Next Steps Initiative*, HC 496, para. 55.
135 *Ibid.*, 'Memorandum submitted by HM Treasury'.
136 Cabinet Office and Office of the Minister for the Civil Service, *Pay and Management Flexibilities, 40 Selected Flexibilities in the Field of Personnel Management, Pay and Allowances Available to Departments and Agencies*, Cabinet Office and Office of the Minister for the Civil Service, 1991.
137 Treasury and Civil Service Committee, Seventh Report, Session 1990–91, *The Next Steps Initiative*, HC 496, Q. 395.
138 Memorandum submitted by the Vehicle Inspectorate Executive Agency,

in Treasury and Civil Service Committee, Fifth Report, Session 1988–89, *Developments in the Next Steps Initiative*, HC 348.

139   Treasury and Civil Service Committee, Seventh Report, Session 1990–91, *The Next Steps Initiative*, HC 496, Q. 16.

140   Treasury and Civil Service Committee, Eighth Report, Session 1987–88, *Civil Service Management Reform*, HC 494 – II, Q. 335.

141   For a history of the Civil Service College, see Dennis L. Bird, *The Civil Service College 1970–1995*, HMSO, 1995.

142   *Civil Service College, Framework Document 1994–1999*, Sunningdale: Civil Service College, 1995.

143   The Rt Hon. David Hunt, Foreword by the Chancellor of the Duchy of Lancaster, *Civil Service College, Framework Document 1994–1999*.

144   Treasury and Civil Service Committee, Fifth Report, Session 1988–89. *Developments in the Next Steps Programme*, HC 348, Q. 236.

145   *Ibid.*, Q. 265.

146   *Civil Service College, Framework Document 1994–1999*, p. 7.

147   *Ibid.*, p. 6.

148   *Ibid.*, p. 6.

149   *Ibid.*, p. 1.

150   Treasury and Civil Service Committee, Sixth Report Session 1992–93, *The Role of the Civil Service: Interim Report, Vol. II, Minutes of Evidence and Appendices*, HC 390-II, HMSO, 1993, p. 166.

151   *Ibid.*, Q. 665.

152   Civil Service College, *Annual Report, 1990–91*, p. 14

153   Civil Service College, *Strategic Plan 1991 to 1995*, Civil Service College, 1991, p. 16.

154   *Civil Service College, Framework Document*, 1989, p. 8.

155   In the first *Framework Document* (para. 5.7), copies were required to be deposited in the libraries of both Houses of Parliament.

156   *Civil Service College, Strategic Plan, 1991 to 1995*, p. 16.

157   *Civil Service College, Framework Document*, p. 9.

158   *Ibid.*, pp. 11–12.

159   *Principal's Annual Report, 1988 to 1989*, Sunningdale: Civil Service College, 1989, p. 13.

160   *Report and Accounts, 1989 to 1990*, Sunningdale: Civil Service College, 1990, p. 1.

161   Civil Service College, *Report and Accounts, 1989 to 1990*, p. 1.

162   *Report and Accounts, 1990 to 1991*, p. 5.

163   Treasury and Civil Service Committee, *The Role of the Civil Service*, HC 390-II, p. 153.

164   BBC Radio interview, 21 June 1990. Quoted in Dennis L. Bird, *The Civil Service College, 1970–1995*, p. 148.

165   *The Civil Service College 1970–71*, HMSO, 1972, p. 3.

166   *Ibid.*, p. 3.

167   *The Civil Service College 1971–72*, HMSO, 1973, p. 3.

168   E. Grebenik, 'The Civil Service College: The First Year', *Public Administration*, 1972, Vol. 50, p. 138.

169   *The Civil Service, Vol. I, Report of the Committee 1966–68*, Cmnd 3638, HMSO, 1968; and Richard A. Chapman and J. R. Greenaway, *The Dynamics of Administrative Reform*, Croom Helm, 1980, pp. 143–58.

170 Sir William Armstrong, 'The Tasks of the Conference', *PAC Bulletin* No. 6, May 1969, pp. 1–7.
171 *Civil Service College, Strategic Plan 1991 to 1995*, pp. 11 and 18.
172 *Ibid.*
173 Civil Service College, *Annual Report 1994–95*, p. 11.
174 *Ibid.*, p. 15.
175 See, for example, *The Times Higher Education Supplement*, 25 July 1993.
176 *Contributions Agency, Framework Document*, Newcastle-upon-Tyne: Contributions Agency, 1991, p. 2.
177 *Contributions Agency, Business Plan 1991/92*, Newcastle-upon-Tyne, Contributions Agency, 1991, pp. 1–2.
178 *The Citizen's Charter*, Cm 1599, HMSO, 1991.
179 *Contributions Agency, Annual Report 1994/95*, Contributions Agency, pp. 6 and 9.
180 *Ibid.*, p. 6.
181 *Contributions Agency, Framework Document 1994*, pp. 4–7.
182 *Ibid.*, p. 4.
183 *Contributions Agency, Business Plan 1995/96*, p. 15.
184 *Contributions Agency, Framework Document*, p. 4.
185 *Ibid.*, p. 6.
186 *Ibid.*, p. 5.
187 *Ibid.*, p. 6.
188 *What's New?*, Contributions Agency, 1991.
189 *Ibid.*; and up to date information from the Contributions Agency.
190 *Contributions Agency, Framework Document (1991)*, p. 15.
191 *What's New?*, Contributions Agency, 1991.
192 *The Royal Mint: A Tradition of Excellence*, Royal Mint, 1990.
193 Government Trading Funds Act 1973, as amended (1990, c. 30) 4 (1).
194 *Royal Mint, Annual Report, 1994–95*, p. 8.
195 *Royal Mint Executive Agency, Framework Document, April 1990*, Royal Mint, 1990, para. 5.3.
196 *The Royal Mint: A Tradition of Excellence.*
197 *Royal Mint, Annual Report, 1994–95*, p. 11.
198 Cabinet Office, *Next Steps: Briefing Note*, 3 January 1992, Cabinet Office (OMCS), 1992.
199 *Royal Mint, Annual Report, 1994–95*, p. 5.
200 *Royal Mint Executive Agency, Framework Document.*
201 *Royal Mint, Annual Report 1989–90*, Royal Mint, 1990, p. 4.
202 *Royal Mint, Annual Report 1990–91*, Royal Mint, 1991.
203 *Improving Management in Government: The Next Steps Agencies: Review 1991*, Cm 1760.
204 *Royal Mint, Annual Report, 1994–95*, p. 13.
205 *The Citizen's Charter*, Cm 1599.
206 HM Treasury, *Competing for Quality*, Cm 1730, HMSO, 1991.
207 *The Citizen's Charter*, Cm 1599, p. 28.
208 *Ibid.*, p. 34.
209 *Ibid.*, p. 35.
210 *Ibid.*, p. 35.
211 *Competing for Quality*, Cm 1730, pp. ii and 1.
212 *Ibid.*, p. 2.

213 *Ibid.*, p. 1.
214 Committee of Public Accounts, Thirty-eighth Report, Session 1988–89, *The Next Steps Initiative*, HC 420, HMSO, 1989, Q. 4049.
215 *The Times*, 14 May 1992.
216 Committee of Public Accounts, Thirty-eighth Report, Session 1988–89, *The Next Steps Initiative*, HC 420, Q. 4049.
217 National Audit Office, *The Vehicle Inspectorate: Progress as the First Executive Agency, Report by the Comptroller and Auditor General*, HMSO, 1992.
218 Dennis L. Bird, *The Civil Service College 1970–1995*, HMSO, 1995, p. 132.
219 Committee of Public Accounts, Thirty-eighth Report, Session 1988–89, *The Next Steps Initiative*, HC 420, Q. 4027.
220 *Government Accounting*, HMSO, 1989, 2.3.3, 2.3.6, 5.1.2, 5.1.1, 5.1.2, 5.1.6.
221 *Ibid.*, 5.2.9.
222 *Ibid.*, 5.2.16.
223 *Ibid.*, Annex 6.1.26.
224 Anne Davies and John William *What Next?*, Institute for Public Policy Research, 1991, p. 43.
225 The Department of Transport, *The Relationship Between the Department of Transport and its Executive Agencies*, Efficiency Scrutiny Report, Department of Transport, 1991, Recommendations 35, 36, 37.
226 Treasury and Civil Service Committee, Seventh Report, Session 1990–91, *The Next Steps Initiative*, HC 496, Q. 64.
227 Nigel Lawson, *The View from No. 11, Memoirs of a Tory Radical*, Bantam Press, 1992, p. 391.
228 *Ibid.*, p. 392.
229 Barry J. O'Toole and Richard A. Chapman, 'Parliamentary Accountability' in Barry J. O'Toole and Grant Jordan (eds), *Next Steps, Improving Management in Government?*, Dartmouth Publishing Co., 1995, p. 118–41.

5 REFLECTIONS

1 Anthony Sampson, *Anatomy of Britain*, Hodder and Stoughton, 1962, p. 270.
2 *Treasury News Release*, 135/96 and 136/96.
3 Sir Ivor Jennings, *Cabinet Government*, Cambridge University Press, 1936 (third edn, 1959).
4 Richard A. Chapman, 'The Rise and Fall of the CSD', *Policy and Politics*, 1983, Vol. 11, pp. 41–61.
5 *The Civil Service, Continuity and Change*, Cm 2627, HMSO, 1994.
6 *Treasury News Release*, 131/96.
7 *Treasury News Release*, 106/96.
8 Rt Hon. Lord Bridges, *The Treasury*, George Allen and Unwin, 1964.
9 Lord Bridges, *The Treasury*, p. 198.
10 *Next Steps Briefing Note*, October 1996, Cabinet Office (OPS), 1996.
11 General Sir John Learmont, *Review of Prison Service Security in England*

and Wales and the Escape from Parkhurst Prison on Tuesday 3rd January 1995, Cm 3021, HMSO, 1995.

12 Lord Bridges, *The Treasury*, p. 198.

13 HM Treasury, *Civil Service Statistics 1994*, HMSO, 1994; cf. *Report of the Royal Commission on the Civil Service, 1929–31* (Tomlin), Cmd 3909, HMSO, 1931; and W. J. M. Mackenzie and J. W. Grove, *Central Administration in Britain*, Longmans, Green and Co., 1957.

14 Richard A. Chapman, 'The End of the Civil Service?', *Teaching Public Administration*, 1992, Vol. 12, pp. 1–5; Richard A. Chapman and Barry J. O'Toole, 'The Role of the Civil Service: A Traditional View in a Period of Change', *Public Policy and Administration*, 1995, Vol. 10, pp. 3–20; Richard A. Chapman, 'Tragedy and Farce: the decision to privatise the RAS agency', *Public Policy and Administration*, 1996, Vol. 11(1), pp. 1–7; and Richard A. Chapman 'The End of the Civil Service' in Peter Barberis (ed.), *The Civil Service in an Era of Change*, Dartmouth Publishing Co., 1997, pp. 23–37.

15 *The Civil Service, Continuity and Change*, Cm 2627, para. 2.7.

16 Lord Bridges, *The Treasury*, p. 203.

17 For comments from civil servants in the 1960s see Richard A. Chapman, 'Profile of a Profession', Memorandum No. 2, in *The Fulton Report, 1966–68, Vol. 3(2), Surveys and Investigations*, HMSO, 1968, pp. 1–29.

18 Peter Hennessy, *Whitehall*, Secker and Warburg, 1989, p. 396.

19 Grant Jordan, *The British Administrative System*, Routledge, 1994, pp. 160–64.

20 Peter Hennessy, *Whitehall*, p. 618.

Index